Looking for Life on the Way to the Grave

Pastoral Journeys amidst the Dying and Grieving

Looking for Life on the Way to the Grave

Pastoral Journeys amidst the Dying and Grieving

Neal R. Sadler

Sigel Press

Looking for Life on the Way to the Grave:
Pastoral Journeys amidst the Dying and Grieving
Copyright @ 2021 by Neal Sadler
ISBN: 978-1-7359934-0-9
Sigel Press
8187 Camp Road
Homerville, OH 44235

Visit us on the World Wide Web at www.sigelpress.com

Cover and Internal Design by Harp Mando
Cover Image: Photograph of Daffodils in Windfall Cemetery by Neal R. Sadler

Printed in the United States of America

Printed on 100% recycled, 100% post-consumer waste paper.

To parishioners who have shared their stories
with me and have encouraged me to share
my stories.

Table of Contents

Foreward

I began writing these stories shortly after retiring from full-time ministry. Writing the stories provided me time to remember, reflect and celebrate 35 years of pastoring churches. As the number of stories began to increase, I was reminded once again of the vast array of situations and wide diversity of people that pastors encounter in ministry. I was also reminded of the many profoundly emotional journeys and deep bonds of trust and friendship in ministry. These shared journeys enriched my life greatly and taught me much about the love and grace of our Lord Jesus Christ. And the stories, though many, reflect only a small sampling from the many more journeys that pastors travel with parishioners.

The stories relate to the themes of aging, grieving and dying, for at these times we seek God most passionately and intensely. As our earthly lives draw to a close, we discard temporal concerns and search for eternal meaning and hope. The resurrection is not just something we sing about on Easter morning but the reality we will soon experience. Our journeys to the grave call forth faith and hope.

In this collection, I changed names, in most cases, to mask the identity of the individuals. Actual names were preserved, with permission of family members, if alive, in Chapters 7, 19, 28, 44, 46, 47, 51, 52, 59, 60, 62, 64, 67, 68, 73, and 78.

I give thanks to my "Shades of Grey" Pastoral Excellence Group and other colleagues who reviewed early manuscripts and gave feedback; to my sister-in-law, Linda, for editing my wordiness and helping me create a more readable book; to the vast number of parishioners who trusted me with their fears, struggles and dreams by inviting me into their journeys; and above all to my wife, Carolyn, whose constant encouragement enabled me to enter and continue in ministry for many years.

About the Author

After initially pursuing a career as an actuary, Neal R. Sadler served churches for more than 35 years as an ordained minister in the United Church of Christ. He journeyed with parishioners in the joys and challenges of seeking to love God and serve one another. His degrees are from the University of Michigan (B.A., MBA), Gordon-Conwell Theological Seminary (M.Div.) and Asbury Theological Seminary (D.Min.). Neal enjoys creating sermons in story form to open listeners to the biblical message. He has a special interest in local and global missions, leading numerous mission trips in the United States and overseas.

Neal and his wife, Carolyn, enjoy long-distance hiking in Europe and exploring America on their tandem bicycle. Carolyn, too, is a former actuary, and happily retired. They have two children, Nathan and Deborah, one grandchild, Anna, and a daughter-in-law, Katelyn, who is also an ordained UCC pastor.

Introduction

I pulled into the driveway of the small house across the road from our church. The church owned the house and used it for Bible studies, fellowship groups and occasional meetings. In a bedroom upstairs was the computer monitor graveyard, where church members sent old computer monitors to die. Actually, our Associate Pastor used the old monitors as replacements in the Sunday School Computer workshop we called Commandments.com. Churches are often the recipients of things no one else wants – old furniture, old computers, old clothes, old appliances. Sometimes we find a use for them around the building. Sometimes we know families needing them. Sometimes we deliver them to Goodwill or Salvation Army. Sometimes we just throw them away.

It was 7:00 am Saturday morning late in August. I fed Spook, the feral cat who waited each morning for my arrival. I put coffee on and unpacked bagels, muffins, orange juice and cream cheese I purchased on the way. The men, mostly middle-aged, soon began to arrive. Each poured a cup of coffee or glass of orange juice and we stood around the kitchen waiting for others. We ate breakfast, then settled in the old living room for our book study. We had come to know each other well. We usually knew what to expect from one another in discussion – usually, but not always – and the surprises energized our gatherings. Each month we wrapped things up sharing the happenings in our lives and families. I think that is why we were really there. We sought human connections and relationships that supported and cared for us. We closed with the Lord's Prayer.

I cleaned the kitchen and walked to the church to meet a teenage boy in our congregation. He was working on his Eagle Scout project, building wooden benches to form a conversation pit among trees on our property. He was organized. Everything seemed under control. A young couple then arrived for their pre-marital counseling appointment. We talked about the upcoming ceremony and reviewed results of their pre-marital assessment tool. I didn't know them well. They were not members of the church. They seemed to have a mature relationship. They listened well to one another and seemed delighted to have found each other. It would be a joy for me to perform their wedding service.

I drove to the home of a young family in a neighboring town. They had been worshipping with us for a couple of months, and now wished to join the church and have their baby baptized. They were leaving a mega-church, wanting a friendlier, more intimate congregation. We talked about joys of being new parents and the meaning of baptism. We talked about life in our church and how it would be different from their previous church. I spoke of the progressive theology of our congregation and the room we offered for individual interpretation of faith and Scripture. It was much different than they were used to.

A couple of parishioners were in the hospital. I stopped to see them after leaving the home of the young family. An elderly man was told by his physician the day before he could not return home unless he had round-the-clock care. It was not safe for him to be alone. He would never be able to live on his own again. The news should not have been a surprise, but the man was denying the severity of his health issues. We discussed loss of independence and the body failing him. We talked about finding care so he could remain at home, which is what he wanted very much. I think the news was a relief. He was worn out. Deep down, he knew he needed help.

The woman in the hospital was recovering well from surgery. We didn't talk much about her physical health. We talked about the ongoing conflict with her daughter. Their relationship was strained, at the breaking point. For years they quarreled and fought. The woman thought she loved and supported her daughter, but the daughter was in constant rebellion. They never conversed without ending in outbursts, accusations and tears.

I barely made it on time to my appointment with a grieving family to plan a memorial service for a woman in the congregation. The woman had been a delight to know. She possessed a strong faith. She and her husband enjoyed a solid, loving relationship. I anticipated the planning would go well and fairly quickly. I was wrong. There were issues among the children I knew nothing about. They could not agree on Scripture, music or if anyone besides myself should speak. The memorial service took shape only amidst tense negotiations. Instead of celebrating the mother's life, they were rekindling old hurts.

Back at the church, I set up coffee for the fellowship time following Sunday's worship. People were delighted to bring food items, serve and clean, but the big coffee makers intimidated them. Non-coffee drinker I was, I made the coffee, regular and decaf, each week. I set up tables and chairs, and set out cups, plates, napkins, creamers, sugar, tea bags, and four kinds of sweeteners (pink, yellow, blue and green). I did a few other routine chores for Sunday worship and went home to pick up my wife, Carolyn.

The congregation had an annual trip to see a local minor league baseball game. It was a fun night. People from eight months old to 88 years old attended. It began with a picnic supper. The game wasn't exciting, but silly antics between innings kept folks happy and entertained. For me, it was a relaxed evening enjoying the company of parishioners, getting to know them in informal, casual conversation. After the game, we watched fireworks.

Back home I reviewed my sermon and worship material. I didn't think too many changes were needed, though maybe I was just tired. It was after 11:00 pm and I had no energy for more edits. I would find out in the morning if the sermon and worship service spoke to the hearts of people.

Then I remembered emails. I hadn't checked emails all day. I should have put them off, but oftentimes someone has a last minute announcement or addition to the prayer list. I quickly discovered a vitriolic string of emails among the Praise Band. They were unhappy with me, the music director, each other, and everyone else. That crisis waited for me in the morning. I didn't look forward to it. Fortunately, it was summertime and I had only one worship service and no 7:30 am Confirmation Class.

This day was not typical in the life of a pastor. We usually do not work 16+ hours. We would wear out quickly if we did. I tell about this day because it illustrates the many relationships pastors move in and out of during a day's time. Some relationships are joyful and uplifting; some stressful and discouraging; some routine and some challenging. We enter lives of parishioners in many and varied ways. We journey with them at birth and death and most significant events in between. We journey closely with some. Others we know very little. Some invite us into the intimate and private recesses of thoughts and feelings. Others are guarded. Some become close friends. Others never want to see us outside of church. We journey uniquely with each parishioner.

Remember the computer monitors in the upstairs bedroom that came to the church to die? Nearly everyone in the congregation, even those not worshipping in years, comes to the church to die. They come partly because of tradition. People have done it for generations. They come also because the church is where people talk most about eternal things. We explore issues of faith, hope, and love. In the church people come to connect with God, however they envision God, and what we commonly call the 'spiritual.' They come looking for meaning and purpose beyond ordinary routines of every day, seeking courage and comfort as they face the greatest journey of their lives.

As pastors, we are usually the ones with whom they connect. Unlike the computer monitors, we seek to treat each person with unique dignity and respect.

Parishioners entrust us with hopes and fears. They share laughter and tears. We guard that sacred trust carefully. We listen and pray. We share the hope of the Christian Church, the promises of God received in Jesus Christ. We are also honest. We do not presume to know what we cannot know. We are not God and cannot pretend to know the mind of God. We are fellow travelers in this adventure of living, anticipating through faith that God has a wonderful surprise on the other side of the door of death.

The stories in this book are journeys I shared with parishioners. The stories revolve around those facing challenges of aging, dying and grieving. At these times we search deeply for meaning and truth. We long fervently for faith and hope. The stories are not just about dying and grieving but also living. In dying we learn best how to live.

Dying and grieving don't happen in isolation. These journeys are mixed with journeys taken throughout our lives – people accompanying us, successes bolstering us, failures defeating us, beliefs surrounding us, regrets nagging us, and dreams lying unfulfilled. Journeys amidst the dying and grieving call forth many stories impacting final journeys. I seek to tell these connected journeys as well.

The stories reveal something of the ministry and calling of a pastor. A pastor's call is not as neatly defined as that of a physician, teacher, carpenter or counselor. A call is personal to a pastor and fluid according to a situation. A pastor's work calls forth more listening and perceptiveness than expertise and advice. The call varies according to gifts, personality, ecclesiastical tradition, local church culture, theology and desires. Through the following stories, I pray readers gain greater awareness of the unique calling of a pastor. Perhaps the stories will answer the perpetual question of all congregants: "What does the pastor do the other six days of the week?"

I pray the stories also elicit from each of us, ordained minister or lay, hopes and fears, dreams and desires, doubt and faith. The issues and questions my parishioners and I encountered and contended with are common to all. I believe God calls us to be growing persons our entire lives and much growth occurs as we see our remaining days among the living diminishing rapidly.

Although the stories touch on failings and frailties in the church, I pray as well the stories also celebrate the goodness of the church. I have spent most of my adult life immersed in this household of faith, believing the church has a unique, precious role connecting seekers to God and one another. As members of Christ's Body, we share the love of Jesus in meaningful and tangible ways. May readers gain a glimpse of God's love made known in Jesus Christ and discover faith that gives courage for final days.

In the end the stories are uniquely mine and my parishioners. They reflect my style, personality, theology and approach to ministry. They reflect my strengths, weaknesses, struggles and faith. They reflect the challenges, dreams, fears, courage, humor and tears of my fellow travelers. I feel blessed to have shared these journeys. These dear folks were patient with my foibles and taught me much about faith, God and myself. They were gracious and kind inviting me into their lives and trusting me with secrets. They gave me meaning and substance, joy and fulfillment, I would never have realized otherwise.

CHAPTER 1

Dad's Dying.
Can You Come Over?

The first ring aroused me from nice quiet slumber into blurry bewilderedness. The second ring cleared my head. I picked up the telephone receiver, "Hello."

"Reverend Sadler? This is Dennis. Dad's dying. Can you come over?"

"I'll be there in a few minutes."

I looked at the alarm clock, 2:30 am ... 2:30 on Sunday morning. I was at my first church after seminary and just received my first 'wake-up' call one month into ministry, the first time I faced the dying and family of the dying as pastor of a church.

When I began ministry, preachers were pastors. Being a pastor meant accompanying your folks as they journeyed in life and, especially, as they journeyed to death. Today preachers no longer seem to be pastors, but leaders, entrepreneurs, strategists, marketers, visionaries, performers, administrators, social workers, activists, counselors, humorists and motivators. Forty years ago, most preachers, certainly small-town preachers, were first and foremost pastors. They dwelled amidst their flock and shared the joys and sorrows of living together in faith communities.

Today we have wonderful resources the hospice community brings to the dying. We know more about ministry at the end of life, taking away physical suffering and tending to emotional and spiritual needs. Then it was primarily pastors, fumbling and bumbling along, seeking to bring hope, comfort and healing to those living in their final days and hours.

Who was I to bring comfort to the dying? What did I know? I was not yet

30 years old. I had read the Bible and studied theology. I had taken pastoral care classes and worked as a hospital chaplain in Clinical Pastoral Education for three months. Yet, I had never sat for hours or days at the bedside of someone dying. Death was more a stranger to me than to the one I sought to minister. What do I say to someone whose existence on this earth will soon come to an end? How do you comfort someone who, from a physical perspective, will soon cease to be? In a few days or hours, they will go from a breathing, feeling, thinking being with fears, hopes, passions and love to who-knows-what.

I knew the promise of the resurrection. The Christian faith proclaims that as Christ has been made alive, we, too, shall live. I believed the promise and proclaimed that hope. But was my faith, though springing deep within my heart, only wishful thinking on my part and millions of pastors proclaiming it before me? Were we honest and forthright to our flocks, or were we simply selling snake oil to those dying? Did this faith ring true among those gasping for breath, those who knew today or tomorrow will be their last day with loved ones?

How do you prepare someone to die when you have never died? How do you assure them of glory when you have never seen glory? How do you tell them the grave is not the end, there is life beyond this life, when you have never ventured there? The Scripture passages for life beyond the grave are beautiful. I cling to them. The resurrection of Jesus to life, eternal life, is the nitty-gritty of Christianity. I cling only because of something I call faith. And what is faith? Is it knowledge? Is it a feeling?

The Bible says "faith is the assurance of things hoped for and the conviction of things not seen." How do I understand this conviction deep within telling me there is more to life than what I see with my eyes and touch with my fingers? Though theologians write with great detail about faith, faith remains the mystery it has always been. Though preachers proclaim the gospel of eternal life in Christ with great aplomb, doubt still creeps into the crevices of our being.

I hung up the phone, dressed, and drove five minutes to the nursing home where Dennis's father, Nick, lay. I visited with Nick on two occasions. He was a retired farmer in his late 80's. His family farmed since they arrived in America more than 100 years before. His son, Dennis, and grandson continued the family tradition, though with machinery and business models that would have marveled and perplexed earlier generations. I was a raw, unseasoned pastor, yet Dennis seemed happy to see me. Keeping vigilance over a dying man, especially your father, is not easy. The experience is meant to be shared.

I was never much of a talker, hard for some to believe about a preacher, but true. I was an actuary before entering ministry and an actuary, according to the old joke, is "someone who wanted to be an accountant but didn't have the personality." One doesn't need to be a good talker among the dying, just a good listener. I asked

Dennis how his dad was doing. He gave me an update on his dad's deteriorating health. Nick's body sank into the bed, sparse and spindly, his cheeks hollow and eyes recessed into the skull. A big change had come upon him in the week since I last saw him. His breathing was shallow. He was unable to speak. I didn't know how much Nick could hear or comprehend. I did not know how long he would be with us, but even from my inexperienced acquaintance with death it couldn't be much longer.

I asked Dennis what he remembered best about his father. He talked about growing up on the farm and his father passing on the love of the soil. He reminisced of the good times he shared with his dad in the fields or barn. He told of challenges in farming, how it was changing and what it would be like for his children and grandchildren. Nick lay on his bed, each breath coming with effort. Did he hear Dennis's stories? His lips were tight and grim, but was he smiling on the inside? Was he rejoicing in the memories? Did he enjoy the familiar farm talk?

A nurse came to care for Nick. Dennis asked questions and I excused myself from the room. It was October and the nursing home was bedecked for Halloween. Cardboard jack-o-lanterns, witches and ghosts hung on walls. Coming from the room of a dying man into the dimly lit hallway of early morning, the cardboard figures evoked more spookiness than cheer. I found the skeletons especially a bit unsettling. They resembled the dying man in the bed too closely. Uncharacteristic for me, I took them off the walls and laid them on the nurse's desk saying, "I think these are a little too realistic for here." She agreed and put them in the waste basket.

I returned to Nick's room. Dennis and I talked less and sat in silence more, watching the rise and fall of his father's chest, listening to each breath. For some reason breathing was coming easier. Nick looked more comfortable and less strained. It seemed death would not arrive in the next few hours. It was about 5:00 on Sunday morning. I had a church to unlock, Sunday School to teach and a sermon to preach in a few hours.

Actually, I had a sermon to finish. Oh, how I struggled creating sermons in those early years of ministry! Thoughts and ideas flew around in my head. When I tried putting them on paper though, they seemed trivial and obvious. Surely there was more I should be saying. What was God's Word for my congregation Sunday morning? I fumed and fussed, ranted and raged, prayed and pleaded, trying to put together a sermon. It wasn't until Sunday morning, after working through the angst, I was finally ready to write, beating it out on a manual typewriter. I went home, took a shower, dressed for Sunday morning, drove to church, and finished my sermon.

Nick died two days later. I met with the family, consulted my "Preparing a Memorial Service" notes from a Pastoral Ministry class in seminary, chose what I thought were appropriate Scriptures and music, prepared a sermon/eulogy, typed up prayers in the little black book that would accompany me to funerals for the next 35 years, and conducted my first funeral. The family seemed satisfied; maybe even a little pleased with my first funeral effort. Dennis invited me to the farm for dinner and the family gathering after the service. The extended family seemed a little uneasy with my appearance. They didn't know what do to with a preacher in their midst and hid beer bottles as I entered the room. When I, too, took a beer, they eased up and invited me into the conversation. I accompanied Dennis as he did his evening 'chores'. They were not the chores I remembered from visits to my uncles' farms growing up. Dennis practiced mechanized farming. 'Chores' meant pushing a few buttons here and there to start electric motors and conveyor belts. Feed dropped from chutes overhead and within a few brief minutes scores of cattle were properly fed.

During the next 35 years of ministry, I would repeat this routine of calling on the dying, preparing a memorial service, and caring for the family hundreds of times. The routine never became routine. No two persons are the same. Everyone's story is different; every life sacred and uniquely celebrated. Each time I enter this holy space I pray, inviting the presence and grace of God so we might honor the dying, comfort the grieving, celebrate life, and instill hope. Experience has made the routine more familiar, but never simple. It shouldn't be easy. Pastors are invited to share a holy moment in the life of a family. We are entrusted with secrets and looked to for guidance and hope with respect to eternal things of this world. We are blessed to share in the journeys. Being a pastor, and not just a preacher, is a precious and holy calling.

CHAPTER 2

Grandpa Is Asleep and Won't Wake Up

I was three months shy of my fourth birthday travelling to my uncle's farm. We parked on Main Street in the center of a small town. My mom, grandma, and aunt shopped in nearby stores. My older brother, who was five and a half, and I stayed in the car with Grandpa. I remember Grandpa laughing. He had a large, contagious laugh, and a red face when he laughed. He laughed a lot. He also ate a lot of bacon, cheese and red meat, and drank a fair amount of beer. He laughed, then suddenly his head snapped back. It went way back because this was in the days before head-rests in cars. I don't know what my brother and I thought at first – perhaps this was a joke by Grandpa. But we quickly knew something wasn't right. I knew because I could tell my older brother was worried as he kept shaking Grandpa saying, "Wake up! Wake up!" Those 20 months difference in our ages meant a lot because he had the wherewithal to go find Mom, Grandma or someone.

I stayed in the back seat, right behind Grandpa in the driver's seat. Grandpa's hat had fallen off and was lying in my lap. The hat wasn't a farmer's cap Grandpa wore working in the fields, but a nice felt dress hat, the kind of hat men used to wear whenever they spiffed up and went to town or someplace a little special. For some reason I felt Grandpa should be wearing his hat. I kept putting it back on, only to have it quickly fall off again. With his head tilted back so far the hat had no chance of staying on, but I kept trying.

Staying with Grandpa in the car was frightening. In my memory the car is dim and shadowy. The longer I sat putting on his hat the more I realized something wasn't right. Grandpa's head looked so unnatural and for him to sit without any sound or movement was unreal. I am not sure what I knew about death at that age, but I was scared because I was pretty sure something big was wrong with Grandpa. Putting Grandpa's hat on again and again kept me occupied until my mom, aunt or someone came rushing to the car.

My brother gave them the news, "Grandpa is asleep and won't wake up." At 59 Grandpa had outlived his brothers. They died of heart disease as younger men. The women knew what happened as they ran to the car. My memories of those first few minutes are vague – my mom, aunt and grandma upset and crying; a police officer coming to help. I was still only three and the world of three-year-olds is self-centered. I felt left out amidst the commotion. I remember seeing on the back seat gum and candy my aunt purchased and being too afraid to ask for a piece, though I really wanted it badly. Even as a three-year-old I knew this wasn't a good time to ask. By coincidence, we were parked outside a funeral home. Grandpa was taken in. I tried to be on my best behavior, staying out of the way and not asking questions.

In the days and weeks following I began to understand a little more about death. I knew Grandpa was gone. He went to heaven and heaven was a good place. I rode with my other grandparents in the long funeral procession winding through the cemetery where Grandpa's body would be buried. I slept at Grandma's farm the summer after Grandpa's death. His tractors and farm machinery were sold at a big auction. Life was changing for Grandma. Death, though, was still a mystery for a young boy not yet four.

Two years later I learned more about death. I was five, almost six. We had a new puppy, a little brown mutt we named "Brownie." Brownie was the smartest, cutest puppy ever. My brother and I played Cowboys and Indians with Brownie. (That is what little boys played then.) We shot and Brownie fell over dead (with a little help from our hands) only to rise and be shot again. We played hard and Brownie played hard. We were all tired. My brother and I sat down in the sand box. Brownie went to lie in the shade of the tire of our neighbor's car. We shared a driveway with the neighbor, so Brownie wasn't far. Our neighbor came out of his house and went to his car. It didn't occur to us immediately we should retrieve Brownie. Then my brother, understanding what was to happen, yelled but the neighbor didn't hear. He started the car and backed up. We watched, and heard the awful squeal of Brownie. We ran to the car. Brownie's little head was squished, his body lifeless.

I learned more about death from Brownie – shock, grief, loss, sadness, anger, regret. I lost something I loved a great deal. Maybe I didn't know much about love at age five, but I lost something bringing happiness and would never have it back. My mother tried to mollify our grief bringing our grandma's dog, Mitzie, to stay with us. Mitzie was a good dog but she was a farm dog. City life wasn't fair to her.

Perhaps children in America learn more about death through pets than family members and friends. Death among young people is thankfully uncommon. Our present graveyards don't have numerous headstones bearing witness to children catching whooping cough, pneumonia or polio and dying at a few days or years, or young mothers dying giving birth. Death takes place in hospitals and nursing facilities, not the home. Many children live long distances from grandparents and great aunts and uncles and are unable to attend memorial services. The first memorial service my wife, Carolyn, attended was Nick's at my first church.

Pets are more a part of the family now than they used to. We fuss over them, giving considerable time caring for them and taking them on walks. We spend much money keeping them happy and healthy. Often through the death of a family dog, cat, guinea pig or hamster, children first encounter death and the finality and ubiquity of death. Something precious, something living, is taken away, and will never come back.

Little by little, children discover not only dogs and cats die, but people die and someday they, too, will die. Death is the final destination of all living things. Death is scary for children to discover. It is scary for all of us, and rightfully so. It is the end of life as we know, the end of conscious existence.

I was told Grandpa went to heaven. I believed it. When we are little, we believe anything our parents tell us. We believe in Santa Claus and the Easter Bunny. We eventually figure out they aren't real, and we aren't too scarred from the discovery. We understand growing up means putting childish things behind.

What about heaven and life after death? Are those childish things we put behind also? Some would say yes. Heaven is something humans made up to cope with mortality. Growing up means facing the stark reality life ends with our last heart beat or final breath. We exist no more after that. The eternal life stuff is only meant to comfort us, to make this life more bearable.

This life after death stuff is still something I can't give up. I remain a child. I understand nothing in physics, biology or chemistry suggests life continues beyond the grave, but I cling to that childish notion. How? Through faith, faith in a loving God, faith God created this beautiful world and will never desert it or the creatures God brought forth. Above all I believe, through faith, in the power of the resurrection of Jesus Christ. Somehow that faith, though absurd and childish, seems very real and true, more real than a life that simply vanishes with its last breath. I don't doubt laws of physics and biology, but there seems to be room for the love of God to enter our world also. And that seems to be truer than anything else.

In faith I am still a child, and will remain a child. Through faith in the grace and love of God I believe each of us is a child and will always be a child, a child of God.

CHAPTER 3

She Died an Hour Ago

Near the end of their studies, most seminarians in mainline denominations serve as chaplain interns at a hospital or other healthcare facility in a Clinical Pastoral Education (CPE) program. The program gives seminarians opportunities to experience real-life situations of grief, death and counseling under the supervision of trained CPE Supervisors and in conversation with other seminarians.

The CPE experience is often intense. It is structured so chaplain interns discover much more about themselves than patients on whom they call. Interns prepare verbatims of conversations of visits and write reflection papers on why 'bad things happen to good people' and other such themes. Papers are discussed with the supervisor and peers. The verbatims and papers do not measure CPE interns' aptitude and competence as much as serving as guides to self-discovery. What are the biases, fears, forgotten experiences, childhood anxieties future pastors bring to ministry? How do these influences affect ability to listen and understand feelings, beliefs and souls of patients/parishioners? Self-discovery happens through pointed and very personal questions directed to CPE interns. Why did the intern respond with those words? What motivated him or her to act in such a manner? The questions strip away protective façades and penetrate into the heart of self-understanding. Angry words are sometimes spoken, emotional meltdowns occur, and tears flow as supervisors enable interns to grow in self-awareness.

During my final summer at seminary, I served as a chaplain intern in a CPE program at a local hospital on the north shore of Boston. I was assigned to call on patients in two areas of the hospital: the Cardiac Care Unit (CCU) and a general medical floor. Each morning I looked at computer printouts of patients in my areas, and planned visits. I served before HIPAA and knew patient's name, address, age and diagnosis. Usually I stopped at the nursing station and asked if there was more I should know.

Patients in CCU had life-threatening illnesses of the heart. I listened to patients' fears but often sought to encourage and focus on the positive. New technologies treating heart diseases were proving successful. Bypass surgery corrected blocked arteries, pig valves replaced old leaky heart valves, pacemakers corrected heart arrhythmia, and new medications helped control congestive heart failure. Patients' deaths, when they occurred in CCU, were sudden. The heart stopped, the monitor flat lined, and a nurse called Code Blue. A team of 10-12 physicians, nurses, therapists and technicians rushed to the patient's room beginning CPR and electrical stimulation to the heart. As chaplain, I sat with family members in the waiting room, offering comfort and hope and keeping them from the frenzied scene unfolding inside CCU. When a patient died, a physician came and broke the news to the family. I was present to help guide family members through the first minutes and hours of grief.

A chaplain's ministry differs from a pastor's. Chaplains minister to strangers at a point of crisis, and usually see them no more. Pastors minister to friends with whom they journeyed prior to the crisis and will continue afterwards. The ministry of pastors flows from relationships nurtured over years.

Patients I visited on the general medical floor generally did not have life-threatening illnesses. Death was not imminent. I went to visit a new elderly female patient with the diagnosis of COPD (Chronic Obstructive Pulmonary Disease), a common diagnosis among the elderly. The condition of patients with COPD varied greatly, somewhat healthy to serious respiratory difficulties. I paused at the closed door. A nurse opened the door and exited, indicating it was okay to visit. The blinds of the window were pulled closed and lights were dimmed. The woman's condition quickly unsettled me. Each breath came with labored effort, her whole body convulsing as she fought for air through the oxygen mask covering her nose and mouth. I stood over her bed and took her hand. She gripped my hand with desperation, squeezing it with surprising strength considering her weakened condition. She clung to it as if her survival depended on it. With COPD she was drowning in her own internal fluid and it was as if my hand were the lifeline to pull her out of the turbulent waters sucking her down. Her eyes revealed fear, pleading with me to rescue her. I can't imagine a more terrifying feeling.

I didn't know what to say. Though I offered my hand, I could not pull her out of the waters engulfing her. I just held her hand and looked into her eyes. I said comforting platitudes. "God is with you." "God will see you through this journey." "God will never leave you." "God loves you and always will." I don't know if she heard the words amidst the noise of the oxygen mask and the convulsions of her body. If she did, I am not sure mere words could bring comfort. What she needed was air. I am not sure anything else mattered. I said prayers for comfort. I prayed she might breathe easier.

The patient, whose name I forgot long ago, wasn't the only one struggling. I was distressed watching her contortions and listening to her gasps knowing there was little I could do. I didn't want to be there. I forced myself to stay perhaps 15 minutes. It felt much, much longer. I needed oxygen, too. I needed to get away from that room and take deep breaths of fresh air myself. I pried her hand off of mine. When I let her hand drop, it felt like tossing the life-saving rope into the waters to let the waters consume their victim. Her eyes seemed to plead with me to stay. I left the room, leaving her to drown alone.

When I returned to the room two hours later, the housekeeping staff was sanitizing it preparing it for the next patient. I asked the nurse in the hallway about the elderly woman. The nurse responded, "She died an hour ago." She probably died alone. I don't know if she had family or friends or anyone who cared about her. Her body was already moved to the morgue. My life intersected with this patient for only 15 minutes. I knew nothing at all about her. She spoke to me only through pleading eyes and a tenacious grip of her hand. I could not shake the belief I failed her in her time of need. I left her to die alone, and no one should have to die alone.

This experience gave rise to many questions in my CPE group. Why was I so uncomfortable at her bedside? Why did I feel I had to leave the room rather than remain? Why did I feel so guilty I had left and she died before I returned? Was I afraid of my own death? Was I afraid of dying alone? I don't remember how I responded to such questions. I could not rid myself of the feeling I deserted a dying woman in need.

We only have one journey to death in this lifetime, and none of us know how this journey will proceed. We cannot schedule the time, or work out the details of this journey in advance. We don't know the cause of death, nor the pain and suffering we will undergo. I pray we all have people with us on this journey, that we do not travel the journey alone.

As a pastor I seek to give more time and care to those travelling alone, those without support of friends and family. In their final weeks and days and hours, I want them to know someone is with them. It is not just my presence but, as a pastor, my presence reminding them of the presence of God. God is on this journey with them. God will never leave them. God's love will embrace and Christ's grace will be sufficient for every need. They do not go on this most important journey by themselves.

CHAPTER 4

Where's the Will?

In the congregations I served I had the joy of offering grieving families a wonderful gift, a funeral dinner – a time to gather after a memorial service and enjoy a meal prepared by volunteers of the church. Tension prior to the memorial service is over. Family and friends relax. People reminisce and share stories of the deceased. Out-of-state family members reconnect with seldom-seen cousins, aunts and uncles. Grieving family members receive love from friends while breaking bread around the table. Hope and joy emerge from the sadness of loss. Celebration of life takes hold.

Funeral dinners are special blessings for pastors because we do so little to make them happen. We call a saint in the church and give her the time and number of people to expect. The volunteers do everything else. On the day of the funeral, a steady procession of dishes arrives – fruit and lettuce salads, pasta and Jello, deviled eggs and baked beans, cookies and brownies, whatever the custom of the church. They fill the counters of the kitchen. People are willing and gracious to provide food for a family experiencing loss.

My first funeral dinner as a pastor came six months after beginning in my first parish. The women prepared an incredibly abundant meal. Family and friends gathered in the fellowship hall on the lower level. The deceased was an elderly woman survived by three children, a number of grandchildren, and a few great-grandchildren. The dinner was a time to celebrate her long life, receive the hospitality of the church, and support one another in a time of loss. But I was apprehensive.

When I arrived at the small membership church, I called on members in their homes. Carolyn and I attended birthday parties and family get-togethers. We quickly grew to know not just parishioners but also children and grandchildren.

We listened to their stories and learned joys and dreams, struggles and challenges. We also learned the conflicts between and within church families.

I came to know this elderly woman and her family also. Not long after our arrival we were invited to her son's farm for her great-grandson's birthday party. My eyes grew wide when I saw the delicious steaks put on the grill. On my limited salary steak was not a typical option for us. Farmers may not have much cash, but they eat well. After a bit of grilling time, I became a little concerned about the fate of my steak. I cautiously suggested I thought my steak was probably done. "Oh no!" was the emphatic response. A little while later I offered the same suggestion. "Oh no, not yet," I was assured. Several minutes later the grandson-in-law took the steaks off the grill, cut into one, and said, "Look at that. Perfect. No pink at all." My heart sunk. I like some 'moo' left in my steaks.

That evening I learned of the estrangement of this family from another in the church. I heard details of the incident causing it and then the ensuing conflict. I sensed they wanted me to hear their side in case I heard another version from the other family. I was learning that in the life of this church dynamics surrounding such relationships influenced vision and policy more than the gospel, Scriptures and certainly the pastor.

I also learned the deep division separating the son and his sister from their other sister. Bitterness and hostility ran deep among the siblings, fueled by a seeming partiality of parents who favored one over the other two. The son grieved the division between the siblings. I grieved for the son and the estrangement caused by his parents' favoritism over the years.

I was soon contacted by his estranged sister, who was not a member of the church, asking if I would help her reconcile with her brother. I was new to ministry. I was naïve. I said, "Yes." I called her brother. He told me pointedly his sister was always pulling such stunts. She had no intention of reconciling. "No," he said, "I will not meet with her." I called his sister and told her I was unable to help. Because of my naiveté she succeeded in getting what she really wanted. She began to tell others how she asked her brother's pastor to help reconcile them and her brother said "No." It gave more fuel to support her own virtue and her brother's stubbornness. The brother wasn't happy with me for being used as a weapon in her arsenal of self-righteousness.

I thought preparations for the memorial service went surprisingly smooth. The siblings spoke cordially to each other. They put aside differences to give their mother a proper farewell. They agreed on details of the arrangements and the content of the service. I was doubtful such civility could continue for long.

Shortly after dinner, while the women of the church were clearing the tables and doing the dishes, one of the sisters, the one who got along with her brother, asked if she could speak with me in private. We went upstairs to my office where she asked, "Where's the will?" I responded I had no idea where it was. She continued, "You have to ask my sister and find the will." I said that wasn't my responsibility. She stormed off. She went downstairs while I stayed in my office. Her brother came up. "Where's the will?" he asked. "I don't know," I said for the second time. "Well, you have to find out. Ask my sister." "I am not going to ask your sister. That is not my place." "As a pastor you can do that for us," he said, returning to fellowship hall.

The next knock on the door brought the sister supposedly in the know of the whereabouts of the will. She was. She said, "I have the will, but it's not signed." "Your brother and sister are looking for it," I said. "What should I do?" she said. "I don't know what you should do," I responded. She opened the office door to leave. Her brother and sister stood there. They confronted her, "Where is the will?" They confronted me, "Make her tell us where it is." I said, "I am a pastor, not an attorney. You need to see your attorneys to work this out." That didn't end the matter. The siblings continued to press me. I kept talking about attorneys. Finally I walked back in my office and shut the door. I probably deserved such treatment for being so naïve in becoming involved in their long running quarrels.

I tried to stay out of family quarrels after that, but it wasn't easy. For example, it seemed like every time I called on one older couple I found myself dragged into the middle of a family disagreement. I tried my best to ask questions that would not side with one or the other, but it was hard. Each visit was a new issue. I quit calling on them. Later the man, who served on Church Council, brought before Council that it was more than a year since I visited in their home. In a small church like ours, that was too long. The Council, he said, should reprimand me for lack of attentiveness to parishioners. I couldn't tell the Council why I no longer called on them. I should have told the couple why I quit calling on them. I doubt if he would have brought it to the Council if I had. I sometimes made trouble for myself in ministry by not speaking more forthrightly.

Nearly three years later, one week before my final Sunday at the church, the brother from the funeral dinner came to my office. He talked about how sad he was I did not support him in his disagreements with his sister. After all, he was a member of the church and his sister wasn't. He also said it always bothered him I started at the church on a Monday. The first day of the week is Sunday. I should have started on Sunday. I explained pastors need time to prepare the Sunday morning worship service and sermon. I also explained my final day would be a Sunday making up for that Sunday three years earlier I missed. He still thought I should have started on Sunday. I think I came to understand why my initial contract stipulated the standard four weeks of vacation per year, but limited Sunday mornings off to only two.

When loved ones die, family and friends bring strength, courage and faith.

Common grief unites and shared love comforts. How sad when we are estranged from the very ones who support us in difficult times. How hard to grieve when animosity and resentment crowd out feelings of loss. What inner sores will fester? What wounds will never heal? In Clinical Pastoral Education, I learned anger is often caused by hurt or fear. What could have healed the hurt in this family so they could put away anger and begin to heal?

When we grieve we deal with much more than immediate feelings. We sift through emotions and hurts brewing for years, perhaps generations. They have all been jumbled together and it is hard to sort out. Grieving is sometimes not very simple.

CHAPTER 5

Today Was the First Morning Henry and I Had Breakfast Alone

"In over 40 years of marriage," Louise said, "today was the first morning Henry and I had breakfast alone." She said it so matter-of-factly the import of the words took a while to settle. The first time in their marriage the two of them shared breakfast alone? Louise was talking about Albert, her brother-in-law. Albert was present at every breakfast since they were married. That is why Louise never had breakfast alone with her husband Henry.

We sat in the kitchen of the old farmhouse, a kitchen changed little in 40 years of marriage. In more than 100 years since the house was built the only changes were electric lights, running water and linoleum on the floor. The kitchen called forth timelessness, and German frugality.

Louise and Henry married late in life. They were both over 40 when they tied the knot. No one expected Henry ever to marry. He and his brother Albert lived on the family farm in the house where they were born. Neither had ever left. When Louise married Henry, it was understood Albert was part of the marriage package. Louise moved in but Albert didn't move out. Henry and Albert would work the farm as always. In Louise, they now had cook and housekeeper.

Louise and I waited for Henry to come in from morning chores. The prior morning he found Albert lying peacefully behind the barn, lying on the land he walked every day of his life. He apparently died instantly. The land had been his life and it received his final breath, perhaps the soil now harvesting his spirit just as he harvested crops from that very soil for so many years. In his chores, Henry was doing what he did every other morning.

When Henry arrived in the kitchen, we talked about Albert and life on the farm. I met Albert briefly once or twice. He was shy and uncomfortable around strangers. Unlike Henry and Louise who attended worship faithfully every week, Albert never did. Henry and Louise said they were fine with whatever I planned for the memorial service. Keep it simple, they said, for Albert was a simple man.

Henry and I went out behind the barn. Henry showed me the spot where he found Albert the previous morning. We walked around the barn and the other outbuildings as Henry talked about life on the farm a long, long time ago, when everything a person needed to eat could be raised on the farm, when life seemed much simpler but probably wasn't. Henry remembered many decades earlier when the first federal highway in the area was laid out about a mile away. Of course, the blockheads in government built the highway on land that flooded every spring. After a few years they finally got wise and re-routed it on higher ground with a new bridge. That was before the bypass was built around the town, which was before the interstate now carrying cars and trucks at speeds Henry would have never imagined when the first highway went in 65 years earlier. Henry was always suspicious of new-fangled inventions and ideas. He was sure every space shot caused it to rain. "How can you put something like that up in the sky without it causing havoc with the weather and the intended way of nature?"

I thought more about Louise's comment, "The first morning that Henry and I had breakfast alone." It didn't just mean Albert at the breakfast table. It also meant no honeymoon, no vacation, not even a weekend away. Life centered on the farm – on land and livestock. Vacations and weekends away were for city folks. They were frivolous, unnecessary. Louise wasn't complaining. She was just stating fact.

Many of us live in a world where our choices seem to have no limits. Our horizons are boundless. We are encouraged to dream, and dream big. We can be anything we want to be. Nothing holds us back. So some of us dream, and follow those dreams. We dare, and venture places far and wide. We have been blessed with education, ambition and freedom to come and go. We skirt about the planet in airplanes, jetting across continents and oceans as if it were just as natural as could be.

Henry and Louise never went further from home than the time it took to return for morning or evening chores. They represent the world in which most of the human race has lived. Opportunities are limited by when and where we are born, parents, economics, common sense and much more. At an early age we make commitments and stick to those commitments. Maybe there are dreams never chased. Maybe dreams are reined in to fit our realm of living. Spending 40 years never having breakfast alone with your husband isn't necessarily a bad thing. Spending 80 years working the same land day in and day out is not lamented but celebrated.

One summer during seminary I served a small 'new church start' in the western mountain area of Maine, a gorgeous spot to live for the summer. We stayed just a couple of miles from the Appalachian Trail. I calculated the average age of the congregation at about 72. Folks in the church were hardy Yankees. The men worked cutting trees in the woods. The women stayed home tending gardens and raising children. Carolyn and I visited with church folks one weekend prior to the summer. We shared a simple Yankee supper of hot dogs and beans with homemade donuts for dessert. After dinner I sat down in the living room expecting discussion about summer plans, instead everyone was quickly out the door. I felt a little embarrassed and asked my host if I said something inappropriate or insulting. "Oh no," she responded, "everyone wanted to get back home in time for Lawrence Welk."

During that summer I got to know some of these hardy Yankees, at least as much as a Midwesterner can get to know Maine Yankees in a summer. One older woman was Lucy. Lucy lived in a simple four-room unpainted cabin. The wood floors of her house were unvarnished and the furniture basic and practical. I didn't see anything frivolous except the piano, which Lucy still played very well. Lucy dressed plainly and, of course, never wore make-up. She pulled her grey hair back in a simple ponytail. On my first visit with Lucy I was amazed. Lucy was anything but a simple widow of a backwoods lumberman. She was well-read in classic literature and voiced thoughtful opinions about world situations. She was sharp and articulate, challenging my own thinking. I didn't expect someone with such an expansive world view living in a cabin in the mountains of Maine.

Why, I thought, did someone of her intellect and interests stay so close to home in the backwoods of Maine? Why hadn't she ventured to the big city, received a college degree and pursued a professional career? Why? Probably because women born in the little towns of Flagstaff and Dead River didn't do that. They married a local boy, settled down and had a family. Lucy did that, but she also explored the world through books, newspapers and magazines.

Roots are important to folks like Henry, Louise, Albert and Lucy. In preparation for an anniversary celebration for the church Henry and Louise attended, I researched and wrote a church history. As soon as Henry read it, he came into my office (the only time I remember him coming to my office) and thanked me profusely. He said I told it just the way it was and he appreciated that. I think what he especially liked was the prologue to the original German Constitution. It had never been translated into English. It was written in an old German script even people fluent in German had difficulty deciphering. I was blessed to find a retired

Lutheran pastor in a nearby nursing home able to translate it. It began as follows:

> *"Brothers are we who are descendants of the German nation. We have left our old fatherland, the sweet Saxon land. Most of us left with bleeding hearts, tore ourselves away from everything that was loveable and dear, and looked far away westward to find a home for the future."*

This devotion to our native land is something many of us today cannot understand. We lack rootedness. We chase dreams searching for the new. When we decide to connect to our roots, we do so through genealogical searches on the web. Henry understood the devotion to roots the church founders possessed and the pain that would come when leaving the place where one was born and raised. For them life wasn't about the number of places visited and sights seen. It wasn't about new experiences and thrills. It was about faithfulness to one's calling, about growing where you are planted.

CHAPTER 6

I Wish You Had Done the Service

"I really wished you had done the service," John said as I visited with him and his wife, Ruth, in their lovely home a few days after the memorial service for John's brother, Dick. John continued, "But our daughter really wanted her pastor. And since she was so close to Dick, I felt we should honor her request." John was too much of a gentleman to speak poorly of someone, but I sensed he was disappointed with the memorial service for his brother. He originally asked if I would perform it. I said, 'yes.' He called later though, and said his daughter's pastor would do it. He still wanted me to participate and asked if I would read a couple of Scriptures. I was happy to help in any way. Dick was not a parishioner. My only contact with him was a visit to the nursing home shortly before his death.

If John was disappointed with the memorial service, I understood why. Dick's name was not mentioned. The service was as generic as could be – generic words of welcome, generic prayers and a generic sermon about the brevity of life and sinfulness of human beings with a come-to-Jesus invitation at the end. I sensed the service was repeated many times. It didn't matter who lay in the casket. After the service, the pastor said to me he once read an obituary at a memorial service and, when reading the names of the children, one young woman cried out in anguish and ran from the funeral parlor. He later learned the young woman was a daughter of the deceased, though estranged from the family. Not expecting her to show, the family intentionally left her name off the obituary. The pastor felt betrayed and embarrassed for being put in such an unpleasant situation. Since then he did not mention the name of the deceased in memorial services.

I assume the pastor's story was true and not an excuse for laziness. But how sad to attend generic memorial services! In a memorial service we grieve the loss of not just anyone, but someone special, someone whom we loved and journeyed with for perhaps many years. Life will be different now. We grieve our loss. Grief is personal and focused. How do we grieve the loss of someone whose life was deeply interwoven with ours in a generic service when no life is generic?

A memorial service is also time to celebrate. We celebrate the life of not just anyone, but someone special. The paths they journeyed are unique, their personality and gifts uniquely theirs, and the legacy they leave is unique. A memorial service celebrates a particular life. The Scriptures, music, eulogies, and prayers are chosen to evoke memories, call forth stories, give voice to deep feelings, and claim God's promises of eternal life for a particular loved one. What a blessing when family members and friends come together to offer glimpses into a loved one's life and tell how they have been touched. Such services comfort, encourage and build one another in faith and hope. Though God's Spirit is strong and works through many types of worship, a memorial service capturing the spirit of a loved one helps grieving to begin in healthy ways.

Creating a memorial service takes time and thought. If we have never known the deceased, we spend time with the family to elicit memories. We encourage close friends and family members to reminisce and tell stories. By spending time with the family, we can uncover some of the stresses and tensions and be sensitive in addressing them during the service. We also uncover the faith language and traditions that speak to them. We select and employ appropriate theological expressions and imagery to minister to the family. Memorial services are not intended to convert the grieving to our theological ways.

I have theological understandings shaping my thinking about God and giving me hope and peace. I am rooted in orthodox Christianity. I proclaim the resurrection of Jesus from the dead and believe we shall be raised with him. I proclaim a God of love, grace and forgiveness, a God welcoming us to our eternal home with a warm embrace, offering hope amidst heartache and faith amidst doubt. I do not, however, impose my theological understandings into the service in opposition to grieving loved ones. Other times in ministry are more appropriate for theological discussion. Memorial services are not about the pastor but the deceased and surviving loved ones. It is sometimes hard because we do not know the families and they may be reticent to share, but we do our best to create a meaningful service.

Attentive and thoughtful pastoral care enables us to create appropriate memorial services. If we journey with parishioners through good times and bad, if we cry with them in grief and celebrate with them in joy, if we share everyday moments of community and togetherness, we are better prepared to create a service celebrating their life and honoring their faith. If we neglect pastoral care, creating a meaningful memorial service is much harder. Hospital and home visits are important to know parishioners and their families.

Our words must have integrity. They capture the essence of a deceased loved one. Eulogizing a saint is a joy, but not everyone we bury is a saint. We do not make them saints if they were not. We must be honest, though not cruel or judgmental. Some misdeeds are left unsaid. Still, we must grieve a realistic portrayal of the deceased, not an idealized one. Only then can healing begin. An unrealistic portrayal conflicts family and loved ones even more. It brings more confusion and dissonance to process before healing proceeds.

I am sad when a family does not wish for any kind of memorial service. I think being with loved ones to remember, grieve, celebrate and hear the promise of life in Jesus Christ is important. It gives comfort and initiates healing. It honors the deceased. Maybe the person was a real scoundrel. Even a scoundrel's life needs to be remembered.

As pastors we have unique opportunities in memorial services to encourage healthy grieving. We remember loved ones in authentic ways, celebrate unique gifts, give thanks for blessings and call forth Scriptures that restore hope. In these ways we invite God's grace to begin its healing work among us.

CHAPTER 7

He Died Doing What He Loved

I sat in my office Sunday morning, undoubtedly stressed as I was every Sunday morning trying to finish my sermon and worship preparations, when the phone rang around 8:00 am. "Neal, this is Mona. They just took Lafe to the hospital. He collapsed in the kitchen when he came in from morning chores. Kendra and Troy were doing CPR on him when the ambulance arrived. I'm sure he will be okay. You don't have to bother going over." It was classic Midwest farm understatement. You were raised to be independent and self-sufficient. You hated to inconvenience anyone else, even if a loved one was dying or dead.

I knew it couldn't be good. Mona was Lafe's daughter-in-law. She and Lafe's son Butch lived with their children across the field from Lafe and his wife, Lucille. Lafe and Butch farmed land that had been in the family for generations. They were devoted farmers, couldn't imagine doing anything else. Farming wasn't a living; it was a calling. It flowed in their veins. Butch was a great basketball player in high school and went to college to play ball. He left after one year; no point going to college just to play basketball. He knew he would return to the farm. Farming was a gift from God. There was no more honorable calling than raising food to feed hungry people.

Several farmers attended my little church. I discovered two types. There were the worriers – not enough rain, too much rain, too cold, too hot, prices too low. Farming was not a love but an affliction or punishment, something they couldn't escape. It was not to be enjoyed but endured. Then there were the Lafes. Farming was a trust they honored with diligence, hard work and wisdom.

In a dreadful drought-stricken year, I remember the patience with which Lafe anticipated a rain that never came. At first, he said, "The roots will go deep looking for water and the plants will be healthier." Then for a long time he said simply, "With a little rain we can still get a good yield." At the end of the season he plowed his fields under because there was nothing to harvest. He talked about spring planting and possibilities for the coming year. "The year following a drought always yields a good crop," he believed.

The hospital was across the street from the church. I walked to the waiting area outside the emergency room. When I saw the faces of the family, I knew immediately Lafe's fate. "Lafe's gone," Lucille wailed. "My man's gone. My man's gone. What am I going to do? What am I going to do?" Lafe did his chores as usual that morning. He came back to the house and hung his hat and coat by the back door. He went into the kitchen for breakfast and fell to the floor. The doctor said he was probably dead before he landed.

There was no suffering, no pain, just instant death. Lafe, strong and fit by every measure except the blood vessels in his heart, died at age 73. His only weakness was revealed through occasional nitro-glycerin pills slipped under his tongue for angina. At the time, being a young whippersnapper of only 30, I thought Lafe lived a full life. I now know he died young.

Lafe never had to discover his purpose in life. From the day he was born to the day he died, he knew it. It was raising crops and livestock. Many of us today spend much time and agony discovering what we are meant to do. We try this, that and the other, things we never imagined. Our lives take twists and turns. Meaning is a lifelong search. We are always looking but never finding. Lafe's purpose in life was always clear: faith, family and farming.

In the following days I heard many times, "He died doing what he loved." Lafe did, right to the final minute of his life. A lot of folks told me they hope to die the same way, going quickly enjoying life to the fullest to the very end. They would be very content to forego the physical pain, mental deterioration and dementia of end-of-life suffering.

Dying suddenly, as Lafe did, is hard on those remaining. When a loved one is taken from us instantly and without warning we are left shocked and crushed. With long terminal illnesses, we do much grieving before death. In sudden death, grief floods us like a torrential downpour.

Though the choice isn't mine, I would like a little time to prepare myself for death. It seems, for life to have its full cycle, time to say goodbye to loved ones and a world that has given us life and sustenance is a good thing. The pains and hurts, maybe even the confusion and loss of memory, enable us to look beyond the present world to the surprise awaiting. Life seems to have a more proper ending if we can say goodbye.

Lafe was a dearly beloved rock of the church, strong and quiet, faithful and giving, selfless and humble. In a family-sized church beset by factions and contentiousness, Lafe was respected by all. I waited until the joys and concerns of prayer time to announce his death. I wasn't up to repeating the story time and again as I greeted the congregation as they entered. A gasp, accompanied by weeping and tears, rolled through the congregation. Most parishioners had grown up in the church. Their families worshipped together for generations. The news stunned Lafe's church family just as it stunned those related to him by blood.

I continued with the sermon and worship service I prepared. I didn't know what else to do. Whatever I preached that day was irrelevant to the feelings of the congregation at that moment, irrelevant to my own feelings. I didn't want to preach it and the congregation didn't want to hear it. We just wanted to grieve. So we grieved as I preached a sermon no one heard. It felt like the longest sermon I ever preached.

Gathering in the sanctuary for the memorial service two days later, we were ready to celebrate Lafe's life. The grandchildren, gifted in music, sang songs and gave testimony to Lafe's enduring spirit and gentle ways. We honored a good life, a true servant of the Lord and an inspiration and model to all, someone who tried to live as Jesus lived. At the cemetery we said our final goodbyes as a cold December wind roared across the frozen fields. Grief and loss was still strong, but joy, hope and thankfulness were rising up and casting out the gloom. The hardy and faithful would persevere and continue. The good news of the resurrection echoed within.

Lafe's farm continues in the family today. His granddaughter and her husband have taken it over. In Lafe's day women weren't farmers, they were farmers' wives. They may have worked in the fields as hard as their husbands, but they were still viewed as "farmers' wives" and not "farmers." Things have changed. Women now are farmers, and sometimes men are farmers' husbands. The farming practices have also changed on Lafe's farm. The focus is no longer on yield and raising grain and beef efficiently. The farm now looks to non-GMO and organic crops and sustainable practices. There is more planning to preserve fertile soils for future generations. Lafe's descendants want to grow the healthiest foods possible for their customers. I think Lafe would approve of the changes. Another Lafe, a young great-grandson of the Lafe who died on the way to the kitchen floor, now lives on the farm. Perhaps another generation of the family will continue Lafe's calling and faithfulness.

CHAPTER 8

I Am Going to Live to Be 100

"How old do you think I am?" Bud asked as we sat in the living room of his castle. It wasn't actually a castle, just an ordinary house, but Bud felt the house was his castle. His wife, a couple of grown daughters and a son-in-law were also present, but Bud reigned over the conversation. A couple of grandchildren ran in and out, hopping on and off Grandpa's lap. Bud had not yet attended worship, but his family was visiting our church regularly. I was trying to know these new folks, although that evening I mostly got to know Bud. That was okay. The family deferred to Bud and if I received his approval, the family would accept me also.

Visitors to our church were rare and visitors who returned a second or third time were even rarer. When I arrived, I looked at the record of new members coming into the church over the past years. Every one entered through marriage or birth. Our congregation was a family, a dysfunctional one, but nevertheless a family. We fought, loved and cared for each other, and then fought some more. Sometimes fights were passed from mother to child to grandchild. I think when visitors entered the sanctuary and saw each family claiming its own pew, usually a safe distance from their nearest antagonist, they sensed maybe this was not the most welcoming congregation.

When I raised the welcoming issue at a Council meeting I was quickly brushed aside. "Of course, we are a friendly congregation," Amos said. "I greet everyone who comes in." And he did. Amos claimed the aisle seat on the pew closest to the back door (quickest exit after the Benediction to beat the Lutherans to the buffet line at the Ponderosa) and nodded to everyone who entered. He never said a word, but in Amos' world a nod conveyed full acceptance and welcome into the church. You don't need to waste time with words when a nod says it all.

"How old do I think you are?" I repeated Bud's question aloud. This was not a time for honesty. "29?" I replied, with a smile on my face. "53," Bud responded. "I don't look it, do I?" "Not at all," I said, again not a time for honesty. "I am going to live to be 100," Bud continued. "I am as strong and fit as ever."

Bud owned a tree trimming business. I sometimes saw him around town standing on a sidewalk or street directing his crew as they lopped off branches high in a tree. I could tell he loved his work. He laughed a lot, was proud of what he did and enjoyed his success. He was pleased with his life. He had a wife and daughters who doted over him, grandkids who admired him, and a tree-trimming business that gave him joy. I must have passed his muster because his family continued to worship with us on Sunday mornings.

Less than two months later I received a call from a volunteer chaplain at the hospital. Bud's family was asking if I could come to the hospital. Bud just died. I couldn't believe it. I had seen him less than two hours earlier directing his crew as usual. "Well," the chaplain said, "maybe you were one of the last to see him alive. His crew found him lying in his truck, dead from a heart attack. There was nothing anyone could do."

I gathered with the family back in the living room of Bud's castle the next day, this time to plan a memorial service for the man who was going to live to 100. Bud was loved and respected by his family, and he loved them. None were ready to say goodbye. Everyone wanted him to live to 100. In the memorial service we honored and celebrated the 53 years Bud did enjoy among us.

We never know when our end here on earth will come. I visited with a woman in my congregation for the first time. A photo on her coffee table showed a young handsome man at the helm of a sailboat. It was a windy day. Whitecaps were on the lake. The man looked confident and in control. I asked my parishioner who he was. She said it was her son. Then she added, "The photo was taken less than 15 minutes before he died." She told the story. He was sailing with his girlfriend on a lake in southern Indiana on a cold, windy March day. They were having a wonderful time. She took his photo. A short time later a wind gust caught the sail and the boom swung free across the back of the boat knocking her son unconscious and into the water. His girlfriend knew little about sailing. By the time she could get the sailboat under control and get help, her son had drowned.

The Psalmist says, "The days of our life are 70 years, perhaps 80 if we are strong." Bud, who was going to live to 100, never saw his 54th birthday. We may wish for long life, but life has no guarantees. Life was good to Bud. He wasn't wealthy in the eyes of the world, but his home was his castle and he felt as rich as a king. He wanted life to go on just as it had for years and years, until he was 100 years old or more. He would never grow tired of it.

Our little church had another new family visiting. A young couple appeared one Sunday, with five children under the age of six. They sat down front where there was plenty of room, filling up the third pew on my left. When they entered, every eye in the sanctuary followed their progress to the front. The young family seemed unaware of the attention. The father appeared shy and backwards, the mother attractive and poised. The whole family, though neat and clean, appeared to wear second-hand clothing that didn't fit quite right.

The children did a remarkable thing. All five sat quietly and attentively the whole worship service, never disrupting or calling attention to themselves. Even the child whom I thought might have ADD was entertained by his mother and never a disruption. Carolyn and I had one son at the time. These five children made less commotion together than our son did by himself. I was amazed.

I was pleased to see the faithful saints in the church greeting the family following the service. Perhaps we were learning to be more welcoming. When I spoke to them, the mother's voice surprised me. In my usual stereotyping, I expected the mountain twang of a family newly arriving from Appalachia. Instead, it was a calm, self-confident voice of an articulate young woman. The voice did not match my prejudice.

The family returned week after week. The women in the church embraced them. I learned a little of their story. The couple was newly married. Each had full custody of children from previous marriages. They were blending five children into one family. They were beginning life anew. The economy in our community was poor and the parents both struggled to find work. They could not afford childcare and needed shifts that didn't overlap. Life was difficult but the mother, who seemed to be the strength in the family, was always positive. The saints in the church helped with groceries and occasionally with childcare. The father's teenage brother also lived with the family since both of his parents were deceased. My heart went out to all of them. Life seemed so hard. I didn't know how they got by.

One day I heard the teenage brother was arrested for shoplifting at the drug store across the street from their house. It didn't seem right. He was a good kid, obedient and quiet, anything but a rebel. I stopped by their house to see how they were doing. The mother was in their tiny living room dwarfed by a big pile of laundry. Children ran in and out of the room. I picked up some children's underwear and T-shirts and began helping her fold. Yes it was true, the young mother said. He was caught shoplifting, nothing more than a couple of candy bars. He did it clumsily, almost like he wanted to be caught.

A bigger difficulty arose because the brother was supposed to be home watching the younger children at the time. His absence meant the children were not supervised. The police reported the situation to the county child and family services department. These young parents, who loved their children so much, were now being investigated for neglect.

The teenage brother was in an upper bunk in the boys' bedroom. I went back and we talked for a bit. He didn't know why he did it. He just had to get out of the house, he said. He was sorry for what he did and for the trouble he was causing the family. I felt sorry for him. Teenagers were supposed to be having fun, not staying home after school watching a house full of little children.

I returned to the pile of laundry and listened some more to the seemingly insurmountable obstacles facing this family. And then this poised, positive young woman broke down in tears. "I can't go on another day," she sobbed. "I can't take it anymore. I can't go on." She buried her face in the laundry and cried. It didn't last long. She got herself together and apologized. I told her how much I admired all she was doing. I assured her life would get better. They would make it through this period in their lives. I told her I didn't know how, only that in some way they would. God knew their pain. I offered a prayer and left wondering how some folks continue under the load they bear.

A short time later the family moved to a nearby town where they had relatives. There they could receive help with childcare and other needs from parents and family members. I lost track of them. I pray they received the strength and hope they sought and deserved.

The little church had two families visiting. In one family, a middle-aged man thought he would live a long time. He looked forward to many more tomorrows because life was so good. He died suddenly, without warning. In the other family a young woman, nearly 30 years younger, wasn't sure she could make it to tomorrow. Life was too overwhelming today. Our perspective of today and tomorrow depends a lot on what we are dealing with in our lives.

Jesus tells us not to worry about tomorrow. It isn't because life will be easier tomorrow. It is because, in Jesus' words, "tomorrow will bring worries of its own." Jesus was a realist. Life is not easy. Our hope is not in an easy life but in a God who cares about us, loves us and will never leave us, especially when life sucks.

CHAPTER 9

Help Me! Someone Please Help Me!

Mary was uncovered once again, lying bare naked on the bed in her room at the nursing home. I didn't blame the staff at the facility. I knew from previous visits Mary thrashed about her bed uncontrollably, covers and clothes quickly discarded. Mary was crying out as she usually did, "Help me! Help me! Please help me! Somebody help me!" During my many years of visiting nursing homes, I heard those words often, sometimes shouted loud and strong from inside a room, sometimes barely audible from a woman with dementia slumped in her wheelchair grabbing my arm as I passed. The words always filled me with guilt. Someone needed my help and I did nothing. I just walked on past. I wasn't much of a pastor.

I walked out of Mary's room to find a nursing assistant to cover her up. Dressing a resident and making her bed was not part of my job as a pastor. More importantly, the Mary I remembered would have been mortified for me to perform such a personal task on her body.

Mary had been a proud lady. She dressed in high-quality timeless fashions, always, even for a trip to the grocery store or gas station. Though her farmhouse had a long gravel driveway her Cadillac shined, always. Her house, with Victorian style furniture and fancy floral carpeting, was spotless, always. Mary told how each week she re-positioned the charming little knick-knacks adorning her end tables after the housekeeper left. I am not sure why someone as fastidious as Mary needed a weekly housekeeper, but Mary took great pride in herself and her world.

Her pride wasn't an arrogant pride. It was an innate pride saying one should present one's self at one's best, always. She wasn't trying to show off or prove herself better than another, nor was she calling attention to herself. It was just the opposite. In being our best we honor those around us, a way of saying we value their company. Our friends are important. We treat them as special people by looking our best and offering them the best we have.

The proud Mary disappeared quickly. Not long before she entered the nursing home, Carolyn and I invited her and a couple of other single elderly women in the church over for dinner on Christmas evening. We were home by ourselves and knew they, too, would be alone on Christmas. Holidays, especially Christmas, are intended to be shared. Mary brought her delicious persimmon pudding to dinner and entertained us with stories of Christmases past.

Priscilla was also at Christmas dinner. Priscilla's farm was across the road from Mary. At one time the infamous Reno Brothers lived there. The Reno Brothers Gang was the original outlaw gang. It terrorized the community for several years after the Civil War. The brothers were responsible for the first successful train robberies. Money they stole was never recovered and every year one or two folks asked Priscilla permission to dig on her property. They were confident they knew where it was hidden. Of course no one ever found the money or, if they did, never told Priscilla.

Neither Mary nor Priscilla ever married. Mary had a boyfriend in another town. They had been dating for over 25 years. Mary loved her freedom and didn't want to give it up for a man. She enjoyed doing as she pleased and going where she wanted without answering to a spouse. She was social, funny and quite capable of carrying out her farm and business affairs herself.

Priscilla was quite the opposite. She was reclusive and withdrawn and felt awkward and adrift in social situations. She never learned to drive and relied on Mary, her lifelong neighbor, to take her places. I picked Priscilla up once per month to help fold and address the church's monthly newsletter. I could have done the work more quickly myself but it was the only activity getting Priscilla out on a regular basis. The church had no secretary and an old hand crank duplicator. Oh, how I used to swear at that machine as I ran off the weekly bulletins and monthly newsletters. I inevitably had purple ink all over my hands. I hoped no parishioners came into the building and heard my curses. Within a month after I left, the church purchased a new copier.

The little church I served went through a pastor about every two years. In each case the pastor was happy to escape and the congregation only too happy to pack him up. Priscilla told me she never voted yes to call a pastor. That way she didn't feel responsible when each one failed. I never asked if she voted for me.

Priscilla's last name was the same as a famous rock star from our town. She was a distant cousin of his, and even more distant in her lifestyle. Although the rock star wrote beautiful songs about the small town he grew up in, I never found anyone in town who predicted his success. Everyone was sure he would never amount to anything. The son of one parishioner had a high school band and rebuffed the future star's attempt to join. It reminded me of Jesus when he said a prophet never has respect in his hometown. Before long Priscilla joined her friend Mary in the nursing home.

The proud, outgoing Mary was gone. The Mary before me, thrashing and yelling, incoherent and unaware of the world passing by, was an unrecognizable lady. Even her once ample frame was emaciated, her sturdy legs nothing but toothpicks. How ashamed Mary would have felt if she knew she would be in such a place before she died.

Her tidy little house was also in disarray. Her niece, her power of attorney and presumably her heir, encamped in her house and appropriated the Cadillac. Her niece said goodbye to her husband and moved her two children, new fiancé and dog into the meticulous rooms of Mary's former abode. When I visited, the house was in an upheaval, a mishmash of half-started building projects, Mary's lovely floral carpet and Victorian furniture covered in sawdust.

Our journey to death may inflict indignities of many kinds. We travel to places we prayed we would never see. We lose remaining fragments of dignity and pride. We become people unrecognizable to family and friends. We listen to the promises of the apostle Paul in II Corinthians, "So we do not lose heart. Even though our outer nature is wasting away, our inner nature is being renewed day by day. For this slight momentary affliction is preparing us for an eternal weight of glory beyond all measure, because we look not at what can be seen but at what cannot be seen; for what can be seen is temporary, but what cannot be seen is eternal." In faith we pray those promises are true.

In those early days of ministry I gave premarital couples a personality assessment to complete. Mary's niece and her fiancé completed the assessment. Upon looking over the results, I was dumbfounded. Each received the highest score possible in Self-Discipline. I didn't understand. These were two wandering, lost people who stumbled upon each other. Their lives appeared to be disasters, unable to hold jobs, maintain relationships, and finish what they started. When we talked about the results in premarital meetings, they acknowledged their lives were somewhat of a mess. They were now trying very conscientiously to find order and direction. They talked a great deal with each other about the need for discipline.

I married them by the persimmon tree behind Mary's farmhouse. I left the church a couple of months later and don't know how their marriage unfolded. One of the drawbacks in ministry is we enter the stories of people's lives but then don't see the story develop and evolve after we leave. On occasion I receive emails from couples to update me on their lives and assure me, despite misgivings I may have felt at the time of their marriage, it worked out just fine. I pray Mary's niece and her new husband discovered the discipline and love they sought and brought some order to their lives and Mary's beautiful house. Mary deserved it. Mary would have been proud of her niece.

CHAPTER 10

Hello, Pastor. It Is So Thoughtful of You to Come

It was an intimate gathering around the gravesite of Kelli – Mom and Dad, Grandma and Grandpa, a couple of aunts, an uncle or two, and some young cousins. I had never seen a baby's casket before. It was so small, almost like a plaything, except the body of a human baby lay inside. Kelli lived less than a month. Her parents received the devastating news at Kelli's birth that her heart was deformed. Doctors could do nothing to fix it. Her heart would soon give out. Kelli would die in a matter of days. She made it 23 days.

I barely knew the parents when I called on them at the Pediatric Intensive Care Unit of the hospital. I was new as Associate Pastor at the church. They were even newer, attended infrequently, and didn't participate in fellowship events for young couples. Many young families attended the church and I was just learning their names and stories, joys and sorrows, dreams and failures, faith and unbelief. At the hospital I expected to find a couple devastated by news of the imminent loss of their precious baby, aching and crying, and angry at God. Instead, I found two young parents delighting in the miracle and blessing of the gift of this small baby, marveling at her little hands, putting their hands through the holes in the incubator to stroke her hair and tickle her feet. Yes, they heard the doctor's diagnosis, but chose to celebrate and love this beautiful gift each day God gave them together.

For several days they filled their lives with the miracle of new life, spending as much time at the hospital as jobs and schedules permitted. Grandma and Grandpa, aunts and uncles, came to visit and adore little Kelli. I could not help but think the baby lay in her protective, life-supporting little bubble in PICU feeling she was the luckiest baby in the world with such loving parents and family. Mourning, crying, and anger were absent at her bedside. There was weeping, sadness and grieving when they left the hospital, but around little Kelli only joy and love.

The memorial service around the little grave celebrated Kelli's brief life. We did not mourn what could have been – joys of a child's laughter, blossoming teen years, the beautiful young woman Kelli would have grown into, children she would have given birth to. We thanked God for the joy of sharing this little spark of delight for 23 days and faith and love that increased and spread because of Kelli. The world was a dearer, more precious place because she came to be with us. We offered Kelli back to her Maker, looking forward to being united with her once again.

* * *

Lindsay was in the springtime of life turning 21 years old. She was pretty, outgoing and smart. Everyone loved Lindsay. It was hard not to. Her smile cheered you, her laughter contagious. Lindsay, though, was not enjoying the pastimes of other college students. Her life was not football games, Saturday night dates and late night chats with girlfriends. Her life was chemotherapy, needles and IV's, feeling tired and worn, losing hair and throwing up lunch. Lindsay was fighting cancer. Her body was losing, but her spirit winning.

I did not know Lindsay well. I visited her on occasion. Others on staff knew her better and did most of the visiting. I saw her big smile on Sunday mornings. I saw her composure and joy as people gathered around to ask how she was doing, and then receive the courage she bestowed in return. I knew it must hurt a great deal to say goodbye to life at such a young age, never enjoy sights and experiences the rest of us take for granted. Amidst that inner sadness, she blessed her family and friends and embraced life to the fullest of her abilities.

* * *

I rang the doorbell and walked through the unlocked front door. "Betty, it's me. Pastor Neal," I announced. "Oh hello, Pastor. It is so thoughtful for you to come. Please sit down and tell me what's happening in the church," Betty smiled welcomingly as I entered the room. I sat in the overstuffed chair across from the couch and told her a little news from the church. I think she knew it all already. Her husband, Bill, and friends from the church kept her well-informed, but it was good to talk about people and activities so much a part of her life. The church and her faith always gave her strength. Bill continued to take her to Sunday morning worship as long as it was possible. She entered with an ever-present smile, greeting friends as she slowly and painfully pushed her walker down the aisle. Bill put wheels on the walker. Though wheels would become standard equipment for walkers in a few years, wheels were a novelty then.

It was difficult for Betty to go out now. Her emphysema was progressing and breathing becoming more and more difficult. Smoking had inflicted its usual damage. For years a tube running from her nose to an oxygen tank gave her lungs needed air. She went nowhere without the tank. Her osteoporosis also seemed more debilitating. Her bones were brittle. Turning over in bed or reaching to flip on a light might crack a rib or vertebrae unless done with gentleness and forethought. Every now and then an involuntary gasp escaped if she moved in a way to ignite pain in one of her many fractures. But Betty regained her composure and the smile quickly returned. Betty was only in her early 60s, but had the body of a much older woman. Her spirit was young and new.

"Now," Betty asked, "how are Carolyn and the kids?" I talked about our lives for a while – our trips, outings, get-togethers, antics of our children. Only then did I ask, "And Betty, how are you doing?" And she would tell me. She gave me the usual gloomy news of her health and doctor visits. She spoke of difficulty breathing and new fractures since my last visit. She did so without lament and complaint, giving me the details to help me understand better what she was experiencing. She did not dwell on her illnesses. We quickly turned to the lives of her children and grandchildren. We talked about life in the old neighborhood of another generation. She told of an older man in our church who, in the days before state-run lotteries, ran a numbers racket. She and other housewives delved into grocery money for a dollar to buy a number when he went door to door. Maybe one week they would win and splurge on a new hat or dress.

Betty did not let her illness define or defeat her. She remained positive in the face of pain and suffering, even knowing her premature death was only a short time away. I left each visit with Betty feeling my faith had been renewed. I was blessed to call on Betty.

*   *   *

So often in ministry our parishioners minister to us. They open us to the workings of God's grace, teach us about hope and faith, and enable us to be better pastors. In my young ministry I saw persons too young to face death or lose a child who faced their challenges with courage. In their dying and grieving, they built the faith of the church and blessed the Body of Christ.

Some people of faith find strength and courage to encounter hardship and trial, even death, with grace, dignity, hopefulness and good humor. For others the trial becomes too much. They question, despair and struggle to find hope in the God in whom they believe. They believe God surrounds them with love and journeys with them into the shadows of death but they cannot discover God's presence in their time of need. I don't know how or why some are able to persevere while others succumb to despair. Is it the depth of prayer, relationships, or this thing called faith? Or is it simply optimism, perseverance, a joyful personality or DNA? We are unique beings and our journeys are all different. We never know for sure how we will face difficult times ahead. I am thankful I have been blessed to have many show me life-giving ways of traveling through trial and death. I pray when my time comes I can proceed with the grace of friends who have gone before.

CHAPTER 11

He Was a Good Man

I knew loud weeping, moaning and a flood of tears were about to begin. I was winding up words of remembrance of the deceased and moving into words of hope and faith, lifting up promises of eternal life in God's presence. Weeping usually started with a large sob from a daughter or sister of the deceased. Wailing then spread through the room like exploding popcorn kernels. Women folk were soon all bound together in uncontrollable mourning, loud involuntary cries erupting and piercing the solemnity of the funeral parlor. They bawled, grief flowing out through tears running down cheeks and soaking hankies, arising deep within from a place they perhaps did not know existed.

Then the men, somber and uncomfortable in their too-small sport coats with the loud colors and wide lapels of the 1970's, clip-on ties dangling from their collars, could not contain their sorrow. Sitting next to their women they, too, joined in the music of heartache. Their sobs burst forth in a cacophony of weeping overtaking the song of the women. I wrapped up my message with proclamations of the resurrection. Nothing – not even death – can separate us from the love of God in Christ Jesus, but my words could not be heard over the weeping filling the room. I said God would wipe away tears from our eyes and there would be weeping and crying no more. Alas, that would have to wait for another time. Right now there was no holding back the flood gates as tears drowned the room.

I performed several funerals following a similar pattern. I met the family for the first time the afternoon before the funeral, arriving shortly before calling hours. The funeral director introduced me to the widow and perhaps a daughter or two who stood guard around the casket. I expressed my sorrow at their loss and offered my assistance. I said I wanted the funeral service to lift up and celebrate the life of their loved one. The women were cordial, polite and respectful. I began to ask more direct questions to learn about the person whose body lay in the casket before us. The responses were vague. The women were tight-lipped about details. I mostly learned he was a "good man."

I went into the family room of the funeral home. Most of the family gathered there, leaning on the counter or sitting at tables drinking Pepsis and smoking Marlboros. The room grew instantly tense and quiet the moment I entered. A well-dressed stranger trespassed in their private space. I introduced myself as the pastor doing the funeral service tomorrow. Silence. I said I wanted the funeral service to lift up and celebrate the life of their loved one and would like to get to know the deceased a little better. Silence. I asked what they would like me to say tomorrow. Silence again. I let the silence linger to the point where everyone fidgeted uncomfortably. Finally, one of the sons spoke up, "He was a good man." Another confirmed that judgment, "Yes, say he was a good man." A couple more spoke up, echoing the same opinion, "A good man." "Yes, he was a good man."

"How was he a good man?" I asked. "He loved us." "Yeah, he loved us. Maybe he never said it. He wasn't a touchy-feely kind of guy, but he loved us." I planted myself on a chair at the counter. The son offered me a cigarette. "I don't smoke, but a Pepsi sounds good." For the next hour or so I sat amidst the cigarette smoke and, little by little, tidbits leaked out. I went back to my study and wrote a eulogy.

Names and families changed, but the routine remained somewhat the same. These funerals were for families with roots in Appalachia. They left the hills to take a factory job in the north, usually a non-union, low-paying job no one else wanted. First, one member of the family moved north, soon the whole clan followed, migrating to an unfamiliar and often inhospitable spot in the big city. They settled together and established neighborhoods to re-create the close-knit communities that sustained them in the backwoods of Kentucky or Tennessee.

The funeral director was a member of our church. His funeral home was a plain, unpretentious house on a busy street in the older part of the city, not far from the Appalachian neighborhoods. The home tended to handle funerals for folks who felt a little uneasy in new, fancy funeral homes. Many didn't have a pastor so the funeral director asked the pastors at his church to help. We did our best to provide a suitable and proper burial for someone we didn't know. We did it because we were pastors not just of the congregation we served but also of the wider community. Everyone deserves a decent sendoff.

Wailing during the service continued to escalate through the prayer of blessing and then crescendo during the final viewing. Grieving loved ones threw themselves on the casket, even on the body of the deceased, chests heaving with great big sobs. Others tried prying them away. Little by little the funeral director and I escorted them out so the casket could be closed, the body exposed to the light of this world for the final time.

At the graveside the men, feeling perhaps a bit embarrassed by their outpouring of emotion, got control and stiffened up as before. The women followed suit. Moaning and tears subsided. As I read the beloved passage from Revelation 21 about God dwelling with us and wiping every tear from our eyes, about death, mourning and crying being no more, perhaps they were hearing the words now. I don't know. One by one they shook my hand and thanked me for the service, loaded into their pickup trucks, and drove off.

We all grieve in our own ways, according to customs, personalities, situations, and many other things, but in some way, somehow, all of us grieve. Some grieve quietly and some grieve for all the world to hear and see. Often we grieve when we least expect it. A story, a word, a remembrance, calls forth feelings and we begin to weep and there is nothing we can do to stop.

To become whole again after a loss we must grieve. We must get in touch with pain within, acknowledge it, and find some way to release it. Sometimes we release it through tears. Sometimes we talk. Sometimes we write, sing, or draw. Sometimes we work it out through physical labor. Sometimes we carry out meaningful rituals. Sometimes we sit in silence with a friend who understands. Sometimes we go on a journey to remember and sometimes we sit at home to remember.

When inward pain and hurt is released, God's peace and hope begins to enter. We have visions of life continuing, of life being good, sweet and kind once again. We trust the fate of our loved one to a God who loves, forgives, accepts and welcomes us home. We begin new relationships and dream new dreams. God embraced our loved one, and God is embracing us.

CHAPTER 12

I Think George Is Dead

The church secretary came into my office looking a little perplexed. "Lois just called," she said. "She sounded confused and distraught. She simply said, 'I think George is dead.' Then she hung up." It was a strange message, but in the ministry we sometimes receive strange messages. George and Lois lived less than a mile away. I quickly got in my car and drove to their apartment. Lois greeted me looking visibly upset. "I think he's dead," she said. "I think he's dead." I walked into the bedroom. There was no doubt George was dead. George lay on the bed with his head back, eyes and mouth wide open, his body stiff, an expression of shock and wonder on his face.

Pastors move around the dead and dying on a regular basis, but we do not often see the starkness of sudden death. When we sit by the bedside of a parishioner passing away, the image of death on the deceased's face tends to be either tiredness or acceptance, not shock and wonder. Death has come slowly. We have sat with them anticipating it for hours, perhaps days. Passing away is a transition, not an abrupt interruption in one's daily routine. But death also comes suddenly. One deceased I called upon lay propped against his bed, one leg in his blue jeans, the other just beginning. The man was starting the day just like any other, when death greeted him suddenly. Rigor mortis set in and he was frozen in a moment of time. Suddenly, without any advanced notification, life as we have known is over.

Most people only see a deceased person lying peacefully in the casket dressed in their Sunday-going-to-church clothes. (Well, what used to be called Sunday-going-to-church clothes. Sunday-going-to-church clothes these days are shorts, blue jeans, soccer uniforms and dance competition outfits.) Hair has been fixed, makeup applied to blemishes, and lips formed into a serene smile. If the undertaker has done a good job a loved one will say, "He looks so peaceful." It seems corny to say those words when we believe only a lifeless physical body remains in the casket and the spirit, or soul, has journeyed onward. Nevertheless, an undertaker able to render a beautiful likeness capturing the essence of the deceased is a real blessing to the family. The peaceful image does wonders helping surviving family members accept the death of a loved one and envision them in a better place.

"I returned after being away all morning shopping and I found him just like this," Lois said. "Have you called 911?" I asked. "No, do you think we should? What are they going to do?" Lois wondered. "It is appropriate when someone dies to call 911," I answered. "It will be okay." I went to the phone and dialed. "I would like to report someone who is dead," I said to the 911 operator. It sounded weird but I didn't know how else to phrase it. "Do you mean you want to report someone who is unconscious?" the operator corrected me. "No, I am pretty sure he is dead. He has been dead for a while, I think." I gave the operator the address. The operator seemed a little suspicious and doubtful of my story. She asked me not to touch anything. Everything should be left as it was. I guess she wanted to make sure no foul play was involved. I told her the little I knew. She finally seemed satisfied and said someone would be there shortly.

Lois and I waited for the first responders to arrive. Lois talked about her morning and how George seemed fine when she left to go shopping. Mostly she cried and told how much George meant to her and how she would never be able to carry on without him. She was always afraid he would go first and leave her alone. She knew his heart problems were serious, but always denied the possibility of sudden death. It was too hard for her to think of living without George.

Firefighters arrived in their big red truck from just around the corner, quickly followed by three ambulances. The township hadn't signed a contract with a specific company so the ambulance companies competed for business. Whoever arrived first got the job. Today they would all be disappointed since there was no trip to the hospital. I went through the same story I told the 911 operator a couple of more times. I did my best to shield Lois from the questioners. She was becoming more and more distraught and the questions intimidated her. Everyone relaxed once we contacted George's cardiologist and he agreed to sign the death certificate for cause of death.

I asked Lois what funeral home she would like to call. She didn't know. I named the local ones and she chose the nearest. I called the home, introduced myself, and asked if they were able to pick up George. Lois began to calm down. We reminisced about their life together. "Is there anyone whom we should call?" I asked her. They had no children, but there were a couple of brothers or sisters she thought should know. She told me where she kept her address book and I found their numbers. I dialed and handed the phone to Lois. She delivered the news short and sweet, "George's dead." Answers to questions were also short and sweet.

"Heart attack." "Just now." "Wasn't home." "Out shopping." Lois was usually a big talker, but not now. I sensed Lois and George were not on cordial terms with their siblings.

The funeral director arrived. We set a time when Lois and I could meet with him to go over arrangements. I took Lois into another room as George's body was removed. I made calls to friends of hers in the church. I explained the situation. They would be happy to come over and spend time with Lois. They would be much better company for Lois than me. They would fix a meal, take care of bed sheets, and talk about old times. They would contact other friends in the church to come and also be with her. They would make sure Lois would not be alone. They would watch out for her in the difficult first days. It was a blessing as a pastor to have such people to call.

Maybe Lois should have called 911 before she called the church. That is the wise thing when we find our spouse unconscious. I am glad, though, she trusted the church and her pastors enough to call them. Pastors are called to do many things –plunging toilets, making coffee, shoveling snow and coaching softball – but the greatest joys are journeying with parishioners in times of need.

For some, church family is their only family. Sunday morning is not only time to worship. It is time to reunite with family members. The church is where they belong, where they are accepted and loved. I know it is not the quality of my preaching or excellence of the worship experience attracting them each Sunday morning. I could put a crash test dummy and tape recorder in the pulpit and they would still come. They come for hugs and smiles and to catch up on news of other family members during coffee hour. Lunch after worship with their church family is a time of holy communion. Often these 'families' have been together for years, even decades. They raised children together, shared photos of grandchildren, and now support one another as they journey toward death. "Blessed be the tie that binds our hearts in Christian love" are more than words in an old hymn. It is what people discover through years of living together as family.

I fear church "families" may be disappearing. Today, we choose a church because of programs and activities meeting our needs at a particular time in life – a single's ministry, good Sunday School for children, charismatic youth leader for teenagers, praise band or choir, senior's travel group. We connect to the program or activity and not to people. Continued involvement in church depends on what we receive and not what we give. Church is changing. I pray we always have a holy place where some folks know church will always be there.

CHAPTER 13

I Am Sorry. These Things Happen

I am not sure how Frank continued day after day. His shrunken frame disappeared into the bed sheets. I barely perceived his breathing. His skin went from jaundiced to yellow and then deep yellow. The whites of his eyes approached the color of mustard. Liver cancer was in its final stages.

Frank was aware. I could see it in his eyes. He heard every word I said, but didn't respond. Perhaps he didn't have strength. Perhaps not the will. Perhaps words at this time of one's life are meaningless. They can't express the deep longings and emotions, maybe deep fears of one's life. But his eyes could speak. It seemed Frank's eyes expressed the longings, emotions and fears his mouth could not utter.

His pastors told him it was okay to die. His lovely wife and three beautiful daughters did the same. It was okay to say goodbye to this world and pass on. Let go. Receive what God has prepared for you. God will embrace you with God's love.

Frank couldn't go though. I don't know why. Perhaps, despite all outward appearances, his body wasn't ready to give up. Perhaps he had a very strong heart. Perhaps, too, it was because Frank was still a young man, in his early 40s, and grieving all he would miss in life – weddings of his daughters, births of grandchildren, pleasures of retirement. Perhaps he worried what would happen to his loved ones after he was gone. (That worry maybe wasn't necessary since three men proposed to his widow as she greeted visitors at the funeral home.) Perhaps he thought a miracle might yet come and save him.

Perhaps also he was afraid to die. We can't blame him. Through faith we believe God has more in store for us when we cross through the door of death. As

Christians we believe that through the resurrection of Jesus Christ we, too, shall be raised from the dead. We believe God will embrace us and set a place for us at the heavenly banquet table. I proclaim this hope at every funeral I perform. Nothing in all creation will separate us from the love of God in Jesus Christ.

But that is faith. There is nothing in the natural world around us to suggest life after death. Every living thing, from the smallest microbe to the tallest tree, is born and will die. Even the universe as we know it will die someday billions of years from now. Death is inevitable. Death is the way of creation. When we as believers proclaim the resurrection, we proclaim what we cannot see. Faith believes something is true even though the world around us suggests otherwise.

It is understandable why someone is afraid to die. Hamlet soliloquized, "To be or not to be, that is the question." Death, if there is no resurrection, is to cease to be. It is to leave this thinking, creative, wonderful body that has given substance to our spirit and venture into nothingness. If there is no resurrection, we are rightfully afraid of death and should fight death with every power and tool we have available. If death leads to nothingness, let us cling to life for as long as we can.

Death has been the foe of human beings since the Garden of Eden. We have created physical monuments to immortalize loved ones. Sometimes, we have sacrificed lives of other living creatures and other human beings so we might prolong our own. We have tried every means to combat disease to increase our years here on earth. Some would say we created religions to give us the veneer of hope to overcome the hopelessness of the words of Ecclesiastes, "Vanity of vanities, all is vanity." Life is nothing but "a chasing after the wind."

Once at a church retreat the priest leading the weekend, unbeknownst to me, invited a friend of his to co-lead the event for 20 or so members of my congregation gathered in the little retreat house. This friend believed in the wholeness of the person, the interrelatedness of body, mind and spirit. A healthy body fosters a healthy spirit and a healthy spirit fosters a healthy body. Our physical debilities and diseases often come from unhealthy spiritual or emotional practices. I certainly agreed.

Then he said he didn't intend to die. Our bodies were created to rejuvenate themselves. If we take care of our bodies – physically, emotionally and spiritually – our bodies will take care of us, forever. Some of us were offended, especially the mother who lost a young daughter to cancer. I appreciated the retreat leader's advocacy of healthy lifestyles, but we live in a world where death still prevails. I have never met anyone whose body will not succumb to the forces of aging and death. I noticed this retreat leader kept sneaking the sinfully rich chocolate brownies our group brought rather than the healthy ones the retreat center provided. Maybe someday he will blame the frailties of his old age on those brownies.

The dying are not the only ones afraid of death. The healthy and strong can be afraid of death also, even those who see it every day. One afternoon, my CPE colleague Paul ducked into the Chaplain's Office looking stressed. He said, "I have a lady in ICU with an inoperable brain aneurysm. She is going to die in a few minutes or maybe an hour or two. Her family has no idea she is so critically ill. The doctor just told them they will do everything they can for her. They're sitting in the waiting room thinking she is going to live." In hospital protocol the attending physician gives diagnoses and prognoses and is also the one to deliver news of death. The chaplain does not counter the words of the physician. The chaplain is a physician of the mind or soul, but not the body. So my friend could not tell the family their loved one would soon die, though the medical and nursing staff in ICU all knew.

An hour later he was looking even more stressed when he stopped in the office. "She died," he said, "but the nurses can't get a doctor to the unit to pronounce her dead. The family keeps asking to go in to visit, but I can't let them see their wife and mother lying there dead. She has been dead for at least half an hour. I can't stall the family forever." Then he went back across the hall to the ICU waiting room.

When Paul returned to the Chaplain's Office a couple hours later, he was livid. Finally, nearly an hour after the woman's death, the nurses found a physician to come to the unit to pronounce her dead. As the physician headed to the waiting room to give the family the unhappy news, he turned to Paul and said, "Okay, this is where you earn your money." Of course, we were unpaid interns. We were paying for this experience.

The physician walked into the waiting room and said to the family, "I'm sorry. These things happen. She had the best of care." Then he left. What he did not tell them in explicit terms was she had died. Their wife and mother was now dead. The first question her son asked Paul when the doctor left the room was "Well, is she going to get better?" And Paul had to explain to the family their loved one died.

Death and talking about death can be unsettling for many of us. We simply cannot do it. Perhaps the physician felt every patient who died was a failure of his and he could not talk about failure. Perhaps he could not handle feelings and emotions of persons who have lost a loved one. Perhaps even after years of practicing medicine, death was still scary for him. The finality of death and the uncertainty of what lies beyond frighten all of us at some time. We prefer to ignore it. Talking about death means facing not only the death of a patient or parishioner, it also means facing our own mortality and our future being or nonbeing.

Perhaps sometime, in the not-so-distant future, we will be able to live what seems almost forever. Genetic research and gene manipulation, biomedical engineering, and a thousand other research breakthroughs may be able to extend our lives for a long, long time. Death at that time will not be any less scary. It may be even more frightful because we will be living with the expectation of continuously healthy bodies indefinitely. When death happens, it will seem even more tragic.

Frank's body eventually gave way, as will each of ours someday, as will the body of the retreat leader who was going to live forever. Sheer will power is not enough to keep us alive forever. Neither is healthy living. We live, and die, by faith in the love of God. I think we always will.

CHAPTER 14

No, No! I Could Never Do That!

As I stood on the front porch, the odor was unmistakable – urine, more urine, and old newspapers. When Helen answered the door and let me in, all I could see was newspapers. Newspapers covered the old linoleum floors from the living room through the little dining room and out the kitchen to the back door. Newspapers were everywhere, even on the faded old sofa and torn easy chair, anywhere little Mabel could go, and even places she couldn't go. Mabel had a drippy bladder and newspapers were there to catch the drips. Helen mentioned Mabel's ill health on her way out of church and I stopped by to see firsthand.

Mabel was a tiny mutt, perhaps eight-ten pounds. If she was ever cute, it was long gone. She was ugly. She was blind. She was deaf. Her legs and hips were full of arthritis. She walked straight-legged with tiny little steps, each step seeming to bring forth pain. Every few steps, she stopped and wheezed, her whole body convulsing. I fully expected each fit to be her last. Surely, she couldn't continue any longer. Surely, she would fall over and die at any moment. But she didn't.

I offered to Helen to take Mabel to the vet to have her put to sleep, to take away her pain. "No, no! I could never do that!" Helen was horrified at the thought and I never offered again. Helen, like Mabel, had some health issues – arthritis, heart concerns and probably other things. Bending over and picking up Mabel to take her outside was painful (and as far as I could tell it didn't do much good). Lifting Mabel up on the sofa so she could lie next to her also was difficult for Helen. But Helen kept on going, caring for Mabel, and coming to church.

The condition of Helen's house revealed what I expected. She was just getting by. Her house was deteriorating. Everything needed to be repaired, replaced, or painted. It was an old house on a busy street in an older part of the city and I wondered if it would be torn down when she moved. Helen, of course, didn't want any help with her house. She would take care of things herself.

As I visited over the months, to my amazement old Mabel kept going. I don't know how, but she did. Yet, old, ugly, blind, deaf, wheezing dogs with dripping bladders will eventually die. Helen grieved but I also sensed a bit of relief. Shortly after Mabel's death, Helen moved out of her house and into a nursing home. She was there not very long until she, too, died, hopefully re-united with her dear Mabel.

After Helen died I realized I had it all wrong. Perhaps it wasn't Helen keeping Mabel alive after all. Maybe it was Mabel keeping Helen alive. Mabel gave Helen a reason to live, a reason to get out of bed. Even more, Mabel gave Helen something to love, something to care for. When Mabel finally died, Helen had permission to die. I wonder if, when I offered to take Mabel to the vet to put her to sleep, perhaps Helen was horrified because she saw her own death in Mabel's. It was as if I were taking her to the grave.

We become very attached to our animal friends. I know losing a dog or a cat is not the same as losing a child or loved one, but people see their animal friends as part of the family. They probably spend more time with their animal friends than they do with family members or human friends. Their animal friends are always with them. They talk to them. They go on walks together. Little Fido or Snowball is the first living thing they see in the morning and the last before going to bed. There is a good chance they even sleep together. No wonder we grieve the loss of an animal friend so deeply. We are losing a living creature nearer to us than any other living thing.

We live less and less in community and more and more in our individual private domains. We rely on our animal friends for companionship. They love us for who we are. They are always there for us. The relationships with our pets are so simple. They give us comfort in a broken world, love in a hateful world, and joy in a dismal world. They always think the best of us. My brother has a pillow with the words, "My goal is to become the person my dog thinks I am." And so, as with Helen and Mabel, we are willing to sacrifice for our animals.

On occasion, though, we lose our bearings in our devotion to our animals. I have visited many homes where the smell of dog or cat was overpowering to me, but oblivious to the owner. We become accustomed to unhealthy living conditions. I was visiting with one couple who had several dogs. The house was somewhat unkempt. Dogs were the first priority. Housecleaning followed far behind. Looking down at one point in our conversation, I saw quick bursts of movement coming from tiny little things jumping around my pant legs. I disregarded it at first, but as it continued, it dawned on me: these quick bursts were fleas. I tried to stay calm as I asked the couple if their dogs ever had problems with fleas. 'Oh, all the time,' they replied.

I wrapped up the conversation rather quickly. I didn't want to take fleas home to our cat, or our children, but I resisted the urge to strip my clothes off in their driveway before stepping into my car. Instead, I drove directly home and stripped in the garage. Carolyn was a little puzzled to see me walk in without my pants on.

We love our animal friends. They are a part of us. Often, they are also our connection with a deceased loved one. Joy, the deceased wife of a young widower, Ron, was a great lover of animals. She was devoted to rescuing and saving all kinds of animals, from cats and dogs to deer and squirrels. When she died, Ron and Joy had two cats and three dogs living with them. They were, of course, animals Joy rescued. The dogs and cats exercised with Ron in the morning, watched television with him in the evening, and went to bed with him at night. Most importantly, they were the comforting presence of his dear Joy. She continued to live with him through their animals. As each one of these dogs and cats passed away in the years following Joy's death, I think Ron felt a little more of Joy slipping away.

I frequently send cards or notes to persons who lose a pet. I try not to minimize the attachment some folks have to their animal friends. Yet, I am afraid I might have done that once in a sermon illustration. The illustration came from an event at a former church Carolyn and I attended. There, I asked Mike, a former parishioner, how Bill was doing. Bill was Mike's pet boa constrictor and I met Bill on a couple of occasions. To his neighbors' dismay, Mike sometimes took Bill out for walks (or slithers?) in the back yard. Sometimes Bill could be found on the curtain rods of the living room, but Bill spent most of his time in his cage. He spent all of his time in the cage when Mike's wife was home.

Well, Bill died. I asked Mike how it happened. He explained Bill was not feeling well and he took him to the vet. The vet said Bill was terminally ill. Mike didn't want to see Bill suffer. Could the vet give Bill a shot and put him to sleep? The vet explained euthanasia for snakes didn't work in the same way as for dogs since they were cold-blooded animals. The most humane way to terminate a snake's life was either to cut off its head or put it in the freezer. So Mike, not able to cut off Bill's head, put him in a bag and stuck him in their freezer. It was a long time before his wife had the courage to open the freezer door again.

I told this story in a sermon at church a week or so later. I used the story to explain how we sometimes are reluctant to end something unpleasant in our life or in the church quickly (cut off the head) and instead we let it chill out gradually (put it in the freezer) until it dies. Maybe the illustration was a bit of a stretch. The congregation paid attention though. I am rarely given a poem inspired by a sermon, but that day two poems about Bill the snake were presented to me as folks left the sanctuary. The tone of the poems made me think maybe I had not given Bill the snake his due respect.

Our relationships with our animal friends have changed over the last generation. Years ago, their lives had little value except how they served us. We rarely had close attachments to animals. Now, they are truly part of the family. Nearly every family with children has pets. Family photos in church directories include many dogs. Parishioners in senior living facilities have cats and small dogs. We fuss over our pets and buy them expensive gifts. The Blessing of the Animals ritual has become quite popular and is a beloved annual event in our ministries. I rejoice we have greater respect for the lives of animals. Some of the love for our pets may reflect an absence of loving relationships with other human beings. Nevertheless I rejoice our animal friends help make this a kinder, gentler world.

CHAPTER 15

I Need a Pastor

"Neal, this is Gene." Gene's voice was breaking badly, but I recognized my friend, the moderator of my former church. He was weeping. Gene was never able to hide his emotions. You knew just how he was feeling. "Joey just killed himself and I need a pastor. We don't have a pastor now. We don't have an interim. We don't even have a supply pastor. I am alone. Can you help me?" It did not surprise me the little church did not have a pastor, nor an interim, nor even a regular supply pastor. Not employing a pastor for a few weeks, or even a few months, was one way the congregation stashed away a little money as a nest egg to pay the next one. They relied on short pastoral vacancies to meet the budget, though of course they didn't have a budget. They just prayed they had enough money in the bank to pay the bills as they came due. If they didn't have the funds, maybe someone would die and leave a little to the church. One of the sayings by the Treasurer was 'if it weren't for the dead we would be in the red.'

Gene knew the ins and outs of pastoral ethics. I, too, knew pastoral ethics well. You don't ask a former pastor to come back and perform a funeral. We say our goodbyes. The congregation promises not to call the pastor for services. The pastor promises not to interfere in the life of the church. Social contact is permitted, after a time, but the pastoral relationship ends. There are times, though, when human need and compassion supersede rules of pastoral ethics. This good friend's son had just killed himself. My friend and former parishioner needed someone to help him journey through an unspeakable tragedy. "Of course, I can help, Gene," I said. "What can I do?"

In my young ministry, I had not yet presided at the funeral of a suicide victim, consoling the anguish of survivors and addressing unanswerable questions of loved ones. Why? Why did he take his life? Did he know how much we loved him? Did he know how much this would hurt us? What kind of pain did he have inside we did not know about? If only we had known, we would have done anything to help. Why? Why?

I didn't know Joey well. Unlike his father who was devoted to the church, Joey had drifted away as a young man. I met him only occasionally at family gatherings. Joey seemed to be doing well. He had a growing and successful heating and air conditioning business and a devoted wife. Joey was a confident young man with purpose and direction. But that morning he was served a warrant for an infraction of the law. He was to be arrested and defend himself in court. The crime seemed minor in the scope of things. That afternoon though he drove his truck into a field, attached flexible tubing to his exhaust pipe (he used what he had available), put the other end through the window, started the truck, and waited for death to come. That night I received the anguished call from Gene.

It seemed out of character for Joey. He seemed like a strong individual, not easily defeated in life, nor controlled by intense feelings and emotions. He didn't have depression or anxieties. Something in him snapped. Perhaps he could not face criminal indictment, perhaps he was disappointed in himself, perhaps he felt he let others down. No one knew, and no one expected he would take his life that afternoon.

Many have said, "Suicide is a permanent solution for a temporary problem." To those considering taking their lives, the pain inside must be so great they long for a permanent solution. In their thoughts a temporary solution is not enough. Something goes on inside those who contemplate suicide the rest of us cannot know. The burden of life is so great they feel they must escape the only way they know how. Of course, suicide is not the solution. Counseling, support, love, and perhaps medication are the solution. But at that moment, it is not possible to convince the distraught person life can be good once again. Those who love the distraught must act to keep them safe. They must keep their surroundings free of potential life-taking drugs or weapons. They must call 911 if there is talk of suicide.

Although a gun did not play a role in this suicide, I have officiated at other services where the deceased took their life by a gun. Tens of thousands of people each year take their lives through a gunshot. I wonder how many deaths could be prevented if a gun were not readily available during a time of intense despair. Gun control laws prevent deaths, especially suicides.

I had a parishioner who, when I went to leave, would reach on top of his cupboard and take down a handgun. "It's loaded," he would say. "I want everyone to know I have a loaded gun in my home and I am willing to use it." The first time he said this I responded that it is far more likely for a gun to be used for something bad than for something good. I think he considered me just a wimpy preacher. He said rather forcefully, "I will protect my family and my property. My grandchildren know it is loaded." Later in ministry I would listen to stories of parents, grandparents and others who kept guns in their homes, usually following the prescribed safety precautions, only to have a loved one use it to end their lives. It was a high price to pay for added protection from theft and break-in.

I began my remarks at Joey's service by saying Joey's death was a tragedy, and there was no reason or explanation for the tragedy. I talked about our hurt and pain, and the hurt and pain of God. I talked a great deal about sharing hurt and pain with others, and finding comfort and hope as we shared memories and talked about our sadness. Gene was from a big family. Every evening at nine, whoever was available would stop by Gene's sister's house for pie, cake or whatever. On occasion when I served their church, I joined them. Now, as they mourned the loss of a young life, they needed support from one another more than ever.

I also talked about the power of God's love to bring healing amidst something as tragic and unimaginable as suicide. God knew what it was like to lose a Son in a tragic way. Healing can come, but usually only with faith, time, and loving relationships. Forgiveness both for oneself and the deceased is needed, trusting God's love can redeem and bring new life out of tragedy. God will never leave us.

I don't know whether I said appropriate words at Joey's service. I don't think words alone could minister to the deep emotions or answer inexplicable questions on all our minds. Gene sobbed a lot during the service. Gene's estranged wife, Joey's mother, seemed to sit there feeling guilty and confused. (One blessing, perhaps hastened by tragedy, was that Gene and his wife re-united a couple of years later.) Gene's young wife sat in shock, probably not hearing a word I said, as she twisted one of Joey's work shirts bearing his name and company logo.

One of the hardest things in ministry is to move from a church and say goodbye to parishioners. They welcome us into their lives, often opening up some of the deepest fears and longings of their hearts. We grow close. To cut ties abruptly and completely when we leave is difficult, for parishioners and the pastor. I understand the reasons and have said 'no' many times when asked to perform funerals or provide pastoral care to friends who are former parishioners. In this case however, I was thankful I could be there for Gene in my feeble way. I wished I was still his pastor to walk with him through the rest of this journey.

CHAPTER 16

This Is What I Have Had to Live with for 50 Years

Ralph and Gladys, married for more than 50 years, both had a dread of dying. They were getting up in age and, in the words of a dear nurse in one of my congregations, were "circling the drain." Medical issues popped up again and again with increasing severity. There was only one way for their health to go, downhill, until they die. Ralph and Gladys, though, each had a tenacious spirit to hold on. Neither wanted to give in to death, not as long as the other was alive. Each was determined not to die first, and thereby open up a possibility of peace and happiness for the other.

Ralph and Gladys hated each other with meanness of spirit I have seen in few people. They despised everything about one another. I don't know how many years fighting had gone on. I guess a long time. No one in the church could remember when they had gotten along. Surely, though, something good and kind had brought them together when they were young. Surely, they must have touched each other's hearts at one time and felt the flush, giddiness and bliss of young love. Surely, they delighted in one another's caress and embrace. If such feelings existed, they had taken the last train years and years ago.

Ralph and Gladys were faithful worship attenders. Every Sunday morning they sat next to one another, hearing the reading of Scripture and proclamation of the gospel as the pastors spoke of love, peace, compassion, forgiveness, mercy and kindness. They listened to hymns extolling the grace of God. They bowed their heads as we humbly lifted up loved ones during pastoral prayers. As far as I could tell though, God's Spirit hadn't yet found a crevice to reach into their hearts. I could detect no feelings of tenderness and love.

Ralph and Gladys dressed fashionably, fashion of 30 years earlier. Folks in the church were friendly toward them, but I didn't know of anyone, in the church or elsewhere, Ralph and Gladys could call friends. I didn't think anyone wanted to be their friend. It would require too much effort. Ralph and Gladys had no children and no family I was aware of. They were together, for life, locked to one another in unbreakable, invisible chains, doomed to share the remainder of their days in the hell of holy matrimony. Neither would consider divorce which might mean happiness and joy for the other. When one was in the hospital, the other would visit the entire day, not out of concern for their well-being, but wanting to deny them a day of quiet.

When I visited with them in their second floor apartment in an older section of the city, I sat in the crossfire of insults and sharply worded barbs. They didn't speak to each other. The scorn and ridicule was spoken to me but intended for the spouse. "This is what I have had to live with for 50 years." "Can you imagine living with that thing for all these years?" It was as if just looking at the other person I should be able to see such disgusting and sinister things they didn't have to say more.

I tried my best to bring civility into the conversation. "You really didn't mean that, Ralph? Did you?" I would ask. "Of course I did or I wouldn't have said it," he replied. "Isn't there something positive you can say about Ralph, Gladys?" I would ask. "Something positive about that good-for-nothing bastard? I don't know what it would be." I failed miserably. They quieted for my prayers, only to hurl the abuse once again after 'Amen.'

An older couple lived beneath the apartment I shared with my brother before I was married. We saw the old guy a lot – a quiet guy, meek and mild. He often stood outside, even in the cold of winter, smoking his pipe. I understand why a wife may want her husband to smoke outside, but I think standing outside smoking his pipe was a refuge, his escape from her. On occasion, her voice pierced the gold shag carpet of our living room. "50 years I have been married to you! I can't believe I have put up with this for 50 years!" I never met her until a package was mistakenly delivered to our apartment. I knocked on their door and she answered. I told her who I was and gave her the package. She thanked me, then said, "Harry and I have been married for more than 50 years, 50 wonderful years. He is such a good man." I wanted to say I had already heard they had been married for 50 years, but I bit my tongue. In contrast, Ralph and Gladys weren't two-faced.

On one hospital visit I found Gladys by herself in the room. I think it was the first time I visited with either one alone. Conversation was difficult without the other one there to insult and provoke. I asked about Ralph's health since he, too, had serious illnesses. I thought I detected some empathy or compassion in her response, something about how difficult it was for him to get around. Then she said how good it was he came to the hospital to see her every day. He didn't have to do that. Wow, I thought, maybe there has been a breakthrough in their relationship. Maybe there is some tenderness and caring beneath the scorn. Ralph then walked in. Gladys greeted him, "Where in the hell have you been you lazy son of a bitch? Your wife's dying and you don't give a damn." He returned the language and they were back at it.

Bickering is a way of life for many couples. That is the way they communicate. They love each other deeply, I think, but their daily conversation is peppered with blunt, caustic remarks. I am uncomfortable around such couples. Again, I think they love each other. For whatever reason, they just aren't able to communicate in civil, proper ways and express their love in tenderness and empathy. I searched hard for love binding Ralph and Gladys and couldn't find it. Arguing, they made all other couples appear as rank amateurs.

In CPE, we heard again and again, when there is anger look for hurt or fear. I wonder how much of the anger of Ralph and Gladys was based on fear, the fear of being left alone. As far as I could tell, Ralph and Gladys had no one else. What would happen if the other died? Did unspoken fear cause the anger?

I didn't find out. I moved on to another pastorate while Ralph and Gladys, circling more rapidly around the drain, continued to stab each other with destructive and slashing words. Those spiteful words seemed to spur them to hang on a little longer. I wonder if, in all my pleas for civility, I ever asked them to say, "I'm sorry." Did I ever ask them to look the other person in the eye and say, "I'm sorry for all the hurtful things I have said to you. I'm sorry for the shameful way I have treated you?" Maybe I did and don't remember. Maybe it wouldn't have made a difference. Those two words have performed remarkable surgery on other couples, usually the first step toward healing. Maybe if I said it to them enough, an "I'm sorry" could sneak in when their defenses were down. I pray they said the words before they entered the final swirling circle and flowed down the drain.

CHAPTER 17

Unknown

Funerals can lead us into the oddest and most bizarre journeys.

I received a call from the hospital chaplain. He sat in the emergency room with Denise. Her husband, Drew, had just died. I was stunned. Denise and Drew were in their late 20s. The chaplain said Denise went home for lunch and found him gone. He had a cold that morning, but nothing more. How strange, I thought. A healthy 27-year-old man dying suddenly from a cold? I went immediately to the hospital.

Denise and Drew lived in town only a short time. Denise worked as a counselor, especially in sexual abuse cases. She visited our church a few times but I hadn't seen her in several weeks. Drew was a free spirit with eclectic interests, very much his own person. He hunted and fished, but also wrote poetry and arranged flowers.

A few months before he died, he penned a poem that became tragically prophetic about his own death. He wrote of the fleetness and brevity of life and the need to "slow down a bit." He said, "Sometimes we find out way too late, We should've listened and taken a break." He pleaded not to let life pass before it's "dust to dust and ashes to ashes."

I met with Denise and Drew's dad, who had come to town. Together, we planned an appropriate service to honor the brief life of Drew. I read his poem. An earlier service for Drew's extended family and friends had already been held in Drew's hometown out of state.

I contacted Denise a couple of times after the memorial service. She didn't attend worship though, and after a while my ties with Denise became infrequent and finally ceased. The funeral director told me the cause of death listed on the death certificate was "Unknown." There was no hint of foul play, no evidence of suicide, no disease or physical ailment. Just "Unknown." Again, rather strange for a healthy 27-year-old man.

A couple of years later I met Denise once again. She spoke at our Ministerial

Association. She talked about Satanic Ritual Abuse (SRA). SRA was abuse inflicted upon persons, especially children, during occult or Satanic rituals. Denise said the occult flourished in our community. Many young people were drawn in. Community leaders were a part of it. Children were captured and abused, some even killed. Often, it was a family member, an uncle or a grandpa, who inflicted abuse on children. Denise and others were re-settling victims of SRA in our community to get them away from their dangerous situations. It sounded alarming, even terrifying.

I didn't believe it. I tend to pooh-pooh conspiracy theories. Yet, in the short time I knew Denise, I discovered her to be rational and practical, not given to flights of religious or other fantasies. I sensed if she was involved there must be a kernel of truth. I also wanted to support her. I had buried her 27-year-old husband dying from an unknown cause just a couple of years earlier.

After the program, I approached Denise about helping. She asked if the church could be used as a 'safe house' on high holy days of the occult. Those wanting to escape the occult needed a safe place to stay overnight while rituals were going on. Otherwise, they would be drawn back to the ritual and abusive relationships. I said 'yes.'

On the next holy day according to the Satanic calendar, Denise's clients began to arrive shortly before sunset, about a dozen in total. They carried blankets and snacks, books and games, like they were coming to an overnight. Most were single women. There were a couple of mothers with children. Some appeared quite normal, some rather bizarre. I settled them into our church's lounge for the night. It had a cushy carpet for those who wanted to sleep. It was Saturday evening. I was preaching the next day and hoping for some shuteye.

Most guests seemed calm and reasonable. They just wanted a place to spend the night where they would be safe. They spread out their blankets and lay down. Others were agitated. I talked with the guests about their experiences. They told convincing stories of abuse by a husband or an ex-boyfriend. Some told of attending satanic rituals as young children when visiting grandparents or an aunt and uncle. Denise, or her partner therapist, uncovered the abuse during counseling sessions. They asked questions that brought out memories. They credited Denise with rescuing them from their satanic families.

As the night went on, some guests started to wander out of the room. I asked where they were going. They were going to a meeting of the occult, they said. I asked where the meeting was. They couldn't tell me. Why? They didn't know where it was. Then how could they get there? They had been programmed by leaders of the occult to recognize signs to take them there. I said I wanted to go to the rituals and see what was going on. Could they tell me signs to look for?

No, they couldn't. It was programmed into their subconscious. A couple of guests appeared to transition through multiple personalities throughout the night. When the sun rose, the guests gathered their things and returned home. I vacuumed the lounge and got ready for my Sunday morning responsibilities.

It was a bizarre night. The guests clearly believed the strange stories they told, but it was all too weird to believe the occult slipped into our homes and communities and was carrying out unimaginable things. Denise gave me a book on SRA to educate me on Satanic signs, practices and types of abuse. She invited me to have lunch with a sheriff deputy from another county who investigated such phenomena. He affirmed SRA was widespread. He had seen evidence. I asked Denise why she uncovered SRA but other therapists didn't. She said she was trained to seek deeper truths through memory recovery methods. Oddly enough, two community leaders the guests alleged to be in the satanic community soon appeared in news stories. A judge was alleged to have sold evidence from the jail in exchange for sexual favors and a former priest was being investigated for child abuse.

The guests came a second night. Again, I spent time talking with them about their experiences. The stories became more outlandish. One guest said she had been at rituals with the Kennedy family. I again pressed for information to locate one of the rituals they were escaping, but none was forthcoming. I began to feel I was being used. I met with Denise again and talked about the weird things. She said she followed an 80/20 rule. Eighty percent of what they said was true, 20% not true. I thought it was probably the opposite. Eighty percent was not true. I said I didn't want to be involved anymore. A week later the sidewalk at our house leading to the front door was filled with dozens of satanic symbols scribbled in chalk. I thought it looked rather childish and washed it off. I didn't want to bother the police. I lost track of Denise and the SRA guests after that.

At first, I dismissed the SRA phenomena as a harmless game played by those leading 'lives of quiet desperation.' They were looking for thrills. The existence of occult rituals, devious mind control and sexual abuse provided excitement. It lifted them out of the ordinary and sent them forth on a unique and dangerous adventure. They were much like those who search the Scriptures and the world news to see evidence of the imminent return of Jesus. We manufacture meaning for our lives.

In the next year though, I received a couple of calls from frantic parents in other states looking for adult children. Their children accused them or another family member of SRA. They left home and broke contact. Parents asked around and thought their children might be in our community. Somehow, they got my name as someone who might have information. They tried calling the therapists but their calls were not returned. Unfortunately, I couldn't help. I told them what I knew.

SRA was not a harmless game after all. It was tearing families apart and perpetrating falsehoods. I think leaders and therapists who 'rescued' victims believed very strongly they were champions of the abused and persecuted. I came to the conclusion they were deceived. They were victims of SRA hysteria and compounded the lies. There was no satanic cult taking over our communities. It was only their imaginations. How easily, even in our desire to do good, we can cause terrible harm. The history of the church reveals terrible abuse and evil by supposedly well-intentioned Christians. How do we make such serious mistakes?

Some of it lies in the quest for excitement and meaning. We are drawn to the bizarre and the weird. We want our life to be different. We try to escape the mundane. We also can be easily controlled by fear, real and imaginary. Fear leads us to believe things our rational mind would not normally believe and do things that go against common sense. Hate, bigotry, racism, and a whole lot of other evils are perpetuated by fear. Unscrupulous leaders are masters at manufacturing fear and then manipulating us through the fear they create.

We can all be manipulated. How important to have friends with courage to question us when we stray to implausible places. How important for us to develop critical minds to question those leading us where we should not go. Blind acceptance of the teachings of unscrupulous or mistaken leaders hurt innocent people. May we always welcome the loving friends who challenge us and help us discover God's way in the confusing dogmas of our world.

CHAPTER 18

I Did It My Way

A sea of blue filled the sanctuary to my left. Perhaps 100 men and women of the city's finest sat properly, soberly and a little uncomfortably in their pressed uniforms. Police officers came to pay tribute to a fellow officer fallen by a single bullet. The bullet, though, did not come from the gun of a bad guy in the course of an arrest or chase. It came from the officer's own gun. He pulled the trigger himself while fellow officers, trained in negotiation, counseling and suicide intervention, stood on the other side of the door trying to persuade him to put the gun down.

I never met the deceased officer, known by his nickname "Butch." I met his widow, Bev, just days earlier, the day after the shooting. She was a friend of a member of the congregation, and needed a pastor and church for the memorial service. My parishioner gave me a brief summary of what unfolded the day of Butch's death. Bev told Butch she was leaving him. She couldn't live with him anymore and was filing for divorce. Butch became very distraught, took out his gun, and threatened to shoot himself if she left. Bev called the police. The standoff between Butch and his fellow officers ensued, tragically ending with Butch pulling the trigger to end his life.

Bev arrived at my office with a male friend. Was he a new boyfriend, or a dear friend to see her through the traumatic ordeal of preparing a memorial service for the husband she was planning to leave? I did not know. Nor did I know why Butch pulled the trigger. He was distraught. He was confused. He was angry. He was hurt. Did he pull the trigger because he felt he could not live without her? Or did he pull the trigger to spite her and inflict her with guilt and shame? Bev did not offer any insight into the why's and it was not my position to ask. Someone died tragically by his own hand. It was a horrific death. My task was to create a service to celebrate

Butch's life while giving an opportunity for the grieving to cry and mourn, reflect and pray, and amidst their confusion and sadness find hope and comfort.

I was thankful the police chief offered to give the eulogy. A police lieutenant and another officer would also participate in the service and offer words of encouragement to their fellow officers. The police chaplain would lead in a prayer. As presiding pastor, I would speak not only to the police officers but especially to Butch's widow, daughter, sisters and friends, none of whom I knew. I would need to do my best, with the guidance and indwelling of God's Spirit, to offer hope and healing amidst an irrational and nonsensical act of violence against oneself. How do you bring God's grace to bear on such an entangled situation?

I talked with Bev about the service. We discussed the role of police officers and went through the order of worship and events. Planning a memorial service for someone who was soon to be her estranged husband was not what Bev wanted to do. But she did what needed to be done, what was appropriate and honorable for Butch. Then she said, "Butch had a request for his memorial service. He always said he wanted "My Way" sung." I am sure I gasped a little at the suggestion. "My Way"? Sung by Frank Sinatra? The song that begins "And now the end is near, and so I face the final curtain. My friends, I'll say it clear. I'll state my case of which I'm certain ... I did it my way."

Bev saw my gasp. She reiterated, "Butch always insisted the song be sung at his service." "My Way" had been sung or played at other memorial services where I presided. It's not a song that reflects my life view but it reflected well the character and philosophy of the deceased, so I thought it appropriate. But for someone who had taken his life in such a manner as Butch? "Do you think it is appropriate?" I asked. "I don't know whether it is appropriate or not," Bev said, "but I have to honor his request." When I talked with the police chief and others on the force, I discovered Butch had discussed "My Way" at his funeral with others. I consented to the song, if we did it at the beginning of the service and not the end.

I looked apprehensively over the sea of blue on the left side of the sanctuary, sober looking officers in their pressed uniforms, as the soloist, a fellow police officer, began to sing "My Way." There was nervousness and fidgeting. As the song progressed though, the discomfort I sensed many were feeling gave way to nodding of heads. They were connecting the song not to his death but his life. I relaxed a little. Butch lived his life 'his way.' Everyone agreed. The chief talked about Butch's service on the force. Others talked about his character and what they liked about him. No one talked about his untimely death. As pastor, that was my task – to face questions that haunt and perplex us, to try to make sense out of senseless acts, to try to find hope amidst life's puzzling dilemmas. My notes began this way:

"There are struggles within each of us that no one else knows ... things too personal to share, too secret to divulge to others, too confusing for even ourselves to understand. Our lives are amazingly complex. We don't know ourselves, but God knows us. God knows us far better than we know ourselves. God knows what lies in the depth of each one's mind, each one's soul. God sees the inner longings of the heart. God hears the unspoken prayers. God listens to the cries for help, the pleas for understanding. There is no place where we can journey in this life of ours where God cannot find us … no place where God's love and grace cannot be experienced … no place where God's forgiveness is not strong enough to heal and restore … no place where the love of Jesus Christ cannot penetrate, no matter how difficult the situation, how tragic the events. God's love is powerful, powerful to redeem, powerful to heal."

I spent a lot of time and prayer preparing the message. I wrote and re-wrote the words. It was a delicate situation, and I didn't know all the dynamics involved. It was not time for simple platitudes. The questions were too imponderable, the pain too deep, the guilt too real. It was important the message connect the grieving family and officers to their God so healing could begin. It was important they find a glimpse of a promise so they could find strength and courage to go forward in faith. Yet, any words I wrote seemed inadequate. As with every sermon, I prayed for God's Spirit to speak where my words fell short.

I talked about our fear, confusion, disjointedness, helplessness, anger, bewilderment and hurt. Then I asked them not to shut God out of their lives, but find a place to invite God in amidst the confusion, anger and hurt. I exhorted them not to doubt the gracious mercy of our God, or underestimate the love of God poured out in Jesus Christ. I ended with a verse I rarely use in memorial services. It is a wonderful verse, but has become so overused as to become trite. I ended with John 3:16, "For God so loved the world that he gave us his Son so that whoever believes in him shall not perish but have everlasting life."

I think the verse was not trite then, but powerful, powerful for people to understand God still reigned. God still loved Butch, and God would be with us as we coped in the days ahead. I sensed the sea of police officers in their pressed blue uniforms walked out of the memorial service a little less sober and uncomfortable, and a little more hopeful. Perhaps a touch of God's grace had gotten through.

In difficult situations of inexplicable tragedy or incomprehensible events, our words are never sufficient. Our words, though, can provide windows for God's Spirit to enter and bring comfort and hope. Understanding may never come, but peace can penetrate clouds of misery and anguish and in time begin to bring light and joy once again.

CHAPTER 19

Two Weddings and a Funeral

There wasn't much in the room to suggest a wedding – no bridesmaids in formal dresses, no groomsmen in tuxes, no sacred symbols of the church, no beautiful decorations, no congregation to observe, not even a photographer to record the event. I wore my white pulpit gown and a white stole around my neck. The bride purchased a pretty new dress and held a small bouquet of flowers. That was all the wedding trappings. There would be no festive reception with dinner and dancing. There would be no honeymoon, not even a wedding night at a local hotel.

Ray, the groom, lay in his hospital bed dressed in a hospital gown, his skin jaundiced, face gaunt, body becoming more emaciated each day. His fiancé, Julia, hoped the wedding would take place in the hospital chapel. It was a pleasant worship space and, if it weren't for its location in a hospital, would be a lovely space for an intimate wedding. Julia planned to adorn it with flowers, candles and ribbons to create a festive setting to say their vows and unite as husband and wife. But Ray's health deteriorated and he was not strong enough to leave his room and venture down the hall, even in a wheel chair. Ray and Julia did not want to put the wedding off any longer. They would forego the frills. They would pull the bed curtains for privacy and say their vows in the hospital room with IV poles and heart monitors as attendants.

I met Ray the previous fall when he began attending our worship services with Julia. Things seemed to be moving rather fast between the two of them and, as Julia's pastor, I became a little uneasy. Ray seemed like a nice guy, but pastors sometimes have a fatherly/motherly concern for single women in our congregations. Julia was hurt by her divorce and I wanted her to be careful before entering into another relationship. Did Julia really know him? Was he a good man? Did he love her as much as she loved him? As Christmas approached, the word engagement was tossed around and, though there was no ring, a wedding was definitely talked about as the New Year dawned.

The New Year also brought abdominal pain to Ray. He was admitted to the hospital for tests. X-rays were performed. Spots were found on the liver, pancreas and lung. Biopsies were taken. I planned a call to Ray's hospital room to follow the physician's visit when Ray would receive news of the biopsies. On the way to Ray's room, I met Sister Camilla, the hospital chaplain. She told me devastating news. Cancer was everywhere. Ray had three months to live. He was 42 years old.

In a few brief days, Ray and Julia changed their horizons from a lifetime together to three months. Three months is not a long time. When you know that is all you have to live, it becomes very precious time. A wedding and marriage were still on the couple's mind. Doctor visits, nursing care, and saying goodbye to three children were a higher priority. Julia moved in with Ray to enable him to remain at home between hospital stays. His body was weakening. Both wanted very much to tie the knot in marriage. Though their days together would be few in number, their love would be sealed forever in holy vows. They would be united as husband and wife and that could never be taken away. So, Ray and Julia said their vows as Ray lay in his hospital bed, an IV in his arm and wires from his chest leading to the heart monitor.

Through my years of ministry, I have found forecasting a time of death is not easy. Some folks add months, years, and even decades on to a prognosis of imminent death. Others meet their end far quicker than the physician imagined. For Ray, the physician had it right to the very day. Ray passed away exactly three months after his diagnosis, just as the doctor had said, and exactly three weeks after he and Julia were united in marriage.

We celebrated Ray's life in a memorial service in our sanctuary. I journeyed to Detroit, to the community where Ray had been raised, the following day to lead a memorial service for Ray's mother and siblings. Though the family made trips to see their dear Ray at his home, his sickness advanced so quickly it was difficult for the family to grasp he was gone. His father died of cancer less than a year earlier.

Life is short. Cancer, heart disease or other destructive illness can make it shorter. We don't know what each New Year will bring. We dream of the years ahead and make plans to enjoy those years, but tomorrow or the next day fate can intervene. We must dream new dreams and fashion a new design for our lives. Love is precious. We can't squander love's hour, but must embrace it now with whatever we have and in whatever way we can.

Sometimes it is not cancer that makes life short and love precious. I called Dale to see if he would be willing to be lay leader in worship on an upcoming Sunday, usually a simple perfunctory call. Dale and his family, however, just returned from California. Dale's wife, Cathy, was a sales representative for a Napa Valley vineyard. Sometimes they were able to vacation in a quaint cottage set amidst the vineyards of the beautiful valley. Dale, Cathy, their 17-year old daughter and 12-year old son were getting ready for bed at the cottage one evening when an intruder broke in. He was armed and waved a handgun at the family. The family was ordered to kneel and the daughter told to tie their hands behind their backs. Dale loved his family and took the role of protector seriously. He was determined his family would not be harmed.

When his daughter tied his hands, he purposely held them apart so he might be able to slip out of the ropes. When his daughter finished tying the hands of his wife and son, Dale made his move. He lunged at the intruder. The gun fired twice. One shot went through his hand. The other shot, he later discovered, grazed his chest, drawing blood but making only a superficial wound. The intruder then subdued Dale and tied him up tightly. He took their money, credit cards, phones and anything he found of value, and left. He let them live. That evening in Napa Valley, life and love became very precious to Dale's family.

I gave Julia a phone call one evening a few months after Ray's services. Julia sounded very happy, almost a bit giddy. She just returned home after a dinner date with David. It was a beautiful evening. She began to talk about David and what a wonderful man he was. It was clear Julia was smitten once again. One date and she was in love? My parental pastoral concern kicked in immediately. Did Julia really know him? After one date? Was he a good man? Did he have the same feelings for her as she had for him? It had not been long since Julia lost a husband to cancer. Julia would later tell me how worried I sounded on the telephone that evening.

David began attending church with Julia. Like an overprotective father I grilled him as to his intentions. He passed the test. He was a good man. He had the same feelings for Julia as Julia had for him. Julia learned you must seize love now for we don't know what tomorrow will bring. I married them two days after Christmas, just eight months after Ray's death. I married a person twice in one year. I never did that again in my ministry. It was the right thing to do. Life is short and love is precious.

CHAPTER 20

It's a Wonderful Life

It was December and I was watching Jimmy Stewart and Donna Reed in the Christmas classic, "It's a Wonderful Life." I saw it for the first time, watching not because the holiday season approached, but because Patrick asked me to watch the film. Though on the membership rolls, I had never seen Patrick in worship. I knew a little about him from his father and other members of the church. Everyone said he came back from Vietnam a different person than when he left. He lived alone in a small apartment walking to his job in the kitchen of a nearby restaurant. He had few friends and generally kept to himself.

I had met Patrick for the first time three weeks earlier. We talked over fountain Cokes. Fountain Cokes, Patrick said, tasted much better than Cokes out of the bottle or can. When I met Patrick, I expected someone withdrawn and reclusive, but Patrick was surprisingly engaging and social. He was thoughtful, giving, trusting, and deeply sensitive. When he received $200 from the state for his service in Vietnam, he gave it away to purchase an artificial leg for a man in Africa. He read widely and we discussed a variety of subjects. I enjoyed our talk. He never brought up Vietnam and neither did I.

Patrick had just found out he had lung cancer. He seemed remarkably calm for such a devastating diagnosis. He was a young man, only 42 years old. He accepted his illness and seemed willing to deal with whatever life might bring. He was not afraid of death. When I asked Patrick if faith helped him face his cancer, he replied a few years ago it would not have but now it did. He then asked if I had seen the movie "It's a Wonderful Life." I confessed I was probably one of only three persons in the country who had not seen it. He said we would talk more about faith after I watched the holiday classic.

Patrick was now dead. He went to the nearby VA hospital for surgery. The surgeon felt confident he could remove the malignant tumor in the lung surgically, giving Patrick an excellent chance of full recovery from the cancer. Something tragic, however, unfolded in the operating room. The surgeon accidentally cut the aorta artery and Patrick bled to death while he lay on the table.

Two days before surgery I took Patrick to get a haircut. He asked if I had watched "It's a Wonderful Life" yet. I confessed I hadn't had time, but it was on my list of things to do. So, in preparation for Patrick's memorial service, I watched George Bailey and his guardian angel, Clarence, for the first time, enjoying the sentimental, yet inspiring story.

In "It's a Wonderful Life," the life of George Bailey (Jimmy Stewart's character) unravels one Christmas Eve in his hometown of Bedford Falls. His savings and loan business is about to go under. He regretfully takes his frustration out on his family. He goes to a bar, becomes drunk, and gets in a fight. He finds himself on a bridge. He is angry and disappointed in himself. His life has been a failure. There is no point continuing. It will be easier if he ends it all. He will throw himself into the river and drown, bringing his misery to its proper finish.

Clarence, his guardian angel, somewhat of a disappointment in heaven, is sent to intervene. Clarence beats George into the water. When George dives in it is not to end his own life but to save another. He rescues Clarence, and through rescuing Clarence, eventually rescues himself. When George tells Clarence he wishes he had never been born, Clarence takes him on a tour of the Bedford Falls that would have been if he had never been born. It is a dreary, mournful place, controlled by the greed of the wealthy. George was unaware of the good he had done, the lives he had touched, the tremendous impact his decency and kindness had on the community. He returns home late on Christmas Eve to a family and town that love him dearly.

I never discussed George Bailey and Bedford Falls with Patrick. I don't know how the movie informed his faith and gave him hope. I don't know what Patrick intended for me to learn from the movie. Maybe it had something to do with guardian angels. God is always watching over and protecting us. We are never alone. Maybe it was a message of hope and faith. Maybe it was about second chances we receive in life. Maybe that we never know the impact or influence we have on others. We touch lives and make a difference but never know. And all of us, from the smallest to the greatest, can change the world for the better. Maybe it was that life is good and we need to open our eyes and see the goodness in ourselves and others.

Perhaps Patrick intended to say he had a wonderful life. To the rest of us, his life seemed plain, unfulfilling, even trivial. He never married, had no children, worked menial jobs, had a very small circle of friends. His pleasures were simple, a fountain Coke. His life passed by with seemingly little significance to the larger world. Yet, perhaps in the goodness, decency and kindness of each day of Patrick's life, the world was a little better. Maybe Patrick walked a different path than we who strive for success, recognition and wealth, but God blessed him and gave him a wonderful life.

In another community, about 15 years after Patrick's death, I attended an "It's a Wonderful Life" celebration. Our neighbor Dan and his wife Sue threw a party for friends and family, thanking them for supporting Dan through his cancer. Dan awoke Easter morning, confused and unstable. Sue called 911. Doctors soon found cancer in the brain. Dan began treatments right away. Treatments were successful and cancer was controlled, for now. No one knew what the morning would bring, but Dan felt thankful to be alive. He wanted to share his joy with others, and planned the celebration.

We all received a set of 'wings' at Dan's party. At the end of "It's a Wonderful Life," a bell rings. George Bailey's daughter says that means an angel earned his wings. Clarence, the guardian angel in the movie, just earned his promotion for saving George. Our wings at Dan's party told us we earned our wings as Dan's guardian angels. Unfortunately, Dan's cancer returned and he passed away a couple of years after we moved from the neighborhood.

Dan was ten years older than Patrick when he discovered he had cancer. His life was much different than Patrick's, one of achievement and success. He was an outstanding athlete in high school. He married a beautiful woman and they had two lovely daughters. Dan ran a thriving business and they lived in a gorgeous house. Dan was respected and admired. He enjoyed all the trappings of American suburban success. Even more, he seemed happy and content. He was a nice guy.

Dan and Patrick, as different as their lives appeared, both discovered the joy of "A Wonderful Life." Each of us is presented with a different canvas to paint our life's story. It is not a blank canvas. Many details have already been filled in – the families into which we are born; the country, culture, socio-economic status with which we begin; natural talents, intelligence and emotional personalities we are given at birth. As we paint our stories, we have disparate opportunities and limited choices. We experience boundaries in our paintings we perhaps cannot cross. We have obstacles and stumbling blocks. Sometimes we have terrible things we have to endure in our painting. The "Wonderful Life" we seek is different for each of us. For some it can be much harder to discover and know. Different as we are and different as our circumstances may be, I pray each of us can taste that "Wonderful Life," at least for a brief time as I think Patrick did, and know something of the goodness and joy in this world.

CHAPTER 21

I Have Nothing

"When I married Herman," Edith said, "he told me I would never have to worry. He said he would take care of me for the rest of my life. Now, I am told there is nothing for me, nothing at all." Herman had been gone for just a couple of weeks. He went to bed one evening prepared for a journey the next day home to his roots in a neighboring state, a journey he made every year. His suitcase packed, his car readied, car keys and billfold neatly laid out on the counter, Herman was a meticulous and particular man. But the suitcase was never loaded into the car and the car never left the garage. Herman never woke up. He took a journey to a different home. He went home to his Creator.

Tears flowed down Edith's cheeks. They were not tears of grief for her late husband, but bitter, angry tears. Edith felt betrayed. She felt foolish having believed his words.

It was the second marriage for both Edith and Herman. They found each other after their first spouses died and tied the knot after a brief courtship. Herman had a nice home and wanted to remain in it. That was okay with Edith. Herman also wanted to keep the furniture and household items that had served the house for many years. Edith wanted to bring some of her things and make it 'their' house and not just 'his.' Herman though was insistent on keeping his things. Edith gave in. She sold her furnishings and moved in with Herman.

The living room was now half-empty. Many pieces of furniture were gone. Herman's only son and daughter-in-law had been there and removed furnishings of greater value. They would gather remaining items later. The house would soon be on the market and Edith would have to move when it sold. She could use the car for a while but that would go to one of Herman's grandchildren. As Edith said, "I have nothing."

Edith said Herman redid his will when they married. Edith never read it, didn't think to have another attorney look it over. She trusted Herman. Herman said she would never have to worry and she believed him. But the will was clear. The house and all the household belongings that were his before the wedding went to his son. All his investments and bank accounts (they didn't even have a joint checking account – Herman paid the bills) went to the son. The car went to a grandchild.

Edith said it hadn't been easy being married to Herman. He was controlling and jealous. She would come home from a walk and be accused of having an affair with a neighbor man half her age. Edith never shared this information with me before. I didn't know Herman and Edith well. They were in church every Sunday, but rarely attended other events.

I received a glimpse into Herman's cheapness once from the chair of our stewardship campaign. The chair was updating me about the progress of the campaign. He was proud of how well the church gave as a whole. "But there is this one guy," he went on, "who is in church every Sunday. He wears dapper clothes and drives a Cadillac. I opened his card and it said $52. At first, I thought it was $52 per week, or maybe a month. I looked again and it was $52 per year. He pledges $1 per week." The Chair shook his head. From his description, I knew he meant Herman.

Edith made plans to move in with her daughter. She didn't know what else to do. Her daughter was happy to have her, but Edith felt she was imposing. Edith had Social Security and a very small pension to live on. She didn't have a car or furniture. She wasn't sure what she could afford. She consulted an attorney about Herman's will, but there wasn't much she could do about changing it. The will was valid and his son was simply getting what was rightfully his. Edith sat there, hurt and angry, feeling betrayed and foolish.

Wills are always important, but especially so when older couples enter a second marriage. It is important couples have new wills created and they read and understand each other's wills. It is also important couples share those wills with their grown children so they, too, know what to expect.

I sat with Art and his two step-daughters in Art's living room planning the service for Jean, Art's wife. I considered myself adept in working with families to create a memorial service honoring the desires of loved ones, the spirit of the deceased, and the character of God. But this afternoon was not going well. Anything Art suggested about the service was quickly vetoed by one of the daughters. When Art expressed reservations about a song or part of the service he felt uncomfortable with, the daughters told him it would be what their mother wanted and he should know that. I was unsure of the reasons for the daughters' hostilities. I was unaware of any hostility in the family before that afternoon. Art and Jean seemed like a happy couple who found love a second time at an older age. Art and Jean, both widowed, met while singing in a church choir. Art was ten years older, but young in spirit. They assumed Art would go first, but it was Jean who got cancer and died.

On a visit with Art a couple of weeks later, Art talked about the hostilities. Things had gotten uglier after the memorial service. Art explained he and Jean had gone to an attorney together before they were married. They updated their wills, living wills and other documents. They agreed they would share expenses equally. They were open and transparent with one another and had no trouble working things out. When Jean died, the daughters went quickly to the attorney and checked the will and finances. They were upset their mother used money from her trust fund for household expenses. Art, as the man, should have covered those. They were upset Jean, as Art did in his will, provided a small monetary amount for her spouse in case of death. That was money they felt they should receive. They were fighting it so Art was giving in.

Again, open communication among all family members is important. A pastoral colleague, upon retirement, put together a notebook with all of the family's finances and legal documents. He gave a copy to each of their children one Christmas and has updated it every Christmas since. He says the children roll their eyes every year when they receive it, but after his death they will be happy he did the necessary planning.

Wills for all of us are important. When Carolyn was expecting our first child, we knew we should have a will, but we didn't want to use our limited resources on an attorney. I went to the library and checked out a write-your-own will book. (This was well before the internet and its resources.) I then consulted the wills of family members and wrote our own. A couple of members of the church witnessed and signed it. That will served us for over 30 years until we took advantage of optional legal benefits through Carolyn's employment and consulted an attorney to replace it.

Chuck, though, didn't have a will at all. He was in his early 50s, and dying. He attended worship as usual on Sunday morning and taught school as usual on Monday. He was not feeling well as he left school and stopped in the emergency room of the nearby hospital. Tests were done. Cancer was in the fluid around Chuck's lungs. He was told he would never go home from the hospital, that he had perhaps only three weeks to live.

On one of my first visits with Chuck after he heard the news, I asked if there was anything I could do. Chuck accepted his diagnosis with amazing grace and calm, but he worried about one thing. He didn't have a will. Did he want me to ask an attorney to come to his hospital room? Yes, he said. I contacted an attorney in the church. He went to Chuck's room the next day and guided Chuck through the process. A couple of days later, as predicted, Chuck's health deteriorated quickly. He could not have completed a will if he had put it off any longer. Chuck's sudden illness and rapid decline were enough for his children to contend with. Having a will spared them some of the aggravation and hassles associated with settling an estate.

Pastors specialize in the 'spiritual' side of the human existence. A little forethought and planning in the practical and legal sides of life can sometimes make the journey on the 'spiritual' side a little smoother and amicable for all.

CHAPTER 22

Welcome Her Home

I stood at Elizabeth's bedside talking. I felt a little foolish. Elizabeth couldn't hear me. Everyone acknowledged that. Ever since her massive stroke a few weeks earlier, she was presumed 'brain-dead.' I repeated to Elizabeth what I said to her every visit. I told Elizabeth she was in everyone's prayers and Charles and her daughters were thinking of her. She had been blessed. She had a good life, a blessed life with a wonderful family. It was now time to say 'goodbye' to this world and 'hello' to the next. God was waiting for her. God had a place prepared for her. Let go. Nurses went in and out as I talked with Elizabeth. I hoped they didn't think I was foolish.

I offered a prayer, though I wasn't sure what to pray for. She was beyond healing. No one wanted her to stay where she was, neither alive nor dead. If she couldn't be healed, it was best she pass on. I could only pray God would take her soon, that God would release her spirit from its imprisonment in a body that no longer served her. So I prayed, "God, You love Elizabeth. You have a place for her in your realm. Welcome her home."

Elizabeth's stroke was severe. According to doctors, it wiped out any ability to think or communicate or experience anything we might call 'human.' She would be what is commonly referred to as a 'vegetable' for as long as she lived. The stroke though hadn't affected her heart and lungs. They were strong for a woman in her mid-70s. If given proper nourishment and water, Elizabeth might live for a long time, probably years, in her 'vegetative' state.

It was the second marriage for Elizabeth and her husband, Charles. They were good friends as couples with their first spouses. When those spouses died, they married and had a good life together. The good life ended the day Elizabeth had a stroke. Charles didn't want to see Elizabeth continue in a comatose state. They had no living wills but they discussed end of life decisions enough for Charles to know

Elizabeth didn't want to exist in such a state either. It was time to let Elizabeth pass on.

The difficulty was Elizabeth breathed well on her own. If a patient is permanently unconscious and a ventilator is breathing for her, the decision to terminate life is easier. Detach the ventilator and the patient usually passes within minutes or hours. The family has clear knowledge the patient was kept alive through artificial means and feels at peace in their decision. They can move forward knowing they have done the right thing for their loved one.

If a person breathes on her own, as Elizabeth did, one must withhold food and water to terminate life. It may take several weeks withholding food for a person to pass away, less time if water is withheld also. Watching a loved one lying in bed slowly deteriorating over a long period of time is emotionally draining. Are they suffering? Is there pain? Was this the right decision?

Withholding nourishment was controversial at the time Elizabeth lay in her bed. Are we hastening an unnatural death if we do so? Are we causing undue suffering? Or, are we artificially prolonging life and causing suffering if we provide nourishment and water? In living wills of most states today, there is usually a separate decision to initial if we do not wish to receive nourishment when permanently unconscious. We struggle with the best decisions for our dying loved ones. We struggle also with what is best for the living.

Charles decided to withhold nourishment shortly after doctors determined Elizabeth was permanently unconscious. Charles was a gentleman and always wanted to do the honorable thing. It was a hard decision to make emotionally, but he believed very strongly it was the right one, right not just for him but also for Elizabeth. Weeks wore on and Elizabeth's continued existence between life and death wore on Charles and everyone else. Visiting Elizabeth became difficult. Twelve weeks after the stroke, after many visits standing by her bedside feeling foolish as I talked and prayed, Elizabeth finally passed away.

Living wills help make difficult decisions easier for our loved ones. They understand better the type of care we desire as we approach death. Since end-of-life decisions are often not clear, it helps also if we have talked about death with our loved ones and verbally let them know our wishes in different situations and the minimum quality of life we believe we would find satisfying. It helps if we assure them we trust their decisions and know they will make the best decision for us when the time comes. They know our wishes and can make difficult decisions with our blessing. We also tell our loved ones our final hope is not in this life and the length of days on earth. Our final hope is in a Savior whom we believe died and was raised from the dead and will come again to take us to our final home.

Charles continued to struggle emotionally after Elizabeth's death. The decision to end Elizabeth's life and weeks spent at her bedside had taken their toll on

Charles. A few months later, though, I sensed Charles' spirits were picking up. The sparkle returned to his eye, the lilt to his walk. He was smiling and laughing again. I was glad Charles was moving forward.

Women (and some men) in our church ran a consignment shop where we sold gently used clothing and household items. The shop was well run and successful. It generated funds for some 'extra' things in the church and a variety of missions in the community. I would often stop in the shop for a few minutes on Monday or Tuesday morning. In part, I was checking to see if they received new clothing in my size. Nearly all my clothes in those days came from the shop. Women's fashions change rapidly and the little shop overflowed with women's clothing. Men usually wear clothes until they are threadbare. Most of my suits and shirts came from men who died.

More importantly at the shop, I was catching up on the 'news' of the church. How was Millie's aunt Martha doing? What about Harold's grandson? Amidst the news was always a little, or maybe a lot, of gossip. As pastor, I always felt I was either the first to know something or the last. Perhaps someone shared with me in confidence and I knew a situation in the church long before anyone else. Or something was happening (an affair, a conflict) and no one had the courage to tell me.

One day a widow, not a member of the church but a volunteer at the shop, talked about plans she and someone named Charles had for the weekend. She spoke in such familiar terms about Charles I assumed he was her boyfriend. When she left the shop, I asked the other ladies, "Who is Charles she is talking about?" Well, it was Elizabeth's widower. After months of mourning, he found a new love interest. Charles was moving forward.

CHAPTER 23

You Knew When to Leave

When a woman loses her husband, other women mobilize. They invite her to luncheons and concerts, book groups and sewing circles, yoga and water aerobics. They chat on the phone and drop off flowers and cookies. They shop together and go for walks. They ask her to come on a bus trip to New York or a week's excursion to France. Women bond together in times of need. They talk about feelings, needs and desires. They don't grieve alone.

Not so with men. When they lose a wife, other men say, "That's too bad." There may be an invitation to a ball game or a golf outing. Perhaps a single phone call or card. Nothing more. Men go on with life, alone. If they talk, it is about Saturday's football game or Sunday's golf match, not about hurt or grief.

Elizabeth's husband, Charles, though, had three other men in our church to journey with him in grief. I don't think they did much talking about feelings, after all they were men, but at least they had lunch together on occasion. They also sat together, in the last pew of the church, always the last pew. One summer, when attendance was light, I roped off the last few pews to encourage folks to sit closer. They just picked up the rope and sat in their usual spot. The rope was put away the following week. I presided over the memorial service for each of their wives.

The four men had been movers and shakers in the community. Charles was the son of a leading industrialist in the city. His family owned a steel mill, one of the economic engines in the region. Charles ran a smaller family company. He grew up in the church and city and was devoted to each.

Fred owned a local insurance agency. He was active in his university's athletics and friends with a big-time national coach. He had a deep bass voice that commanded attention. Folks in the church talked about his late wife, Lucille, with fondness. She died of cancer shortly after I arrived. She was viewed as a very 'spiritual' person. You had to look hard for a 'spiritual' bone in Fred's body.

Ernest owned a local grocery store. Long after national chains moved into town, Ernest ran a small, successful family-owned grocery through attention to personal service. Everyone was greeted by name. His wife, Marilyn, was one of the sweetest, caring ladies I ever met. Although she never smoked, she died of smoker's lung cancer. Ernest loved racing and owned race cars.

Ken was a noted attorney in town, tall and distinguished looking. He served in the state legislature and considered a run for Governor. He prided himself on being a wordsmith and orator. He hadn't attended worship for many years until a serious illness put him in the hospital. I visited him. Ken always said what he liked about me was not just that I visited him but, in his words, "You knew when to leave." I think he meant I didn't intrude where I wasn't wanted. I respected his space and his feelings. I took cues from him and didn't press my agenda. Ken's wife, June, was an elegant and gracious lady, a Christian Scientist. She, too, died of cancer. Ken didn't care for the Christian Science readings so he asked me to preside over her service and offer a eulogy.

These men, movers and shakers around the community, were doers. They prided themselves on getting things done. They were also good talkers. Conversation with them was spirited and fun. They didn't talk about feelings. They didn't talk about grief, loneliness, inward hurt and pain. They didn't talk about these things, but they felt them. I discovered that their feelings, as with most men, were usually revealed in silences. You didn't have to verbalize. Silence spoke more profoundly than words. Words got in the way and were inadequate. We would sit in silence and let the silence say what needed to be said.

These men also coveted prayer. In prayer I could verbalize feelings not expressed in regular conversation. In prayer I could express their longings for God's peace and strength. Prayer gave them comfort and hope for the grief that, though not always expressed on their lips, lay heavy on their hearts. Prayer was serious stuff for them. Prayer should not reduce God to their best friend or buddy, thereby trivializing or diminishing the greatness of God. God was always more than we could know or experience. God's holiness, majesty and mystery evoked wonder, and could not be captured in simple platitudes.

Delbert was a member of a different church I served. He lived in a nursing home in another city. Because of the long drive, I saw him only on occasion and listened to his stories. He was a master storyteller and I didn't mind hearing some for the third or fourth time. He began speaking before I sat down. He was still going when I walked out the door an hour later. Another man in our congregation was very faithful to call Delbert every few weeks to catch up. When we checked notes, we usually heard the same stories. When I asked Delbert one day if this man was still calling, Delbert said to me, "Yes, he says I am the only friend he has." I found it hard to believe. This man lived in the same community his entire life and his only friend is the elderly gentleman in the nursing home he occasionally calls on the phone? Maybe it was true. Men have a hard time making friendships.

The best support I have seen men offer one another has come in small groups organized just for men. The men meet regularly, usually have food, and explore the Bible or faith-related themes. At one church we had a small men's group of about eight who met one Saturday morning per month for breakfast and study. The group attracted few newcomers but those who came usually didn't leave. Over the years we came to know each other well, at times we thought too well. We talked about our work, our kids, and sometimes our wives. We would sometimes share things that were hurting and grieving us also. What we shared was always considered confidential.

Within a year three wives, all in their 50's, started battles with cancer. Two would lose their battles a few months apart. A fourth man in the group would lose his son to suicide. I pray those many Saturday mornings where we had eaten, studied and prayed together helped the men through these difficult times. They were there for one another as they suffered loss, and also as they put their lives back together.

Men may voice their fears and hurts in different ways than women. They may be more reluctant to reach out for help or offer help to others. The need for support, companionship and comfort, though, is just as real for men as women. Men voice feelings and longings in prayers, not in casual conversation. Much can be left unsaid because it is already understood. Honesty and transparency is expressed in our emotions. Love and empathy is felt, though not always verbalized.

I was glad these four men, former movers and shakers of the community, sat together every Sunday in the back pew, even when I tried to rope it off. I am glad they joked, teased each other and reminisced about old times. I am glad they ate lunch together. Men have a hard time making friendships. I rejoice when they do. Good friends lift our spirits and give us comfort and hope as we journey through the valleys of life.

CHAPTER 24

I Didn't Think You Had It in You

I stopped to see David's widow, Rose, a few days after his memorial service. They lived in a beautiful home with wonderful pieces of artwork, most created by Rose. Rose gave me tours of her art studio on previous visits. Pieces of wood or blocks of stone sat around uncut. Rose said she waited for the wood or stone to tell her what lay inside. Only once the stone spoke could she begin to cut. I once asked her to design the cover of the bulletin for a celebration Sunday in the church. It was a simple task, I thought, considering her abilities, but she agonized over the cover for weeks. Her artistic expression could not be easily corralled. It flowed spontaneously from her inner spirit.

We sat in a large sunroom. The windows looked onto a country club fairway. When David asked the architect to design the sunroom he told him the windows had to stand up to the impact of golf balls. The architect said they would. When the room was completed, David took out his driver, stood in his back yard, and unleashed a drive into the window from 30 feet. The window withstood the impact and David wrote out a check.

"The service for David couldn't have been any better. I didn't think you had it in you. " Rose said to me in her usual direct style of speaking. I thought it was a compliment and said, "Thank you." David's family owned the local newspaper and he served as publisher for more than 40 years. Ninety-seven per cent of the city subscribed to it, the highest percentage of any newspaper in the country. David was an influential voice in the community. Through his leadership in national newspaper associations, David was also an influential voice well beyond our little city. He was an important person, a man of great resolve and determination. He and Rose demanded a lot from themselves. They demanded a lot from others. And they voiced their displeasure when they were disappointed. Rose believed in a previous life she had been a Viking warrior.

I was a young pastor in my 30s, somewhat reserved and shy. I must have been in the bathroom when God passed out charisma because I didn't have any. I was not an impressive preaching personality gaining followers and attracting crowds. My ministry flowed from perceptive listening, building consensus and respect, understanding and knowing my parishioners, out-of-sight organization, attention to details, and just plain hard work. I was adept working with the creative energies of others to shape programs and worship services that ministered effectively to those our congregation served. Those types of gifts don't win awards in dynamism and popularity. Fortunately, those gifts were needed at the church at that time. The church was growing and prospering after a disastrous period of decline. So, Rose wondered if I were up to the task of a memorial service to give David a fitting sendoff. I guess I passed the test.

When I arrived at the church, Rose attended faithfully. David had not worshipped for many years. When he was hospitalized with significant health issues, I made calls and prayed for his recovery. He survived the scare and returned home. He started to attend worship, every week. I thought it wouldn't last. I saw others in my ministry who, after an illness or unnerving life event, return to worship but quickly fade out of sight.

I was especially suspicious because the church I served was called the 'Country Club' church at one time. Men joined because it offered connections to other men of stature in the community. A previous minister offered a prayer early Sunday morning in the country club locker room. The 'Country Club' reputation helped build the church for generations. I think it also helped lead to its rapid decline in the years before I arrived. David was from the generation of 'Country Club' men. The 'Country Club' model didn't seem appropriate to me for a church following a Savior who sacrificed and died for us.

I was suspicious also because I had once inadvertently seen a list of pledging amounts. Despite considerable resources, David's pledge was less than half the congregation's average. I was dubious of David's prolonged involvement.

I was wrong. From then on David was a regular worshipper on Sunday mornings the six months a year not in Florida. Maybe his life slowed and he had time. Perhaps he was getting up in years and things of God were more relevant. I sensed he was honestly seeking to know and serve God.

David occasionally stopped in my office with a question, always a focused question. At first, the questions didn't relate to faith or theology. They were about practical things around the church, things like, "Our sanctuary is a disaster, when are we going to fix it up? How much money do we need?" or "How many new members do we get a year? Is that enough to sustain the church?" On occasion, he would ask me to lunch, not to the country club but the hot dog diner. Something was on his mind. He wanted to know what I thought. His faith was hands-on, but every now and then he surprised me with a question about what I meant in a sermon, a belief of the church or a teaching of the Bible.

At one of those hot dog lunches, David acknowledged he didn't give much to the church. He also said he wasn't going to give any more than he did toward the operating budget. But he wanted to help. Let him know when there were building needs. I held him to that promise and he came through with substantial leading gifts for capital campaigns.

I would have liked to learn more about David. He led an interesting life. He possessed a wonderful history of the community. He also did some wacky things, like drive the car when barnstorming stunt pilot Mike Murphy took off and landed an airplane on a moving vehicle for the first time in history. But David refused to talk about himself. He was business-like. He didn't tell stories or dabble in trivialities. I think he took his publishing responsibility very seriously. One time he opened up a little of his inner feelings when he said he felt a tremendous burden lift when the newspaper was sold. Pleasing family members with financial interest in the newspaper was the most difficult aspect of the job.

David died suddenly of a heart attack. He was 78 and appeared to be in excellent health. When I went over the morning of his death, his body was still in bed, reading light on and a book at his side. He appeared to die peacefully for a man who lived with so much energy and resolve.

When I met with Rose and her sons to plan the memorial service, many ideas were considered. The family members wanted so much included – poems and music, tributes by children and grandchildren, liturgy, Scriptures and prayers. Talking about the service may have seemed a bit chaotic to Rose. She probably had a difficult time understanding how it all could come together in a unified whole, but it apparently did. She was pleasantly surprised. Perhaps I should have shared with her that putting together a worship service or writing a sermon is like creating a work of art. We look at material we have to work with – Scriptures, music, stories – and keep looking until our inner spirit speaks and tells us the form it should take.

I think Rose and I were both guilty of misjudgment. I misjudged David and she misjudged me. So often we judge others not for who they are. We judge from feeble first impressions, past prejudices or erroneous stereotypes. Judgments reveal more about us than the person we are judging. How often others surprise and delight us when we cast off misconceptions and learn to know the uniqueness of each person.

CHAPTER 25

Get Out! And Never Come Back!

"Get out!" Clarence exploded as I entered his hospital room. "Get out! I don't need you! You come in every day and say your damn little prayers, but you don't know how I feel. You don't know the pain I have. You don't know what I am going through. Get out, and never come back!" I turned around and walked out.

I should have been expecting the outburst. In previous visits I listened as Clarence chewed out the nurse, nursing assistant, respiratory therapist, even the housekeeper. Now it was my turn to bear the wrath of Clarence's anger.

Clarence was angry at the world. He had congestive heart failure. This once active man now spent his life attached to an oxygen tank through a long tube from his nose. Laboring for breath is a horrible struggle. I sensed though there was more to Clarence's anger. Even before Clarence's health deteriorated, he was out of sorts with the world. In retirement, before his health issues, he and his wife Ruby had the financial means to travel literally around the world, more than once. They enjoyed the good things of life. Why was he so angry?

Clarence's hands always caught my attention. They were large hands, rough and strong, hands of someone who had worked hard all his life, hands that were not idle. Clarence was like his hands, a little rough and tough.

Clarence had always been a fighter. Though he came from humble means he had ambitions for success. As a young man he rented 1200 acres and started a large hog operation. He worked hard and his business flourished. When a fall broke his back and he could no longer handle the physically demanding farm work, he sold the hogs and went on the road selling. Once again, he was successful.

Then Clarence and Ruby received phone calls from neighbors of Ruby's family.

Ruby's family had considerable land, money and influence in the area. Ruby's father and brother were drinking heavily, the neighbors said. They were squandering the family's wealth accumulated over generations. If there was going to be anything left, the neighbors said, Ruby better come home and let Clarence take over the family business. Clarence and Ruby returned to Ruby's roots. Clarence managed the business and the farm turned around.

Clarence and Ruby were devoted to one another but seemed to have few friends. They travelled by themselves. They ate out by themselves. They were not blessed with children. A couple of nephews called on occasion. Clarence dismissed their visits as simply checking on their inheritance.

I sensed Clarence nurtured resentment for giving up a successful career to take over the farming business of Ruby's family. I think he felt people in the community viewed him as a moocher or freeloader, living off the considerable means of his wife's family, not someone who was successful on his own. I think that bothered Clarence deeply. He was a proud, successful, self-made man. He didn't need to rely on his wife's money. He took over his wife's family business out of a sense of duty, not to sponge. He was anything but a sponge. It hurt Clarence people might think that.

About this time I visited a young girl at the hospital. It was an odd visit. I received a call from the chaplain's office of someone asking for me to stop by. I knew my congregation well and it was not a name associated with the congregation. Since this occurred before HIPAA, I could check the hospital admissions list for additional information. I saw the person was a ten-year old girl. Again, I was puzzled who this might be. Her room was outside a nurse's station and I waited as a physician completed his visit.

It seems I spent a lot of time waiting in hospital hallways. Most of my ministry was before cell phones. So, I would listen, observe, pray, and look at my watch. I also looked up at ceiling tiles and wondered about the myriad of tubes, pipes and gadgets embedded in the ceiling.

I walked in and introduced myself. Again, I was puzzled. I did not recognize the girl. Very awkwardly I apologized and asked if we had met. Oh, she said, her family had visited the church last Sunday for the first time. I have never been a pied piper of children but I did my best to relate. I asked what brought her to the hospital. She talked about getting sick Sunday evening. Her appendix was the problem and she had surgery to remove it. I asked if it hurt and she said yes. I asked if it still hurt a little and she said yes. We talked about children in the church she knew and about her brother and sister. We had a prayer. As I left the room I thought to myself it had been a clumsy visit. I hadn't done a very good job of connecting with this little girl.

The physician who had just seen the girl got on the elevator with me. He was at the nurse's station and apparently overheard our visit. He was a young surgeon people in town respected. As the elevator doors closed, he said to me, "Never ask a child if they are in pain. If they are in pain, they will tell you. Don't put ideas into their heads." He got off at the next floor and I stood stunned in the elevator. "Never ask a child if they are in pain?" Those words of advice haunted me the next couple of days.

I called the parents of the little girl after she was home, to ask how she was doing. Her mother said she was doing fine. Then she added her daughter kept talking about my visit. It was the highlight of her stay in the hospital. When the family returned to worship, she gave me a big hug. Again, her parents told me how much the visit meant to their daughter.

It had been an odd visit, I thought, not at all special. I was surprised it meant that much. Why? I wondered if it was because I asked if she hurt and believed her when she said it did. Someone understood her. It is awful to be in pain and not have others acknowledge it, to suffer alone. I decided I wouldn't follow the advice of the young surgeon. Pain was meant to be shared, including the pain of children.

I thought of the visit to this girl as I reflected on Clarence's outburst, ordering me out of the room and telling me never to come back. Clarence was in pain, physically and emotionally. He was also alone. His pain needed to be shared. Maybe I was not listening closely. Maybe my hospital visits were too perfunctory.

I returned to Clarence's room the next day. He never said a word about his outburst. Neither did I. I continued to return and say my 'damn little prayers' with him. I also tried to listen a little more carefully. I tried to understand his pain and his suffering the best I could.

Clarence's congestive heart failure became worse. He and Ruby moved into assisted living. Ruby showed signs of dementia and moved into a skilled nursing unit. I continued to visit Clarence and he began to mellow. I sensed he no longer had to be the tough guy. We had wonderful conversations. Clarence no longer hid his tender emotions and often began to cry during our visits. Nearly every visit he would tell me no one cared about him except me. Besides his wife's nephews, I was the only one who came to see him. He was alone and our time together meant a lot.

Clarence's mind stayed sharp until the day of his death. I called on him at the hospital one morning and, though Clarence appeared to understand all I said, he was too weak to respond. Thinking death might be imminent, I returned that afternoon. When I walked into the room I could see he had passed away. I went to the nurse's station and asked if she knew. Yes, she said, they had found him dead less than five minutes earlier. I went back into Clarence's room to wait the arrival of a nephew. I am glad I didn't give up on Clarence when he ordered me out of his room, and I am glad Clarence didn't give up on me.

CHAPTER 26

Reminds Me of a Boy Scout

I knew Stanley's house would be bad, but not this bad. I had seen cluttered and dirty houses, even disgusting houses. I had been in the homes of hoarders. This was far beyond those, beyond filthy and uninhabitable. Stanley apparently lived in a wretched lounge chair in front of the television. One small path led from the chair through the dining room to the refrigerator in the kitchen. Another path led to the bathroom. That was the only passable floor space. Trash filled the rest of the house, at least 5-6 feet high – junk mail and old newspapers, soup cans, discarded take-out dinner cartons, and who knows what else. The neighbor who led me through the house said he had taken away and burned piles of porn videos. The bathroom looked worse than an outhouse. Piles of human feces is too nice of a description. It was full of shit.

Stanley had fallen in the house, broken his ankle and couldn't walk. He was forced to call 911. I don't know what unfolded between the police and the county's office for older adults, but it didn't take much to determine Stanley could no longer live in the house. He was moved into a nursing home. Piles of clutter grew around his bed there. The neighbor and the neighbor's family agreed to declutter his house and prepare it for market in exchange for anything of value inside. They ended up with a truck full of antique furniture to sell as compensation for the disgusting hours they spent clearing out the house. I have no idea whether it paid for their time.

Although I stood on the front porch many times, I had never been inside the house before. When I arrived at the church, I made attempts to get to know Stanley and his sister, Clara. I called at their house, a house reminding me of Boo Radley's in *To Kill a Mockingbird*, but without the trees. I knocked on the front door, stood back, then waited on the porch. No one answered. After a couple of knocks, I would see a curtain move slightly and a face glance out the window. Still no one answered. I left my card and returned to my car.

The neighbor, who gave me the tour, greeted me on one visit when I went to leave. He said ten years earlier neighbors got together and cleaned out Stanley and Clara's house. They filled two large dumpsters with clutter, including a couple of sex dolls. The mess quickly returned and the neighbors vowed not to undertake another cleaning. I gave him my card in case he ever needed to reach me.

Clara's health began failing perhaps 20 years earlier. She was confined to her house. Though I never visited with her inside her home, Clara called me at the church on occasion, usually after one of my futile attempts to visit at the house. Clara loved talking on the phone. She cued me in on the history of the community and gossip of years past. She would say outrageous things trying to provoke reactions. She offered her opinion on just about everything. Our conversations sometimes lasted an hour. They were never boring and never predictable. I sensed she called when Stanley was not home.

As Clara's health deteriorated, she entered a nursing home where we were able to visit face to face. On one visit she received a call from a brother who lived out of state. I excused myself and as I walked out the door I heard her say to her brother, "That was the preacher – kind of reminds me of a Boy Scout." Her brother Stanley often visited her in the nursing home. His visits became more closely monitored, however, after a nurse walked in and found Stanley and Clara engaged in a sex act.

After Clara's death I continued to call on Stanley. When I knocked on the door, the curtain moved and a face appeared as before. Then Stanley would open the door, just the slightest crack, and slip out onto the porch. In that brief moment an overwhelming stench slipped out the door with Stanley. It was all I could do to remain on the porch. We visited on the porch no matter what the temperature, even when the thermometer dipped below freezing. I knew his living conditions must be deplorable but I was cautious about intruding into his life. I offered to help in any way possible. Stanley, of course, turned down offers. He was getting along quite well by himself. I struggled whether to report Stanley to the authorities. Instead, I tried to gain his trust to see if he might seek help voluntarily. Finally, Stanley broke his ankle and the situation took care of itself.

I don't know what kept Stanley in that abominable house all those years. Perhaps because the house was the only one he ever lived in. He didn't know what else to do. Perhaps too, his addiction to porn kept him there. I don't know what demons dwelled in Stanley's past. He never spoke about them. Often, our lives start down a road and we just don't know how to get off that road, as bad as it may be.

Stanley seemed happy in the nursing home. After his broken ankle healed, he really didn't need nursing home care for his physical needs but he stayed. I guess the county didn't know what else to do with Stanley. Maybe he had money to pay for the room. I wasn't sure. He seemed to enjoy three meals per day, clean sheets and people coming to wait on him at the press of a call button. He argued with the nursing staff constantly about the amount of clutter around his bed, but that was his biggest complaint. I wondered whether I should have reported Stanley to authorities years earlier. He could have enjoyed the comforts longer.

On one visit I was surprised to find a woman taking dictation from Stanley. Apparently Stanley advertised in the newspaper and a stenographer answered the ad. She looked uncomfortable being there. I gave her my card and said she could give me a call. She did. She didn't quite know what was going on with Stanley. Most of his dictation was high-sounding words, but gibberish. She felt kind of creepy there. Besides, she hadn't been paid yet. I told her she probably wouldn't get paid and she may want to quit before she invested any more time.

Sometimes in the ministry, we enter situations where it is difficult to find signs of redemption. In all of my visits with Stanley I don't think I ever heard a word of caring or sympathy for another. Stanley seemed unable to respond to other human beings in loving and giving ways. He lived in a weird, dysfunctional world, seemingly devoid of the redeeming grace of Jesus and the renewing power of the Holy Spirit. And yet, I believe Stanley, like all of us, bore the image of his Creator. Somewhere in his narrow and self-absorbed world, God's light was trying to shine. It was hard for me to imagine the beautiful person God intended Stanley to be. Somehow though, I believe God's grace doesn't give up. If life continues beyond the grave, as I proclaim, then God's grace extends beyond the grave. We cling to the hope of a better life for some, if only through our faith in what is yet to come.

CHAPTER 27

It Isn't Fair. It Isn't Fair

"It isn't fair. It isn't fair." Arlene lamented as I approached her a few minutes before the public viewing. Bob's body was in the front of the sanctuary, before the beautiful altar where he presided over communion for 20 years and next to the pulpit where he proclaimed God's Word faithfully and eloquently Sunday after Sunday. The body was dressed in the gray preaching robe he always wore in worship. Hundreds of parishioners would soon arrive. They would line back the center aisle of the sanctuary and out the front door, supporting Bob's wife, Arlene, and expressing their love to Bob. Less than a month earlier, I attended a huge retirement dinner for Bob. It was a festive, joyful occasion. The congregation honored his diligent and loving years of service.

The church was Bob's life. He served as a pastor for 40 years, devoted to his congregations, devoted to serving his God. He worked long hours visiting the sick, preparing sermons, studying the Scriptures, teaching Bible studies and overseeing all the details of the church. He was on call 24 hours a day. Other than vacations, he rarely took a day off. I had the privilege of serving as his Associate Pastor for four years. The church was the heart of Bob's family life as well. Arlene served as Director of the Preschool, his daughter as Church Secretary at one time. His son mowed the lawn before his tragic death in a car accident.

Besides the church, Bob had another great passion, fishing. In particular, he loved fishing in his beloved lakes in the north woods of Wisconsin. When I served with him, all his vacation time was spent at his lake cabin there. He relaxed, taking his little fishing boat out every day to cast for northern pike, walleye and bass.

Bob and Arlene loaned their cabin to our family for a week one summer. Two large smallmouth bass were mounted on the wall. On our return, I commented on them and asked Bob where he caught them. Bob grew sheepish. Well, Arlene caught them, not he. One morning he and Arlene pushed away from their dock. While he was busy fidgeting with the motor, Arlene cast her line by the rocks on the shoreline. In less than five minutes she brought in the two big bass.

After his final Sunday, Bob and Arlene hitched their boat to the car and drove to northern Wisconsin with their daughter, Linda, and son-in-law, Eric. They would begin retirement doing what they loved best, fishing and enjoying the beauty of the northern lakes with their family. They backed their boat into the lake. Arlene and Linda drove to the cabin as Bob and Eric prepared to take the boat around by water. Bob pulled the cord to start the engine and fell to the bottom of the boat, dying instantly of a heart attack. He was retired less than two weeks.

And so, Arlene greeted me with the words, "It isn't fair. It isn't fair." Bob worked long hours for many years. Now was his time to enjoy fishing and the beauty of the lakes, to take life at a more leisurely pace … and he died before the first line was cast.

One of the important things pastors, and all of us, learn is that life is not fair. We do not live in a world of perfect karma. Rewards and punishments are not meted out with justice and fairness. The bad often prosper and the good sometimes die young. Babies are born deformed, children contract leukemia, non-smokers get lung cancer, and teenagers die tragically in accidents. Life is not fair, never has been. When unfairness strikes home and we or loved ones become victims, we feel the injustice of life. "It isn't fair."

I spoke with Bob a couple of times as his retirement approached. Rather than looking forward to the good life and a well-deserved rest, he was apprehensive. He was anxious about what he would do with his time, what his purpose would be, anxious because all his friends were in the church and he would need to observe pastoral boundaries. He wasn't sure he was ready for retirement, but he was 65. It was time for him to retire and time for the church to have a new pastor. Yes, he loved fishing. He looked forward to more fishing and the quiet and peacefulness of the northern lakes. But that was a diversion, a pastime. He was a pastor at heart. Caring for his flock, preaching and teaching God's Word, celebrating the sacraments, was the essence of his life. He couldn't imagine life without these devotions.

I remembered a conversation I had with Bob shortly after I arrived as his Associate Pastor. He talked about the death of his son Kevin. Kevin died in a freak auto accident in a popular nearby state park. Bob said the only thing that pulled him through that difficult time was the promise of the resurrection in Jesus Christ. In faith, he believed Kevin had a new body, a resurrected body, and he lived in the presence of his God. The promise of the resurrection was his only comfort.

Bob knew too well life was not fair. Sons are taken away from their fathers suddenly and without reason. We hunger for fairness and justice, but we must look for goodness and grace wherever we can. Otherwise, our faith and being is destroyed by the unfairness of life around us. Despite his reservations, I think Bob would have enjoyed retirement. He would have loved days of fishing. He would have found opportunities to serve as a pastor, either informally or occasionally filling in. I think Bob, through his faith, was not dismayed by the unfairness of life here on earth. Instead, he believed God's love and mercy are greater than the uncertainty and fickleness of life. He embraced the resurrection and took comfort in knowing God's grace is sufficient in all things.

If there is no resurrection, then death is the greatest unfairness of life. We are born into an incredible world. We experience love, joy and beauty. We enter into special and precious relationships. We believe we have souls that have eternal value. We think there is meaning and purpose to life. We seek to live in kindness and justice. If there is no resurrection, the grave the end of our existence and the world itself ceasing to be at some time in the distant future, then it all seems unfair. We have been given this glimpse of something magnificent, but it is only an illusion. In the blinking of an eye it will all be gone and exist no more. In that case, life seems like a cruel joke. The apostle Paul writes, "If for this life only we have hoped in Christ, we are of all people most to be pitied."

As Christians, though, we believe there is more to life than meets the eye, "in fact Christ has been raised from the dead, the first fruits of those who have died." We believe the love of God shown in the resurrection of Jesus will overcome the unfairness in the world. Grace and joy will win the day. God's love is eternal. Our destination is the loving arms of God.

Bob was a big hugger in his ministry. At Bob's committal service I said God stretched out God's arms and wrapped them around Bob, embracing him, and welcoming him home with the biggest bear hug ever. Bob was receiving his well-deserved rest.

CHAPTER 28

Two Things I Have Done

Estella lay still in her bed, her breathing so shallow I thought at first she had passed away. Her slight frame, now even thinner as she refused food and began to wait for death, disappeared under the bedding. Estella's voice, though weak, still carried the quiet determination and resolve that made her, in my mind, a remarkable person. "Two things I have done in this life," Estella said. "I kept an alcoholic man sober and I gave a young man a home."

The alcoholic was her husband. Estella met him at a Salvation Army treatment house. Estella was an officer in the Salvation Army and crossed the clear boundaries the Army expected and needed out of its officers. She began to date one of the residents in its program. I don't know if he captured her heart, if impassioned love, common to us all, flooded in and filled her, or whether other reasons, perhaps unknown even to her, caused her to disobey Army regulations and marry an alcoholic. Her husband died years before my arrival at the church and Estella didn't talk to me about him. Gossip among ladies at the church who knew him said he was a little rough and gruff and didn't treat Estella as well as she deserved. Estella never complained about him to me, though.

The young man to whom she gave a home was a story I knew well. Estella had no biological children but opened her home to care for foster children. Over many years, dozens of children found safety and love in her house while county authorities did their best to make decisions of custody with the best interests of the children in mind. Some stayed with Estella for a few days, others for years.

One Sunday evening Estella was watching the CBS news program "60 Minutes." They were interviewing Vietnam Vets serving time behind bars. One young vet, convicted of rape, was incarcerated in a neighboring state. His name, Wayne, was the same as a young boy she cared for years before. The age of the inmate, she guessed, would match the present age of her Wayne. As she watched the program, examining features of the young man's face and observing his habits and mannerisms, she became convinced this young man had been one of her foster children.

Estella wrote the prison warden giving information she remembered about Wayne. The prison officials consulted with Wayne and Estella was right. Wayne had been her foster son. "Could she write to him?" Estella asked. "Yes" was the response. Estella wrote. Wayne wrote back. Letters began to flow. "Could she visit with him?" Estella asked. "Yes" was the response once again. Each month, church women drove Estella the four hour journey to the prison. The women were happy to help Estella but wary of this young man behind bars. Tender-hearted Estella, they believed, could be easy prey for an opportunistic convict.

Undaunted by fears of others and determined to give Wayne a good life, Estella began to write Wayne's parole board. "Would they parole Wayne and release him into her care?" She would provide him with food, shelter, love and a family. "No," the answer came again and again. Wayne was not ready for parole. Estella had no legal relationship with Wayne. Besides, he would have to serve parole in the state of his crime and incarceration.

Estella was stubborn and persistent. She continued writing. Finally, the parole board said, "Yes." I asked Estella again and again if she were ready for a young man convicted of rape to move in with her. Did she know the risks? "Yes," she said. She had plenty of room in her little trailer. She could give him a new home, an opportunity to begin again.

Estella lived in a small single-wide trailer. In my priggishness I referred to her little trailer park as dumpy. Everyone would certainly have called it untidy. We set a bed and dresser up for Wayne in the tiny second bedroom of the trailer. I never saw Estella happier than when Wayne moved in. He was her 'son' and she was so proud of him. She was proud he went out and found a job quickly. She was proud of his 'fiancé', a young lady he met and moved in to live with them a short time after his arrival. Estella switched bedrooms so the two of them could have the larger room. She spoke fondly of Wayne and how well her son was doing. She transferred title of the car into his name. Her health was declining and she should not be driving anymore, she reasoned. She transferred the deed to the little trailer into his name. He would inherit it when she died, so why not do it now, she reasoned once again.

It began to appear Estella's death may come sooner than any of us expected. Her health was declining rapidly. She spent long days and even weeks at the hospital. Wayne never visited her, not even once. When I asked Estella about it, she just brushed it aside. He was too busy working. She was in his prayers. That is what really mattered. She was just as proud of him as ever. I stopped at the trailer and talked to Wayne about it, how much it would mean to Estella if he would visit her at the hospital. He said hospitals made him sick. He had bad experiences there and he couldn't go back.

Finally, Estella moved into a nursing home to receive daily care she needed. She was too weak and ill to return to her trailer. Still, Wayne did not visit. I left messages for him to stop by, but even as weeks in the nursing home turned into months, Wayne never came. The women in the church disparaged him. With all Estella did for him, why couldn't he stop and pay a visit? I don't know why Wayne could not bring himself to visit Estella. It bothered me a great deal. It didn't make sense. By the time Estella passed away, Wayne had left town. No one knew where he went.

Had Wayne used Estella for his own benefit? That is what we all thought, but none of us knew what lay in Wayne's mind, the trials he had undergone or the experiences that shaped him. Estella never talked about his absence. Wayne had his own life to live and she was proud of him for living it. And so, as she lay dying, the two things giving her the most satisfaction in life were the sobriety of an alcoholic husband and a home for a prodigal son. Both things represented stubborn acts of rebellion on Estella's part – things she did against the sound judgment of others. There was a spunkiness in Estella that belied her demure size, her holy prayers, and her pious reading of the Bible. She went her own way and did her own thing. In the end she was proudest of the times she had rebelled.

I shouldn't have been surprised the two things that gratified Estella most defied the expectations of others. Estella was a rebel at heart. She was a rebel because she followed Jesus. She took his words literally. When Jesus said, "Do not worry about tomorrow," Estella thought he meant it. When Jesus said, "Give to everyone who begs from you, and do not refuse anyone who wants to borrow from you," Estella thought he meant that also.

If I visited Estella around 3:00 in the afternoon after school let out, I would find children from the trailer park sitting around her kitchen table enjoying milk and cookies. If I showed up around 5:00 in the evening, I would find 8 – 10 feral cats gathering outside waiting for an evening meal. Estella lived on $600/month from Social Security. The church Financial Secretary told me a check for $60 showed up in the offering plate the first of every month. She tithed religiously. With cookies she provided the neighboring children and food she fed the feral cats, along with other beneficiaries of her generosity, she ran out of money, and groceries, every month. Women in the church saw her empty refrigerator and bare cupboards, and dropped off a sack of groceries. They lectured her, telling her she needed to use her money for herself. Estella never once asked for assistance.

I admired Estella's willingness to be vulnerable for Jesus, to be a rebel for Jesus, to care for the least among us, to give sacrificially without regard for her own well-being. She did not give lip service to following Jesus. She joined in his rebellion.

Sometimes in Bible Study, some women would complain about rising taxes or welfare for the poor. Estella would simply say, "If Jesus were alive today, he would be a Democrat." She meant Christian politicians should support government programs that reach out to the lost and poor, those whom others ignored and rejected. That is the way she lived her life. Jesus said it would be harder for a rich man to enter the kingdom of God than for a camel to go through the eye of a needle. Estella believed that, and it made her a rebel, a piously praying, Bible-quoting rebel.

CHAPTER 29

What Is My Purpose in Life?

When my daughter, Debby, was young, we followed a routine one day each week. I picked her up at Preschool in the downtown YMCA and we walked a couple of blocks to Jamie's Soda Fountain. We ordered a cheeseburger basket and peanut butter shake. As we waited for the food, Debby showed me her artwork and chatted about morning adventures with her friends. Her eyelids started to close and her head droop, landing on the table about the time food arrived. She roused sufficiently for perhaps one bite of the cheeseburger, one fry, and two sips of the shake. Then she curled up in the booth with her head on my lap fast asleep. I finished the cheeseburger, fries and shake, gathered up Debby, and carried her to the car. I fastened her in the car seat, drove home, carried her into the house, and put her in bed.

A short time later she appeared wanting her cheeseburger and fries. I explained she fell asleep at the soda fountain and I ate them. She protested adamantly, "I wasn't sleeping." I asked how she got home and to bed. Well, she didn't know how she got home, but she wasn't sleeping. I fixed her another lunch, and then we visited homebound members of the church.

Sometimes I felt a bit guilty combining family and work in this way, day care and visiting parishioners. I tried to be sensitive to Debby's feelings. If she didn't want to go, I wouldn't take her. But she always looked forward to the visits. Maybe she liked the older folks fussing over her. Maybe she enjoyed stories they told. She still remembers some of the people and their tales. Older folks loved it when I brought Debby. They seemed disappointed when I showed up alone.

Connecting generations is important. Children learn and experience much through hearing stories of those who went before. Their lives and perspectives are broadened and enriched by hearing history first hand. They discover, though technology and pastimes change, longings and ambitions, feelings and passions, do not. And older folks delight to hear the talk of young children. They remember their own childhoods and are given hope for the future. I think the faith of both is strengthened. Small churches lend themselves to interaction between generations naturally. In large churches, generations are divided and ministry takes place in separate settings. One sad aspect of mega-churches is people spend time only with like-minded folks in similar situations of life. They do not receive wisdom and perspective from those of differing ages and faith.

One church I served had a Reverse Trick or Treat ministry. At Halloween children dressed in costume and delivered home-made crafts to homebound members of the congregation. Children continued to visit in other seasons of the year. Friendships developed lasting for years, and sometimes children attended visitation hours or memorial services when their elderly friend died.

Generally I think it is good when children attend memorial services. The unknown is usually scarier than the known. If children feel consciously excluded, more questions and fears arise in their minds. If parents go through a healthy, faith-filled grieving process, children learn to grieve in positive ways also.

One of the homebound parishioners Debby and I visited on a regular basis was Margaret. Margaret loved the visits. Debby and Margaret bonded quickly. Debby not only tolerated Margaret's hugs and kisses, but enjoyed them. And Margaret loved to kiss.

I remember my first visit with her, sitting around the kitchen table her beloved late husband built. I asked if she would like prayer. "Oh yes," she said, and then reached out, grasped my hands and held them tightly, as if they were a direct connection to heaven. I said a prayer. I thought it was a pretty nice prayer, but Margaret wouldn't let go of my hands. Her grip tightened, and she began to pray, to pray for me as I began my ministry at the church, to pray for the church, to pray for her friends and loved ones. She prayed passionately, her voice breaking up, tears streaming down her cheeks. Even when the words stopped, she wasn't finished. She clung to my hands until I made it clear I was ready to go. Still, Margaret wasn't through. She drew my head down to hers and gave me a kiss, a big wet smacker on the mouth. Prayer with Margaret was never perfunctory, always fervent and impassioned.

On most of our visits she pleaded with me, "What's my purpose in life? I must have a purpose. If God has something He wants me to do I wish He would tell me. If not, I'm ready to go. He can take me tonight." I talked about her ardent prayer life. Every Sunday morning as our worship began she prayed for me and the congregation. Her prayers every day blessed others in ways she would never know. She was never satisfied with my answers. She was looking for more.

We need a purpose for living. When we no longer have purpose, we feel it is time to die. For most of us, that purpose lies in doing – making, providing, achieving, staying busy, completing our checklist for the day. Purpose is tied to activity. Margaret's health was frail. There was little she could do physically. She relied on someone else to bathe her, dress her and feed her. She no longer felt able to serve and care for others. It was time for her life on this earth to come to an end.

A jovial, take-charge African-American woman by the name of Minnie cared for Margaret. Minnie cooked her meals, cleaned her house, bathed her, dressed her, and supervised medications. She also listened, encouraged, comforted, scolded, corrected and gave Margaret the will to carry on. She enabled Margaret to remain in her house for many years and eventually die there. The Minnies of this world are wonderful blessings. They work long hours giving dignity and grace to those in need, often for very little pay. We take them for granted. I pray they have a special place in God's reign.

Minnie joined Margaret and me for communion. Caring for Margaret prevented her from attending her own church and receiving the sacrament there. Communion was a special time for the three of us. When Debby began coming with me, she joined us at the table. It felt unchristian to exclude her simply because she was too young. I was raised in a tradition where children did not participate in communion until Confirmation in the eighth grade. Only then were they old enough to understand the Lord's Supper. Communion was serious stuff and belonged to the adult realm.

Debby's presence on my visits changed my views on children and communion. Jesus said, "Let the children come to me for to such belong the kingdom of God." We are all children at the Lord's Table. Do any of us really understand the mystery of the bread and the cup, how Christ's body and blood can dwell within and through such common elements? At the Great Banquet in God's heavenly realm people come from the north and south, east and west. Surely, children will be there. Christ's love breaks down all barriers and unites us in the Holy Spirit.

A friend told me of a retiring pastor entering a pastors' gathering and holding up a home communion set. "Anyone want it?" he asked. "As far as I can tell it hasn't done anyone any good in the last 40 years." I found just the opposite experience in ministry. Somehow, in the simple act of home communion, hearts open to God and God's grace flows in. Partaking of the cup and bread connects us to God in ways I will never understand.

Holy Communion appears to do nothing to address the world's great problems of hunger, shelter, health care and peace. Yet, in that simple sacrament of communion we discover the purpose for which we are born, "to glorify God and enjoy Him forever." In the Christian faith, we worship a "three-in-one" Triune God. Relationships lie at the heart of God's identity. Created in God's image, relationships lie also at the heart of our identity.

Debby lifted Margaret's spirits. Instead of dwelling on herself and the search for God's purpose in her life, which she did when I visited alone, Margaret's attention was on Debby. Debby talked about her activities at school, stuffed animals, and friends. She brought joy to Margaret I never could bring myself. When it was time to leave, Margaret hugged Debby and planted wet kisses on her lips. Neither wanted to say goodbye.

Sometimes purpose lies not in doing and accomplishing but in relating and communing, simply being with those we love and care for. As we grow older, our doing and achieving becomes less and less. We discover joy and fulfillment in relationships more and more. What a blessing when in our later years we can share time and affection with family, friends, caregivers and 'adopted' grandchildren.

Debby continued to visit Margaret several more years, until Margaret passed away when Debby was nine. Debby attended her memorial service and said goodbye to a dear friend. There were no wet kisses there.

CHAPTER 30

May Success and Happiness Greet You Today

The voice on the answering machine took me by surprise. "Hi, this is Tim with Success Dynamics (or Success Now or Success Today or Success Always or whatever it was) wishing you a happy, successful day. Our proven program at Success Dynamics will guarantee success for your business, school or corporate office. If you want to be among our growing list of successful clients, leave your name and number and I will give you a call just as soon as I can. May success and happiness greet you today." The voice was filled with confidence and conviction, the voice of someone living a happy, productive, fruitful life. I left my name and number for Tim and said I would enjoy taking him to lunch.

At lunch Tim talked nonstop about clients, perhaps more accurately, potential clients. He named local school systems and large corporations. He was sure they would sign contracts very soon. His system of obtaining success, whatever the field, whatever the pursuit, was guaranteed. It was by far the best program out there. "Was the church interested?" he asked. "No," I replied, "we wouldn't have the funds." Passionate and enthusiastic, Tim never slowed down. I didn't have the heart to interrupt and bring up issues I was asked to talk about.

I had lunch with Tim because his mother, Doris, asked me to 'have a little talk' with him. Pastors are often asked to 'have a little talk' with someone. Usually we are asked by a well-meaning parent, child, or friend to say things they can't say or things they have tried to say but couldn't get through. As pastors, they think, we have divine powers of persuasion to bring some sense to their child or friend. Maybe we can help them understand things about their life no one else can get them to see. I am convinced I don't have such powers of persuasion and never look forward to these 'little talks.' They are never 'little talks.' They are talks about issues cutting deeply to the heart of a person's identity and self-worth, issues they avoid, issues they are quite content to leave unexplored with questions unasked.

Tim was in his late 30's. Despite the bravado of the voice on his answering machine, he was still on his mother's dole. She paid rent on his apartment and insurance for his car. Each morning he dropped by her house. She gave him lunch, gas and cigarette money. She even paid his office rent and the phone bill for his message of success. Many mornings they argued because he wanted more or she didn't want to give him any. Doris was nearly 70 and wanted to retire but couldn't because she was supporting Tim. She fretted about the situation constantly. She lost sleep. She loved Tim and didn't want to cut him off but she also couldn't continue the handouts. Her own health was beginning to fail. Tim's father died in a plane accident when Tim was only three. Doris never remarried and raised Tim and his sister herself. She always felt responsible for him.

I didn't know Tim well. I talked to him occasionally when he picked up his son at church events. Doris made sure church was a significant part of her grandson's life. He attended Sunday School and other youth activities. Tim's son was a good kid. He lived with his mother. He and Tim seemed to have a good relationship. Tim seemed to have a good relationship with his ex-wife as well. I think she left because she could no longer support Tim and his failed dreams.

A huge disconnect existed in Tim. There was the personification of a prosperous entrepreneur selling success over lunch. There was also the mooching, uptight, angry young man arguing with his mother each morning. The two personalities living together in Tim must have caused painful emotional distress. Finally, Tim succumbed to his mother's pressure. He left 'Success Whatever' behind and found gainful employment.

Tim was a dreamer, a big dreamer. He didn't want to be content with the ordinary and accomplish what anyone could. He wanted success on a grand scale. His dreams gave him energy and hope. Dreams offered motivation for striving, living, and getting out of bed in the morning.

Success never caught up with Tim, but smoking did. He got cancer. His health deteriorated quickly. He never made a fortune, or achieved a semblance of success in the business world, success he craved so much. In his final years though, he had a fiancé who loved him, knew all his failures, disappointments and losses, and still loved him. She also knew not to loan him any money. While succumbing to cancer, Tim received a harvest of love and was blessed with a devoted mate who enabled him to die with dignity.

When I met with Tim's fiancé to prepare his memorial service, she revealed a side of Tim I had not seen before – a meditative, poetic side. Some years earlier, before cancer and 'Success Whatever,' Tim compiled a little booklet of poetry he had written. He called it *Quotes in the Key of Life*. He said it was "a collection of quotes, poems, thoughts, and phrases to help guide us through the mysterious adventure called life." The poems revealed Tim thought about much more than financial gain and material success. He also drifted to the ethereal and divine. I read one of the poems at his memorial service where he spoke of joining "in the communion of life," "touching the face of God," and "holding hands with the universe."

Here was another apparent divide in Tim's life, besides the fabricated image of success and the irresponsible young man. Here was the thoughtful voice of a seeker after truth, who sought communion with the Eternal, interested not in fame and fortune but the face of God. We never know what lies in the hearts of people.

In his final days Tim wrote a paragraph he wanted me to read at his memorial service:

> "We have come together in this lifetime for a reason, a purpose yet to be discovered. There is something to be learned from our togetherness. The learning might be finished in minutes, days, or perhaps a lifetime. But when we have learned what there is to be learned we will move on into the next phase of our life. But do not despair, we will meet again on another level of consciousness, maybe in a different way, and maybe in a different lifetime – as many times as needed to learn the lessons to be learned and to put them to use. Be careful in your travels and wisely make use of the wisdom you are attaining. We will meet again."

Tim understood he was still a growing person, still learning and seeking. He seemed much more comfortable and content with the person he had become.

As a follower of Jesus, I believe God's measure of success is very different from the world's measure. God looks at our faithfulness in walking the way of the Lord. Success is counting others more important and loving our neighbors as ourselves. Success is praying for our enemies and doing unto others as we would have them do unto us. And in the end success is not what matters most, but grace, God's grace poured out to each of us through God's eternal love in Jesus Christ.

Since the beginning of my ministry I have had a poem on my office wall. It reads as follows:

> "I asked God for strength, that I might achieve
> I was made weak, that I might humbly learn to obey.
> I asked God for health, that I might do greater things
> I was given infirmity, that I might do better things.

I asked for riches, that I might be happy
I was given poverty that I might be wise.

I asked for power, that I might have the praise of men
I was given weakness, that I might feel the need of God.

I asked for all things, that I might enjoy life
I was given life that I might enjoy all things.

I got nothing I asked for – yet everything I had hoped for
Almost despite myself my unspoken prayers were answered.

I am among men most richly blessed."

Perhaps the theology of this prayer could be picked apart and found wanting, but the Psalms teach us we pray with our heart and not our head. The poem in my office reminds me I do not always desire and seek what is best for me. I find blessings in my disappointments and failures, in the very things I try to avoid. We discover joy not in the successes and amusements we chase but in the grace we discover along life's way. I pray that was the case with Tim.

CHAPTER 31

Sex, Drugs, and Rock 'n Roll

Our custodian, Marvin, was a character, in a church of characters. We were a conglomeration of odd, quirky personalities striving to be the Body of Christ, a visible representation of God's grace and love in our community. I often thought the peculiarity of our church showed God had a sense of humor, though a bizarre sense of humor. No two people thought alike. If ten were gathered together, we offered 20 different opinions. Sometimes we didn't give people space to be weird, but sometimes we did. I remember one contentious vote on a budget issue at a congregational meeting. I stood in the back and observed. When hands were raised for the vote, most of the married couples split, husband and wife on different sides.

The church hired Marvin as custodian nearly 20 years before my arrival. He was an institution of the church, part of our weird identity. Marvin was living in a halfway house after a nervous breakdown. He found out his wife was having an affair and lost it. He ended up hospitalized for mental illness. I heard many times the church took Marvin on as a mission. They gave him a full-time job, health and dental benefits, and a pension plan. They did away with the dental plan shortly after I arrived, however. Marvin had all his teeth pulled and was outfitted with dentures. When the dentures didn't fit properly, rather than having them adjusted, he just gave up and went toothless – no need for a dental plan if there were no teeth.

Although he was on the church premises for the 40 hours we paid him, I am not sure how many hours Marvin actually worked each week. I know in training vacation substitutes, he always told them the best places to hang out where the pastor wouldn't see them goofing off. The Women's Fellowship hired a separate cleaning lady to attend to the kitchen, lounge and nursery, places they fussed about most. Of course, Marvin never thought I did any real work. I sat in my office, working on the computer, talking on the phone and passing time with people who stopped by. None of that was real work.

I could write a book about my experiences with Marvin. That is not necessary, though, since Marvin wrote his own book. His book told the precise details of his daily routines during three vacations in Knoxville, Tennessee. He travelled there by bus, checked into a hotel, and then asked the church to send him Bibles. I shipped a box to his hotel. Marvin put a dollar bill inside each, and then roamed the streets passing them out to homeless people. He called his self-published book *Kindness of the Heart*. To promote his book, he sold T-shirts with those words printed on the front. I wear my "Kindness of the Heart" T-shirt on mission trips so I can tell others the story of Marvin. Marvin always dreamed a movie would be made out of his book. Tom Hanks would play Marvin in the starring role.

Marvin had two children. His son, Scott, lived in town. He was a hard-working, steady young man who slogged through life providing for his family while following the straight and narrow. Like his father, he was socially backwards. He didn't have many friends. However, he found a young lady. They admired and respected each other and felt blessed to be together. I married them. They gave each other company, contentedness and a baby.

Marvin's daughter, Lori, lived out of town. Marvin talked about her with a great deal of pride. She was a straight "A" student at the university majoring in philosophy and anthropology. Scott talked about his sister differently, as someone pursuing, in his words, "sex, drugs and rock 'n roll." One night, while she was presumably high, she fell down a stairway. I met her for the first time in the Intensive Care Unit of a hospital in a nearby city. She was comatose, her face battered and bruised, wires, tubes and monitors everywhere, nurses and doctors coming and going. A ventilator breathed for her. Most likely she would not live. If she lived, she would remain a vegetable. The medical staff doubted she would ever walk, talk or feed herself again.

Lori surprised everyone. She came out of the coma. She was weaned from the ventilator. Her injuries meant she would have to relearn everything from walking and talking to even thinking. Long days, months and years of therapy ensued, every kind of therapy imaginable. When I visited Lori at the rehabilitation hospital, she was usually in therapy, and always angry. She was angry at the therapists for prodding her on. She was angry she could not walk, talk or think as she once had. She was angry she was still alive. She didn't want to live like this. But angry as she was, she kept working. She kept striving. She kept trying to do more and more. And she did. Lori kept surprising everyone.

Eventually Lori recovered sufficiently to live in an apartment alone. She made remarkable, unimaginable, progress, but she was still angry. Angry because she would never be as pretty as she once was, because she would never walk or talk as she once did, because she would never again have the intellectual acumen that earned her straight 'A's in college. She talked about not wanting to live. She called her brother and talked about suicide. Scott was not trained in suicide prevention and did not know how to respond when she called. Besides, Lori always called back. She was okay. She apologized for worrying him.

One Friday night Lori called Scott to say "goodbye." She had just taken a bottle of pills. Scott wasn't sure what to do but Lori called back as she always did. She had thrown up and would be okay. Don't worry about her. And Scott didn't. He didn't tell anyone. When Lori's mother arrived on Sunday evening, after a weekend away, she found Lori's body in her chair, already beginning to decompose.

Accusations and insinuations filled the room before the memorial service. Why hadn't Scott called 911? Why had her mother left town for the weekend without anyone to check on Lori? Where was Marvin when Lori needed him? Questions to deflect the hurt, pain and guilt each one felt. They could not share grief or be supportive in their common love for Lori. Years of dysfunction and acrimony, punctuated by a tragic death with unanswerable questions, caused each to put the blame on another.

In the funeral message I talked about how we would love to protect our children forever, to keep out all the evils of this world. No mishap, no accident would ever befall them. No disease, no illness would ever strike their body. They would not have to hear unkind remarks or see thoughtless and selfish acts. The enticements of this world that promise so much but deliver so little would never tempt them. How we would love to keep our children young, innocent and safe forever!

I said there is no protective blanket for our children to keep out hurts, calamities and sufferings that fill this earth. Our children can't remain young, innocent and safe forever. Every parent has the scary task of watching their child venture out into the world and choose their own way. Lori chose her own way and charted her own path. No one could do it for her.

We all wish Lori was still among us, I said. We wish the tragic fall that changed her life forever never happened. We wish we could change the events of last Friday evening. We wish Lori could have been freed from the pain, anger and frustration of her emotional prison. We wish she could have found hope and courage in her time of need. Such wishes are vain. We cannot change the past.

We can change the future though, I continued, becoming a bit preachy. The past may not be what we want it to be. But the past doesn't have to determine the future. In Jesus Christ, God shows us the way in which the future can be different from the past. As we have been stung by the arrows of others, our own arrows have inflicted pain on them. Forgiveness and grace, love and mercy, can redeem the past. It can open for us a way of hope and courage. That's what God has done in Jesus Christ. That is what we can do for one another.

I talked about our common love for Lori and Lori's love for us. I talked about how special she was and how in some way we were all blessed by her. I talked about Lori now with her Creator, her pain and trauma over. She had rest, eternal rest, for her troubled soul. She was in God's arms. She was now young, innocent and safe forever.

I don't know if anyone heard me. I still heard grumblings as we proceeded to the graveside and then again after the committal service. As the funeral director drove me away, we passed the grave of another rebel, James Dean, the iconic movie star of the 1950's. Souvenir seekers chipped away much of the gravestone. James Dean was the poster child for young rebellion in movies like *East of Eden* and *Rebel without a Cause*. He, too, died a tragic death at a young age. I thought James Dean would be good company for Lori.

CHAPTER 32

He Is Here to Look at My Stamp Collection

I was visiting with Paul and Walter, bachelor brothers in our congregation. Paul had just returned home following heart surgery and I made an unannounced pastoral call to see how he was doing. The doorbell rang. Walter quickly rose and went to the front door off the sunroom. As he let his guest into the house, I heard him say from the other room, "My minister is visiting with Paul. I will have to make up a reason why you are here." Walter and his guest walked into the living room where Paul and I were seated. Walter said, "This is Brian. He is here to look at my stamp collection," and they went upstairs. Brian appeared to be in his early 20s (almost young enough to be Walter's grandson), athletically built with model-quality good looks. He was dressed in baggy red silk shorts and a glossy black short-sleeved top, no coat, and it was a cold day in December.

In my travels I have seen female prostitutes advertising their wares on big city street corners and red light districts. This was the first time I thought I saw a gay male prostitute. I felt uncomfortable very quickly, bothered and upset. I sensed the house was unclean and wanted to leave. I politely ended my visit with Paul. I think he sensed my discomfort. We had a short prayer and I left.

People in the congregation told me Paul and Walter were gay. I didn't know whether it was true for Paul. He was soft-spoken, loved sports, and dressed in plain, drab clothes. Walter fit my gay stereotypes quite well. He loved fashion and had an eye for beautiful things. He sported a nice hair piece, spoke in feminine tones, and worked in gift and jewelry shops. Their parents were veterans of Vaudeville and ran a theater downtown in the classic age of movies. Walter and Paul grew up immersed in the arts. They still lived in the house where they were raised.

This was before same-sex marriage was widely discussed. Gay rights were just beginning to be recognized. I was struggling whether same sex relationships could be compatible with the teachings of Scripture. I wanted to accept gays and affirm same sex relationships, but believed I could not do so and remain faithful to the Bible. Honest discussion and debate on the issue seemed impossible. One side shouted 'apostate.' The other responded 'homophobic.' The topic divided churches, denominations, families and friends, and still does to this day.

I tried to understand my discomfort with the prostitute. Was it because he was gay? What if a voluptuous young woman in short shorts and a halter top had entered? Would I have felt the same discomfort? Or would I think, "Wow, I didn't know Walter had it in him?" Instead of Walter, what if it were an older woman with the young man in the red silk shorts? Again, would I have the same discomfort? Or would I think, "You go, girl!"?

Or, was my discomfort more because the young man was a prostitute? The Bible vilifies prostitution. And yet, in the Bible's subversive ways, prostitutes also emerge as heroes. They are a part of Jesus' lineage. I heard frequent rumors a man in our congregation ran a brothel for public officials and others. It was a way to buy favor for public contracts. That corruption bothered me much more than what was going on upstairs.

Sex, in my understanding, was not a commodity to be sold but an expression of love between two people deeply committed to one another. It was best expressed between a man and a woman, two people joined together as husband and wife. But again, I knew when we read the Bible with a mind open to God's leading and without our personal biases, God doesn't speak as definitively as we would like. It is never as simple as "The Bible says it. I believe it. That's it." The Bible, taken in its entirety, is far more complex and nuanced than our own belief systems might want it to be. And grace and forgiveness seem to have the final say.

This was spinning around in my head after the visit with Paul and Walter. I was trying to sort out my own beliefs. What was faithfulness to God? What was God's view on sexuality? Where did I stand? Why? The debate raging within me turned my focus inward. It made me lose sight of Walter and, unfortunately, I forgot about Walter's needs.

Amidst my inner fretting and confusion, I forgot what Walter told me before the doorbell rang. They found a mass in his lungs. They were to biopsy it in a couple of days to see whether the mass was malignant. He said it so nonchalantly, perhaps I didn't pick up on it as I should have. Or perhaps, the young man in silk shorts distracted me from remembering Walter's condition. I didn't remember Walter's biopsy until the following week when I learned through other church members the biopsy report came back positive for cancer. If I had been paying attention to Walter's needs and not struggling with my own feelings and theological and cultural understandings, I would have followed up with a phone call and heard the news directly from Walter. I let my own inner conflict blind me to my call as Walter's pastor. I was not attentive to my parishioner's condition.

In the next 9 – 10 months before his passing, Walter and I had many good talks in the sun room where Walter cautioned the young man of my presence. Walter was fun to talk with. He brought a theatrical flair to the conversation. We talked about music and movies. In one Sunday morning sermon I mentioned a film I had seen in a Doctor of Ministry preaching class. I asked the congregation if anyone had seen it. Only Walter raised his hand. We talked about Walter's involvement in his family theater and its history in the community. We talked about preserving God's creation and caring for the least of God's people. Walter was committed to the good stewardship of God's good earth. We laughed when I barely recognized him in the hospital without his teeth and hair piece. We also talked about faith and God. Of course, we prayed together every visit. We never talked about the young man in the red silk shorts. I grew to like Walter and I think Walter grew to trust me. I sensed Walter wasn't afraid to die. He seemed at peace with his God.

As pastors, we bring a lot of "junk" to our ministry preventing us from seeing people as Jesus sees them. Rather than seeing through the grace of God, we look through prejudices and stereotypes we have learned and developed through a lifetime of experiences. We judge and draw conclusions before we listen and understand. We twist the Scriptures to fit our world views rather than permitting God's Spirit to shape our understanding of Scripture from God's perspective. We miss the deeper needs of our parishioners and are unable to respond with kindness and compassion. Thus we may fail to love when our parishioners need it most. Difficulties in my ministry arising from pastoral care situations have come because I withheld grace, not because I extended it too freely.

Years later I received a call from a former member of the church I served. He now lived in Florida. His gay partner of more than 25 years took his own life. He wanted to have the memorial service in their home town. Would I be willing to do the service? I could tell he was very cautious with his words, not knowing me or how I might respond to their relationship. Would I be receptive and understanding, or distant and cold? Perhaps he was used to judgment and not grace. I think I was able to respond appropriately by then. I could understand better the love and bond between two persons of the same sex deeply committed to one another. I could mourn with him the tragic death of a loved one, someone with whom he was united in mutual love and commitment, and plan a memorial service honoring his loved one's life.

We are all growing and learning. Our understanding of God and God's grace changes. Where we are today is not where we will be tomorrow. People change. I change. And the church changes.

CHAPTER 33

Make Sure They Put Me in the Right Drawer

"This isn't it. This isn't the way. I know it isn't," Maggie kept repeating as we followed the cemetery worker from the chapel to the clusters of mausoleum crypts that surrounded it. Her daughter, Susan, patient, loving Susan, tried to reassure her mother this was the way. The cemetery worker knew what he was doing. But Maggie kept saying, "No, it's not." Maggie had always been a little ditzy. Now, in the beginning stages of dementia, she was very ditzy. She got confused all the time.

Committal services for those whose bodies were interred in a mausoleum crypt, rather than buried in the ground, usually occurred in the cemetery chapel. The family didn't stay to see the body interred in the crypt. The cemetery would take care of that. Watching a coffin slide into an opening on the side of a building doesn't offer comfort or closure, so we skip it.

But not for Vernon, Maggie's dear late husband. Vernon had been insistent. "Watch them," he warned, "and make sure they put me in the right drawer. They're going to mess it up. I know it. I will be in the wrong drawer and no one will know where I am." In honor of Vernon's request, we walked to witness the interring of his body in the right 'drawer.'

As we walked among identical buildings with identical crypts on all sides, Maggie was adamant, "This is not the way." Finally, the funeral director and I asked the cemetery worker to check the paperwork and make sure we were putting Vernon in the right drawer. The worker, insulted and mistreated, shuffled away. He returned in a few minutes looking sheepish. Sure enough, they opened the wrong crypt. They were at the correct spot on the wall and at the proper side, but at the wrong building.

We waited as the worker returned to get his tools and open the correct crypt. He undid the screws and threw in the bearings. We slid the casket in the right drawer. All the time we could see Vernon looking down on us saying, "I told you so. I told you so."

Funeral directors tell me it is not uncommon for cemeteries to make mistakes. They open the wrong grave, set the vault, and lower the casket. No family member is around to tell them otherwise. The mistake is not discovered until the grave is re-opened many years later for the body matching the name on the headstone to be interred. Then the real mystery begins. Whose body is buried in the wrong grave?

I wandered around the cemetery after one committal service looking at names of the deceased's family members buried nearby. I found the gravestone of his sister with her dates of birth and death. Unfortunately, she was not yet dead. She was 99 and didn't have too many years left, but she was still quite alive. Knowing her well, she probably would have had a good laugh and quoted Mark Twain who, upon hearing news of his death, said, "The reports of my death have been greatly exaggerated." The cemetery and monument company didn't laugh when they were asked to fix it. A woman with the same name died and they confused her with my parishioner.

When I read the Easter story from the Gospel of Luke, I think of Maggie and Vernon. "An idle tale." That is what the disciples thought of the news Mary Magdalene and the other women brought from the garden tomb on that first Easter morning. Jesus, risen from the dead? Jesus, crucified on the cross on Friday, now alive? Nothing more than an idle tale, nonsense from nonsensical women. We don't listen to women, especially ditzy women such as Maggie or Mary Magdalene. But idle words from a ditzy woman walking to the wrong drawer turned out to be true, just as idle words from Mary Magdalene, a woman from whom seven demons had been cast, were also true. The grave was empty and Jesus, their friend, was risen from the dead.

In the first chapter of 1 Corinthians, Paul talks about the foolishness of the cross. The resurrection is even greater foolishness. The dead don't rise. It has never happened, and will never happen. Everything that lives, dies. But Christians have the audacity to say Christ is raised from the dead and we shall be raised with him. It's foolishness, absurd.

On a family vacation I looked at the stack of books our son, Nathan, brought along to read in the van. While our children were growing up, our vacations were epic camping adventures exploring the national parks and treasures of our country. A fair amount of time was spent in the van and Nathan was prepared with books to read. He got his fill of changing scenery rather quickly, then buried his head in a book. One book was about a conference at Harvard University on space abductions. (I am sure there must have been fine print that said although the conference was held at Harvard, the university was not a sponsor and certainly didn't endorse the ideas espoused there.) The book was filled with experiences of those abducted by space aliens and then returned to earth. As I read the premise of the book, I thought, this was absurd. Who in their right mind would believe in the abduction of human beings by aliens? Then I remembered I believed a dead man had been raised to life. Who in their right mind would believe that?

Christianity is a faith. We believe things that cannot be proven by empirical science and reason. I know people say they come to Jesus because they are persuaded by the facts of the resurrection, but I don't believe it. We believe a dead man is raised to life and no matter what anyone says, that is absurd. It goes against the fabric of nature where every living thing must die.

We are all like Maggie and Mary Magdalene. We are a little ditzy, believing in the resurrection. We believe because, despite the cycle of life and death, the beauty of this world testifies to a Creator. We believe because we think there is a God who is greater than this world we see around us. We believe because we have experienced the goodness of God. We believe because, in ways we can't fully understand, God's grace and forgiveness renews us. We believe because we think God's Spirit, what we call the Holy Spirit, in some mysterious way dwells within us.

Still, we who follow the resurrected Christ are all a little ditzy. There is a little bit of 'ditziness' in faith.

CHAPTER 34

I Only Die Once

Gerald was alone in the beautiful funeral parlor. He lay in a top-of-the-line mahogany casket surrounded by gorgeous displays of flowers. Gerald preplanned and prepaid his funeral arrangements and chose the best. It was okay if that meant less money for his children. As Gerald told me, "I only die once."

His children were greeting guests in the hallway of the funeral home, outside of the parlor and away from the lovely flowers and Gerald. Was that distance accidental, I wondered, or was the setting intentional? I knew some in the family did not want to be too close to Gerald. They had enough of him while he was alive. Let him lie in the casket by himself. Then everyone can have peace.

While family visited in the hallway, I kept Gerald company reading the names of those who sent flowers. I felt the presence of someone in the parlor. I turned around and was surprised to see a familiar person paying her respects to Gerald, a former housekeeper of his. I hadn't expected to see her. It took courage for her to visit. Gerald's children probably thought it took a lot of gall. She was perhaps one reason Gerald lay alone in the parlor while his children were in the hallway. I don't know all the other reasons. I could only guess. Who knows what Gerald had said or done? It was easier to be Gerald's pastor than his child.

The housekeeper worked for Gerald for many years. She started when Gerald's wife, Hazel, was alive. After Hazel died, Gerald called on her to do more and more. Gerald wasn't fond of cleaning, cooking and laundry. The housekeeper's husband also helped doing things Gerald couldn't or no longer wanted to do. Gerald became dependent on them and attached to their whole family. Did he become attached because he had difficulties with his own family? Again, I didn't know.

I first visited Gerald and Hazel years earlier, shortly after I arrived at the church. I quickly realized I was unable to carry on a conversation with the two together.

I had one conversation with Hazel and simultaneously a separate conversation with Gerald. That was okay. I had practice in my ministry perfecting this style of conversation with similar couples. During the visit Gerald always wanted to please, making sure I was happy and had everything I needed. He was like a mother hovering over her son who just returned home for Christmas after being away at college or in the service and needed fattening up. Would I like a coke? How about a cookie? A piece of pie? Though Gerald offered food, it was always Hazel who served me. At 5:00 pm Gerald offered me a martini, which I respectfully declined.

The visit lasted much longer than I anticipated. Gerald had a lot of stories to share — stories about his son's athletic achievements, stories about the war and bombs dropped and men killed. He especially had stories about former ministers. Each story was a wonderful tale with funny embellishments and sarcastic wit. When I checked the details, a former minister told me it didn't happen quite the way Gerald said. Gerald was marvelously entertaining, unpredictable and a little raunchy. Members of the church told me Gerald had a wandering eye for women and marital fidelity was not something he took really seriously.

I visited Hazel and Gerald frequently over the years. They had medical problem upon medical problem, in and out of hospitals on a regular basis. "What can I say? Just one thing after another," Gerald told me again and again. Gerald was attentive to Hazel through it all, her congestive heart failure, cancer and other illnesses. Despite Gerald's contrary and grumbling ways, Gerald and Hazel seemed devoted to one another. If there were issues in the past, they had worked out the differences.

Gerald always said, "I only die once." Gerald actually died twice. One evening I received a call from a church member that Gerald had a heart attack at a local restaurant and was taken to the hospital. I found Gerald in the Cardiac Care Unit attached to every conceivable tube and monitor. His legs and arms thrashed and jerked involuntarily. His face winced in pain. The nurse told me his heart stopped at the restaurant and the emergency response team used a defibrillator to start it again. He was 'dead' for several minutes. I sat by Gerald's bed waiting for his son to arrive. It was difficult for me to watch him.

His son, a physician, arrived a few hours later. The attending physician in the emergency room told him there was no hurry. His father would not be alive by the time he reached the hospital from the city where he lived. But Gerald, tenacious and determined, was still alive. His son began to mention funeral arrangements. I told him in the hours I was there I felt Gerald had improved. His breathing was more regular and he was less fitful. I thought he might make it. And he did. Gerald spent weeks unconscious in the hospital and months in rehabilitation. He never returned to his condominium, but he regained some quality of life. He died a couple of years later from prostate cancer.

During those months of recovery, his son took over Gerald's finances. He discovered Gerald passed a quarter million dollars to the housekeeper and her family, the housekeeper who came to the funeral parlor to pay her respects. He bought them a house, a car and much more. He was not tricked. Gerald was sharp and wary of any scam. I think he not only did it willingly, but gladly, probably offering the money. His son was upset and consulted an attorney, but there was not a case for return or repayment of the money. Gerald did not have control of his money after that time. He was never happy about that.

Family dynamics are complex and convoluted. I am sure over the years Gerald's infidelity, sarcastic wit and crude humor strained family relationships. Perhaps these gifts to the housekeeper and her family were the breaking straw. It maybe was especially irksome to the family because much of Gerald's wealth came from Hazel. Her family owned the town's department store and Gerald had managed the store. People in town said he did a surprisingly good job. But national chains and shopping centers brought an end to small, family-owned, downtown department stores with elevator ladies and sales clerks who knew customers by name and called everyone Mr. or Mrs.

Gerald's two daughters could have used the money as much as the housekeeper. The daughter who lived close spent much time visiting her dad and arranging for his care. Neither daughter spoke ill of their father. The daughter-in-law, who didn't need the money, no longer talked to Gerald. Gerald admired and loved his son but wondered whether his son visited only out of obligation and to manage his business. So, at the funeral home, Gerald lay by himself in the parlor while the family greeted visitors in the hallway, and I am not sure of all the reasons. Maybe they were just allergic to flowers.

At the memorial service, I could tell it was painful for the daughter-in-law to be present. She sat in the front row, head bowed, visibly upset, and not by grief. She did not want to be there. She did not want to mourn someone who probably insulted or offended her in ways I did not know. Through the opening words, prayers and Scripture, she never lifted her head. The family asked me to read the obituary, which I usually do not do, feeling it is often somewhat impersonal. Perhaps they didn't know what else I would say. But Gerald and I had become close over many years and I had much to say.

I began saying Gerald was unique. I shook my head and repeated with a little laugh that, if nothing else, Gerald was unique. I saw the daughter-in-law's head raise just a little. I talked about that first visit with Gerald and Hazel and what a character Gerald was. I also said in those visits with Gerald I got to see a side others did not see. Gerald wanted ... needed ... to be liked , to be loved. But his mouth and words often got in the way. He wasn't able to express his love for others in words. His sarcastic wit, his penchant to shock, masked a softer heart underneath. I tried my best to portray the real Gerald, neither saint, nor sinner, but someone struggling to find his way just like all of us. As I talked, the daughter-in-law's eyes now engaged mine. She nodded her head and a little smile curled at the corner of her mouth.

I spoke about Gerald's softer side. When we prayed together on our first visits, prayer was something we did because I was a preacher and preachers pray. As time went on, prayer became Gerald's passion. He grabbed my hands and asked for prayers because he needed them. At times he would shed a tear or two. He openly confessed his faith in Jesus Christ as Savior and Lord. Faith gave him comfort and hope. He talked about death openly and a little too directly at times, saying more than I wanted to hear, but that was Gerald.

After the service, tension that filled the room before the service was alleviated. The family was relaxed. His son came to me and said, "I have been to two of your services and you do your job well."

Grieving is necessary, even for someone we don't like, someone who has offended us and perhaps even betrayed us. And, sometimes in that grieving, we can begin to find forgiveness and understanding.

CHAPTER 35

You Have to Save Her!

Helen's daughter took me out of Helen's hospital room to speak to me away from Helen's other children. "You have to save her," she pleaded with me. "She has never accepted Jesus Christ as her personal Savior. I can't bear the thought of my mother spending eternity in hell. She only has 48 hours to live! You have to do it! You have to save her!" What happened in the next 48 hours would determine the eternal fate of her mother. If she could just say a few simple words, "Jesus, I accept you into my heart," she would live forever in heaven, in the presence of God. If she couldn't say these words, she was destined for hell, the absence of God. As her pastor, it was my responsibility to coax these words out of her. If she couldn't say these words, I failed her. If she did, I gave her life. I bore the burden for the final resting place of her soul. That was the faith of Helen's daughter.

I don't know the exact words I said to Helen's daughter. I told her I rejoice when people commit their lives to Jesus. I told her I believe we worship a good and gracious God, who forgives all our sins and grants us the gift of life. None of us, though, knows what lies in the heart of another person. Judgment belongs to God, not to us. Each person has their unique relationship with God and we don't know what that is. I tried to be gentle and understanding but I know my voice sounded like I was irritated. And I was. I was irritated her daughter, who I viewed as harsh and judgmental, cold and unsympathetic, was confident she was going to heaven. Her mother, who in my years knowing her, was kind and compassionate, patient and giving, was not going to make it unless I pulled out a winning, game-ending touchdown. I know her daughter was not satisfied with my answer. She said very pointedly, "You have to get her to pray the prayer of salvation and ask Jesus into her heart." I bristled when she said that.

As I minister to dying persons I try to understand the faith or tradition that gives them strength and hope. I choose words, ideas, and Scriptures consistent with my understanding of their faith. The words and Scriptures which bring me comfort and peace can be different from those that speak to others. Death is a time for someone to embrace the faith God has given them. I needed to minister to Helen in ways that expressed her faith and not her daughter's.

Knowing well the evangelical faith Helen's daughter proclaimed, I understood the urgency of her request. I had been a part of the evangelical faith community. I asked others to pray that prayer. I went to an evangelical seminary. In her faith, and in the faith of much of America, Christian belief is wrapped in this one prayer. Worship services, Bible studies, and evangelism efforts focus on people "getting saved." Altar calls, evangelism tracts, revivals, crusades, prayer groups and much, much more are dedicated to "being born again." Signs at football games and golf tournaments read "John 3:16." Billboards and sides of barn say, "You must be born again." The essence of faith is expressed through this one prayer. Pray it and live forever. Don't pray it and you will perish eternally.

I understood well where Helen's daughter was coming from. I should be respectful of her faith and sensitive to her concerns. I should be diplomatic and talk about the love she expressed for her mother and how she wanted the very best for her mother, including salvation. But I couldn't. In part, I couldn't relate to the daughter as I should because I was dealing with hurts and insults from past encounters. Others, from traditions similar to Helen's daughter, called my faith into question, challenging whether I was a believer in Jesus Christ. I had deserted the Bible and grieved the Holy Spirit, they said. The daughter not only challenged her mother's faith, but mine as well. If I didn't impress upon her mother the importance of this prayer, my own faith was lacking and I probably wasn't much of a pastor. I usually relate to people from a wide variety of faith traditions, but at that moment I could not relate to her.

As a minister of the gospel of Jesus Christ, I want people to commit their lives to Christ. When I baptize infants I ask parents if they profess Jesus as Savior and Lord. We spend considerable time and effort teaching young people about the Christian faith. As they confirm their faith or are baptized, they confess Jesus as Savior and Lord. When we receive new members into the life of the church, we ask if they profess Jesus as their Savior and Lord. I rejoice when people of every age commit their lives to God by praying and receiving Jesus into their hearts.

Where I differ with evangelicals such as Helen's daughter is I try not to judge others if they follow another path. I will not presume to be God and Judge of good and evil, right and wrong. I have no right to condemn another person to hell through my words or actions because they do not believe as I. That is arrogance and leads to bigoted religions. I think too many in America are drawn to a church because there is a message, usually subliminal and seemingly innocuous, saying, "Because I believe this way, I am better than others." We should always pause in prayer whenever we begin to think, "I am going to heaven and you're not."

Our encounter with God should be humbling. We deceive ourselves when we pretend we know intimate things of God with great clarity and certainty. We diminish the majesty and wonder of our Creator. The simple fact is most of theology, no matter what the tradition, reflects our own desires and wants. We create God the way we want God to be. I am just as guilty as other Christians (and adherents of other faith traditions) in this regard. I talk a great deal about a good and gracious God, a forgiving and loving God, because that is what I want God to be. I also think it is the God revealed in Jesus Christ and the Bible. Of course, God is God, and not my creation or anyone else's.

I also believe an undue emphasis on getting "nonbelievers to pray the prayer" leads to a trivialization of the gospel of Jesus Christ. Often, even in my congregations, I hear the phrase, "Well, I accepted Jesus as my Lord and Savior and that is the important thing." The gospel is much deeper and richer than a simple prayer. Following Jesus is much more. It takes a lifetime, and more, to discover the riches of God, to learn how to live as a follower of Jesus. When we place so much emphasis on the "decision" again and again, we diminish the faith.

A great emphasis on the salvation prayer leads to conflict in people. Rather than experiencing the blessings of God's peace, they wonder whether they have really prayed the prayer. Are they really saved? The prayer becomes a salvation based on works and words, not grace.

I believe those who talk about God with humility and reserve have greater faith than those who seem certain of the intimate secrets of God. Folks with a humble faith cannot talk about "being saved" and "born again" with absolute conviction because they feel it is an intrusion into God's sovereignty. They can't presume to know God's grace. They simply put their care and destiny into the hands of their Creator. This was Helen. Helen couldn't say a simple prayer and claim she now had a seat at God's banquet table. She hoped she would feast with the saints, but she wouldn't encroach on God's ground. She loved and respected God too much.

I wasn't going to ask Helen, "Have you received Jesus into your heart?" That would be an insult to the faith she expressed over 70 years of living. I asked if her faith gave her hope and strength and she thought it did. Was she at peace with God? She thought so. Was she scared of dying? No, she said. She trusted in God's love and grace.

At Helen's service I quoted from Paul's letter to Titus. Paul writes, "Remind them (the followers of Jesus) ... to speak evil of no one, to avoid quarreling, to be gentle and to show every courtesy to everyone." I said this is the way Christians should act. There is a reason, Paul goes on to say, why Christians should act this way. It is because of what God, in God's goodness and love, has done for us. God saved us, gave us eternal life, not because we have done anything to deserve it, but because God loves us. We are to conduct ourselves toward others with kindness, gentleness and compassion because this is the way God reaches out to us.

I talked about ways Helen exemplified this in her life, through her social consciousness and concern for justice, rooting for the underdog, wanting a better world for all people, a world of fairness and equity. I talked about her compassion and kind, gentle treatment of all. I concluded with words that Helen is now with her Creator. Because we know the grace, mercy and love of our Lord, we know Helen is in good hands. I talked about resurrection and how Christ shows us life on the other side of death. Christ has prepared a place for each of us so through faith in Jesus Christ we can experience all the joys of everlasting life. I concluded that as we rejoice in Helen's life among us, we rejoice in her life in the presence of her God. I didn't say Helen accepted Jesus as her Savior and Lord in her dying days.

Helen's daughter refused to talk to me after the service. In her view I failed. More importantly, I failed her mother. She didn't expect to see her mother in heaven. I pray God's grace is greater than her daughter's faith.

CHAPTER 36

It Still Hurts Today

Hugh and I walked in the five-acre park behind his house. It was not a public park, but Hugh's private park fashioned on his own land. Hugh was proud of it and rightfully so, though he never called it a park, just 'the woods behind my house.' For decades he cut dead trees and planted new ones, shaped and groomed trails, and banked the creek to prevent erosion. In his mid-80s, he still worked there every day, splitting logs and hauling wood chips to keep weeds off the paths. I assumed the woods were no more than a pastime for Hugh. Outdoor work kept him fit, busy and out of his wife's hair. But I discovered that day the woods were his passion and love. It was very beautiful. For some reason we never ventured into the woods on my previous visits. Perhaps I never asked. Traipsing beside Hugh, experiencing his little piece of paradise carved out with the help of the Creator, was a joy and honor.

Hugh was a straight-forward, unhurried kind of guy with a dry wit, a retired mechanical engineer. He loved to tell stories and, as he spoke rather leisurely, stories could continue for some time. Often, a story ended with an unexpected twist. Hugh's eye would twinkle and his mouth divulge a small smile. Hugh served as captain in the army during World War II. He didn't talk much about the war but he talked a great deal of life in Germany following. As captain, he had oversight of a German town. He treated people with respect and he and the townspeople grew very fond of each other. Knowing Hugh's love for trains (his father had been an engineer on the railroad), they presented him with a replica of a locomotive when his assignment was over.

Every now and then Hugh made a beeline for me after worship. I could easily see he was agitated. Something in my sermon disturbed him. Usually Hugh was upset because he felt I championed a liberal cause and he wanted me to hear the other side. We would have a brief discussion while others waited in line, exchange viewpoints, and come to an understanding. I always viewed Hugh as very conservative.

On the walk in the woods, we talked about his declining health and how he would not be able to maintain the park much longer. The woods was his joy and he worried some developer would simply tear it down to build large ostentatious houses. I asked if he considered donating it to the community. He had given it a little thought, he said, but wasn't sure how that would be done or whether it was what his family wanted.

Our talk then turned to Camp Tycony. Camp Tycony was a YMCA Day Camp on the outskirts of town, not far from Hugh's house. In the early 1950's our church was deeded 25 acres. The church, not sure what use they had for the property, rented it to the YMCA for 99 years for the princely sum of $1. The YMCA constructed a lovely day camp popular with children in the community. It was a wonderful, park-like property. Our church celebrated worship and held a picnic there every June.

The Camp Tycony land, though, had a dubious history. In the 1920's, the Ku Klux Klan held a large national rally there. Older folks in the congregation, children in the 1920's, remembered the lines of Model T's filing through town on their way to the gathering. Thousands attended the rally. When the church received the land, remains of the infamous lighted crosses of the KKK were still scattered about the property. The church quickly disposed of them.

Hugh then said, "My parents were members of the Klan." I never heard anyone before say they or anyone in their family had been a member of the notorious organization. In my view, membership in the Klan was not something to be proud of. I wondered if this connection was where Hugh got his conservative ideas. Hugh continued, "I told my mother the Klan was evil and she and dad shouldn't belong. My mother smacked me across the face and exclaimed, 'I never want to hear you say that again!'" Hugh paused, "It was the only time my mother ever hit me." A tear formed in old Hugh's eye. He continued, "My cheek still hurts today." I was proud of my right-wing parishioner who stood up to his parents and denounced their racism and bigotry, and bore the pain of that conviction his whole life.

When I meet an older person in my parish, it is hard to envision them as a small child or even a young man or woman. I think of them as always being 80 years old with grey hair and wrinkles, arthritis and poor hearing. It is hard to imagine them as young, energetic children skipping to school and running with friends on the playground. The small child never leaves though. He or she is always there, with the dreams, disappointments, hurts and even tears of childhood.

As a pastor, I see people during one small slice of life, perhaps ten years. I don't know the journey they undertook. Stories can help turn back the clock and give me a glimpse into their lives at an earlier time. In a small way, stories take me along their journeys and open for me the hopes and fears, sadness and joy, that molded and formed them into the people they are today.

Hugh died while I was away on vacation. A former pastor of the church was in the area and did his memorial service. I don't know that I would have mentioned the slap from his mother in the eulogy, but I know it influenced how I viewed Hugh. I was glad Hugh and I went for the walk in the woods that day. I saw not just the outward beauty of the land, but an inward beauty and courage in Hugh I had not seen before.

A short time later the KKK announced they would have a rally in our city. They said they were going back to the property where the infamous rally was held in the 1920's. I wrote a letter to the editor assuring the community the church owned the land and there was no way we would permit the Klan to spew forth their hatred on our property. Churches of the community came together and organized a Day of Unity the day the Klan came to town. The celebration was held in a park near where many African-Americans lived. It was a fun day of games and music for families and children. Whites and blacks, Catholics and Protestants, came together in a spirit of togetherness as a testimony to the love of Jesus Christ. The Klan held their rally, corralled to a corner of the downtown square, enclosed by a circle of police.

I remembered Hugh that day and all others who resisted the tyranny of fear and intolerance. I was reminded I, too, must speak out against hatred and bigotry wherever and however it is perpetrated.

CHAPTER 37

You Almost Killed My Son

Jack was on the phone. "Randy just died," he said. "Oh no, I am so sorry to hear that," I replied. "Are you home? I will be right over."

I hopped into my car and left the church parking lot, my mind undoubtedly on Randy, Jack and his wife, Frances. There were confusing construction markers on the main street. I looked closely and pulled out slowly. I turned onto Jack and Frances' street and parked across from their house. When I got out of my car, a woman in a passing car rolled down her window and shouted at me, "You almost killed my son." I looked in the back seat of the car and saw a young child strapped into a car seat. They apparently followed me down the side street to chew me out. "If you had hurt our son, we would have sued you for everything you had," her husband, the driver, added. I said I was sorry. There had been no honking horns nor screeching brakes. I couldn't imagine it had been a close call and their son's life was in danger. The couple wasn't finished, "You better be careful. We're watching for you." They sped off. I walked to the house and rang the doorbell.

Randy was Jack and Frances' 33-year-old son and a handful since he was a young boy. He had ADD which led to an assortment of behavior issues at school. He also had severe asthma which led to life-threatening health concerns. As Randy grew, he carved his own path. The path unfortunately travelled through drug addictions, paternity suits and encounters with law enforcement. The path skirted around wise decisions, steady employment and healthy relationships. He was a constant source of worry for his parents. Lectures, threats, counseling and tough love seemed to have little impact on Randy for long.

I performed a wedding for Randy six years earlier. His girlfriend was very pregnant. They decided to become husband and wife before the baby arrived. Randy, with glassy eyes, appeared a little stoned at premarital sessions, and even on his wedding day. His first marriage ended, but the product of their union, Johnny, was a great source of joy for Randy. Little Johnny loved his dad. Randy and Johnny were buddies.

It was easy to like Randy. He had a ready laugh and an ever-present smile, a kind and gentle heart, and an eagerness to help anyone in need, even when he had nothing. He possessed a naiveté and happy-go-lucky spirit. He never worried about the future. He accepted others as they were and accumulated a motley collection of friends. He just needed a dog and a few buddies.

Jack and Frances loved Randy despite his faults. His antics exasperated them and his waywardness broke their hearts, again and again, but they never gave up on Randy, as much as they might have wanted to. They were desperate to find help. Maybe next time things would work out better.

Randy, after all these years, was finally getting order and structure to his life. Things seemed to be working out better. Little Johnny, whom he saw on weekends, gave Randy purpose and a reason to get his life together. Someone looked up to him. A friend of Jack's gave Randy employment in the parts department of his auto dealership. Randy loved the job. He was a gearhead. He loved tearing engines apart, though he wasn't particularly adept at putting them together again. Recently Randy met a young woman and was engaged. His fiancé, too, seemed to have a positive influence on him.

Nearly all parents love their children. No matter what they do, how many times they disappoint us or break our hearts, we love them and always will. They are a part of us. We can't divorce a child. Though counselors tell us it isn't healthy, we long for their happiness more than our own. There is practically nothing a child can do to break the bond of parental love.

King David's son, Absalom, raised an army and led an insurrection to depose his father. Absalom would have gladly had his father's head. Yet, David, upon hearing news of Absalom's death in battle, went into his bedroom and wept, "O my son Absalom, my son, my son Absalom! Would I had died instead of you. O Absalom, my son, my son!" Nearly all are like the loving father in the Parable of the Prodigal Son. We are always ready to welcome rebellious children home.

I called on another father of a wayward son. His son, Rodney, was arrested for a third time. Each time it was something stupid. Rodney's father was agitated and anxious. I suggested we walk around the block to work off some nervousness. This father loved his son and as we walked he talked about things they did together as Rodney was growing up. He talked about special moments when he felt they were bonding. Every now and then as he talked he would interject, "Damn you, Rodney. Damn you." The words expressed both his deep love and deep hurt for his son. Rodney not only hurt himself with idiotic behavior, he wounded his dad deeply. His dad wanted so much for Rodney to have a good life, a happy and productive life. He would do anything to make that happen, but again and again, Rodney dashed his hopes.

Visiting a child behind bars must be one of the hardest things a parent can do. It is unsettling for me, as a pastor, to visit parishioners in jail – armed guards, orange jumpsuits, conversation through bullet-proof glass. Above all, it is the awful clanging of the steel doors echoing in bare steel hallways, locking a loved one in and the world out. Such times deepen grief and sadness we already feel for our wayward son or daughter, and oddly, these times increase our love. Seeing their anguish, we experience the anguish and hurt of our own soul more deeply. That anguish draws out even more love for our child.

At the service for Randy, I talked about how God made us all unique and how each has something worthy to be discovered totally different from everyone else. Throughout Randy's life just about everyone wanted to change him. Things undoubtedly needed changing. Randy walked to the beat of his own drummer and was usually out of step with the rest of the world. He created his own rhythm and beat. He was on his own time clock.

Though there were things we would like to change, I said there was so much about Randy we would never want to change. I talked about his gentleness and kindness, his easy laugh and the simplicity of his demands on life. He wanted to please others and make them happy but he was always upended. Nothing quite turned out the way he planned. I encouraged his family and friends to celebrate the Randy we knew and not the Randy we sometimes wanted to create.

Our children, no matter how disappointing or rebellious, are still our children. We will never let them go. Sometimes we see our own hurts and failures in them and want badly to spare them pain that we, or others, have gone through. But we can't do that. Each being is created uniquely and travels their own path. We pray for them, counsel them, and are there when they fall. We love them as best we can. But we can never protect them from all the slings and arrows of life.

I suppose the couple who followed me and castigated me for almost killing their son was just protecting their precious little child. Perhaps they did it in the only words they knew.

CHAPTER 38

Short and to the Point, Just like My Life

The AIDS epidemic in New York City came home to our congregation. Brian came back to die at the age of 28. Brian was raised in the church and community. After graduation from high school, he left for Disney World. He loved it, finding a place where he was accepted. On he went to New York City to pursue his dream of acting. He loved the excitement, hustle and bustle of New York. He enjoyed seeing the country as part of travelling theatre groups but always looked forward to returning to the city. Brian loved being part of the vibrant gay community there. He could express his true self. He was accepted dressing the way he liked to dress, walking and talking the way he liked to walk and talk.

Brian was from a working class family with working class values. His parents were employed in the automotive plants and lived in a nice, solid, traditional, working-class neighborhood. His parents probably never fully understood Brian's sexual orientation and the life style he lived in New York. But they loved Brian.

I never knew Brian. He left our community before I arrived. I didn't know his parents well. They attended Christmas and Easter, if that. From all reports Brian was a good kid, a kind kid. Because his sexual orientation made him different from his hometown peers, he had a heart for others who were different or spurned. He took an unattractive, heavy-set girl to the prom. He befriended the social outcast. People said Brian always had the courage to face life head on. He had the courage to go against expectations of others, the courage to be himself regardless of what others thought.

AIDS was at epidemic proportions among the gay community in New York

City at the time. Many people, especially Christians, felt it was God's judgment on what they believed to be a perverted, unnatural lifestyle. It is easy to stereotype when it is a nameless, unknown face in the news. It is not so easy when the face becomes someone we know and love. It was hard for those who knew Brian to say AIDS was God's judgment. Brian was no worse than any of us.

Brian had a loving partner, Rick. They had been together a few years. They seemed to care for each other a great deal. Brian's sister though said to me Brian would call her and confide, "I have been sleeping with other guys. I love Rick but there are just so many hot guys I can't control myself." The AIDS epidemic in New York had been around long enough so that everyone was aware of risks of sleeping with people you didn't know and having unprotected sex. You were endangering your life and lives of others. Brian's promiscuous lifestyle was not only unfaithfulness to Rick, it was very dangerous, and Brian knew it.

Most gay couples I know have loving, faithful and monogamous relationships for many years. Their relationships are steady and life-giving and do not appear much different from heterosexual couples. At the time of Brian's AIDS, however, there was much talk about promiscuity in the gay community. Even some gay leaders said gay men weren't meant to be monogamous. I don't know if promiscuity among gays was any more prevalent than among heterosexuals. It all added fuel to the homosexuality debate.

Brian lived on the edge. He lived dangerously. He craved highs he received in physical, sexual contact. Addictions gain control over our lives and lead us to unhealthy and dangerous decisions. Addictions destroy common sense and reason. A pathologist in my congregation chain-smoked as he examined cancer biopsies. A psychiatrist specializing in alcohol addiction imbibed multiple alcoholic beverages each lunch hour. Pious, Bible-quoting, silver-haired ladies fed their retirement savings into slot machines. Addictions are hard to face and even harder to quit.

I remember church annual meetings conducted in smoke-filled fellowship halls, smoke from nurses' lounges filling hospital hallways, and physicians smoking while calling on patients. These good folks smoked, knowing full well the dangers of cigarettes. I have officiated at many memorial services where the deceased died of cancer or emphysema caused by tobacco. When I visited them, they took their oxygen tube out with one hand and puffed a cigarette with the other. Like those addicted to sex, heroin, alcohol or thrill-seeking, they were willing to risk injury, disease, and even death for the pleasure of a long drag on a cigarette.

Chad was a recovering drug addict who stopped by my office frequently. The church hired him for painting and other small jobs around the building. Chad was outgoing and fun, a good worker, also a great manipulator. I never knew when he was telling the truth, never sure when he was back on drugs. One morning we discovered a window smashed and our preschool office broken into. Tuition payments were stolen from the locked desk drawer. The police thought it was an inside job. We suspected Chad and the police found the stolen checks in his apartment. When I called on Chad at the jail a few days later, Chad said he had no memory of ever breaking in. He must have been high.

I attended Chad's sentencing hearing. The judge was familiar with his history of drug addiction. Before sentencing Chad, he spoke about the need for education and treatment programs. Jail time did not reform or cure addicts. He sentenced Chad to jail not because it would cure him but because state statute demanded it. Addiction is not simply a moral failing, conquered through moral resolve and discipline. It is far more complex.

Maybe we are learning. As I write, an opioid epidemic is plaguing nearly every community in our country. We are working to educate communities about its dangers. We are warning against its use. We are providing treatment centers and trying to care for the addict. We are not branding the opioid overdose victim as someone evil or sinful but someone who made risky choices about their lifestyle.

Brian faced death head on, with humor and courage, just as he lived life. He talked to his family about things he wanted – a black casket with silver handles, white roses, and angels on his headstone. He wanted to be buried with Harvey, the stuffed hippo his grandmother made for him when he was two years old. When asked about the funeral service, he said, "Short and to the point, just like my life."

CHAPTER 39

The Three Bricks of Nantucket

I looked around on Lillian's front porch. It could use a little attention. Spiders had added another web or two since my last visit two weeks earlier. Lillian's elegant house, yard and landscaping were always immaculate, but neither the gardener nor housekeeper checked the front porch. If Lillian had seen the webs, she would have gotten out her broom and attacked them with a vengeance. Spiders wouldn't dare rebuild them. Neither Lillian, who had been fighting cancer for several months, nor anyone else used the front door much. In fact, no one seems to use front doors anymore. Mostly we enter through garage doors.

Lillian's front doors reminded me of front doors of many churches I have entered, even churches I have served. Only visitors entered through the front doors. Members knew short cuts through back doors and back hallways. In the downtown church where I grew up, everyone entered through the alley door. People met and greeted there. The business and gossip of the church centered on the alley door. One pastor wanted a name for the alley door, something bright and positive, so "alley door" wouldn't appear so often in the church newsletter. The congregation voted on names. "Alley door" won by a landslide. At the last church I served nearly everyone entered through the "back door," where you immediately negotiated a steep stairway. We spent over $1 million to turn that "back door" into a beautiful, welcoming and accessible "front door."

Lillian's daughter answered the door and invited me inside. She was appreciative I was able to come. I told her I was sorry for her loss and wanted very much to do her mother's memorial service. I had been in the living room many times on my visits with Lillian. It was a beautiful room with many family heirlooms. For the first time though, I noticed the painting over the fireplace. "The Three Bricks of Nantucket," I said to Lillian's daughter. I was surprised to see the painting hanging there. "Yes," she responded, "my mother was descended from the Starbucks."

"The Three Bricks of Nantucket" are three beautiful brick Georgian-style homes on the island of Nantucket, just off Cape Cod. They were built by whale oil merchant Joseph Starbucks for his three sons in the middle of the 19th century. Although Nantucket is now a playground of the wealthy, then it was the whaling capital of the world. The joke on the island today is, "You can't miss our house. It is the grey one with white shutters." Just about every house on Nantucket is grey with white shutters, so the "Three Bricks," side by side on Main Street, command attention.

I had seen the "Three Bricks" just the day before. Our family was camping on Cape Cod and we took our bicycles on the ferry to Nantucket for the day. We learned a little history of the island, including the history of the "Three Bricks." Though Joseph Starbucks was head of the whaling operation, his wife, we discovered, was the real power in the family. It didn't surprise me Lillian was descended from such a woman.

I left my family on Cape Cod to return home to officiate at the funeral, the only time I remember interrupting a vacation for pastoral duties. Vacations are sacred times for pastors. We are on call 24 hours per day, seven days per week. Vacations are opportunities to relax without the urgency of responding to phone and email messages. At that time our family took a three week vacation nearly every year exploring a new region of the country. I treasured that time and planned well in advance. I left a detailed itinerary with staff, church leaders, and funeral directors where I might be reached in case of an emergency, and told them to get in touch if there was something I needed to know. They respected my time with the family and rarely contacted me.

When the call about Lillian's passing came, we were staying at my old seminary in the Boston area. During the summer they rent dorm rooms to alumni at a rate much cheaper than local hotels. The kids and I picked up Carolyn at the airport (due to her work she was unable to be with us the first week of vacation) and enjoyed dinner at our favorite seafood restaurant from seminary days. We returned to the seminary late in the evening.

A security guard knocked on our door with news that someone was trying to reach me. The name was a funeral director, good friend and member of the church. This was in the days when cell phones were called car phones. I had one but it was not working for one reason or another so I trudged up the hill to use a pay phone by the student mail boxes. I was reminded of the many hours Carolyn and I used this pay phone when I was first in seminary, before car phones and long before cell phones.

Going to seminary to study for the ministry had been a difficult and risky decision, the result of years of questioning and seeking. My brother and I loaded all the personal items Carolyn and I owned in a U-Haul. In the midst of a blizzard, Carolyn and I left early one January morning to drive nearly 900 miles east to begin a new life "preparing to serve the Lord." We had been married less than six months. My mother stood at the front door crying while I backed the U-Haul truck out of the driveway. Carolyn followed in our VW Rabbit with the cat. Our parents had been unable to persuade us this seminary/ministry thing was a hair-brained idea. I was giving up a secure and well-paying job as an actuary. We had no idea what we were doing. Our parents were right, but we went. Through days of snow storms and aggravation of three truck breakdowns, we arrived at our new place at 3:00 am three days later.

During our first months at seminary, we used this pay phone to call our parents on Sunday afternoon to let them know we were still alive. We had no phone in our house. We were renting a house only temporarily and installation charges for phones were steep. I thought we could do without one for a few months. The house didn't have a mailbox either and rather than install one we received mail by General Delivery. If someone needed to reach us they had to call the seminary and have a note left in my student mailbox. The house also didn't come with a refrigerator in the kitchen, so we used an old dorm refrigerator which worked okay except for frozen items. We kept those in a cooler in the breezeway. That worked fine until we had a thaw in early March. Carolyn came home from work one day to find me gulping down a half gallon of ice cream before it melted.

I spoke to the funeral director. As expected, Lillian, a long-time prominent member of the church, had died. Her daughter asked if I could do the service. I said 'yes.' The funeral wasn't scheduled for a few more days. I could continue with our vacation, fly home, officiate at the funeral, and return to Boston. I would be gone from family for only a day and a half. The next day our family walked the Freedom Trail in Boston. The thermometer was well above 90 degrees and we walked all the way to the ship, The Constitution, and then to Bunker Hill. The kids complained the whole time we were torturing them. We were walking the "Freedom Trail." They shouldn't be forced to walk the "Freedom Trail," especially in such heat. The bike trip on Nantucket went much better.

At the memorial service, I spoke about Lillian's gritty determination. She was widowed at age 34 with two young children. I talked about her service to the church and community and some awards she had been presented. Eleanor Roosevelt was one of her heroes. I quoted Adlai Stevenson, who said of Eleanor, "She would

rather light candles than curse the darkness and her glow has warmed the world."
I thought the same applied to Lillian. I talked about Lillian's outspokenness. One
Sunday morning she left the service saying, "Good sermon. I disagree with you,
but good sermon." Lillian had strong opinions, but she was secure in her beliefs.
You didn't have to worry about hurting her feelings, and your feelings weren't hurt
when she disagreed with you. I didn't mention in the eulogy one time when she
spoke at a congregational meeting. Her brother mentioned his mother lived to 103.
He planned to do so also, and hoped he, too, would be the oldest member in the
church. Lillian, who was just a year older, raised her voice and said to her brother,
"Thanks. You want me to die before you."

Having just returned from the Freedom Trail, I mentioned her independent
spirit and the spirit of the revolution that still lived in Lillian. Having seen the
painting of the "Three Bricks" hanging over her fireplace the day before, I talked
about the strength and resolve in her life she received from her Starbucks lineage.
I was glad the funeral director called and I was able to celebrate the life of this
tenacious woman.

CHAPTER 40

This Isn't Going to Be Pretty

I sat in the living room of the cheery little bungalow having a cup of tea with Virginia. She insisted on tea. She knew I didn't drink coffee. She wished she had pastries on hand, but she didn't. She had cookies. Would I like a cookie? No, I said. It was early morning and Virginia was in her bathrobe. Her husband, Russell, lay on the bathroom floor upstairs, dead of a heart attack. She apologized profusely for getting me out of bed so early. I assured her I was already awake. Virginia was always gracious and hospitable, even less than an hour after learning of the death of her husband of more than 50 years.

Virginia was recovering from knee surgery and unable to negotiate the steep narrow stairway to their bedroom. She was sleeping on the downstairs couch until her knee healed. When she awoke that morning her beloved Russell was not downstairs yet. She didn't hear him rustling around upstairs either. She called up the stairs and there was no answer. She was pretty sure what happened.

Russell had heart difficulties for many years. Some years ago he died on the operating table during heart surgery. He was resuscitated and, after 23 hours in the operating room, the surgeon appeared. He had good news. The surgery was a success and Russell should recover. His heart was weak but the surgeon felt Russell would have a few more good years. Virginia was mystified to see the surgeon looking amazingly refreshed after nearly a full day in the operating room. She commented on it to the surgeon. "That is because," the surgeon said, "the surgery was a success. If we had lost Russell, I can guarantee you I would not appear so well."

I often thought of the surgeon's comment in the context of ministry. The long hours and seven-day-a-week schedule doesn't wear me down. Sitting by the bedside of a dying parishioner doesn't burn me out. Nor does caring for the hurting and grieving. Failures take their toll – stagnant or declining Sunday morning attendance, Bible studies with few participants, stewardship campaigns falling short, members leaving in a huff, members leaving unnoticed, and potential members who never join. Pettiness takes its toll– toilets that don't flush, boilers that break, people upset over dirty carpets and bathroom fixtures that don't match. Unmet expectations take their toll. I can't be the world's best preacher, singer, counselor, motivator, evangelist, Bible scholar, pied piper of youth and so forth. I can never meet everyone's expectations and I feel every day the burden of having let people down. Above all, conflict takes its toll – snippy comments and demeaning remarks, arrogant and selfish people grasping for control, childish behavior from supposedly mature adults. These are the things that burn a pastor out.

Certainly the hospitality and graciousness I received in the cheery living room of the cute little bungalow did not. It refreshed me. It was easy to minister to someone who offered you tea and cookies even while her husband lay dead in the bathroom upstairs. Virginia talked, as she often did, about being thankful for those years following Russell's surgery. She considered them bonus years. They were a precious time to enjoy life together. She and Russell both knew this day was coming. She will miss Russell, she said, but he is in a better place. As we talked, Virginia comforted me amidst my grief.

Feeling certain what had happened during the night, Virginia called her good friend and mine, the funeral director, rather than 911. Bill came over right away, went upstairs, and found Russell lying dead on the bathroom floor. He apparently died the evening before while getting ready for bed. Bill came down the stairs and asked if I could help him. Not knowing what he would find he had not brought an assistant along. I followed him up, and saw the body of Russell already zipped into a body bag. Russell was a big man, 6 feet 7 inches tall and probably pushing 300 pounds. He filled the bag.

"This isn't going to be pretty," Bill said, "but there isn't any other way. The stairway is too narrow for the gurney." Bill took the feet of Russell and started down the steps. I followed with his head. Russell had a lot of weight. We couldn't lift him so we bounced him down the steps, one at a time. Bump, bump, bump, all the way down, each step seemed to echo in the stairwell. We struggled to get him on the gurney and then out the door to the hearse. Listening to the grunting and groaning (and perhaps occasional cursing) of two men wrestling a big body down the stairs and into the hearse would not have been pleasant for Virginia. When I returned to Virginia after the struggle, however, she didn't say a word. She continued to be gracious.

I knew many other widows or widowers who would not have been as understanding. My ears would have burned when I returned. I understand. The body of a deceased deserves respect. It held the spirit of that person for many years. I am thankful Virginia chose to be gracious rather than angry.

Early in my ministry I was in a funeral home before calling hours waiting for the family to arrive. The family was delayed because the skies had opened up and a torrent of rain dropped out of heaven and flooded the streets and bridges. I was alone in the parlor with the body. The parlor had a decorative little niche where the casket was displayed. Suddenly, the ceiling above the casket opened and water started pouring onto the body. I quickly moved the casket out of the way and fetched the funeral director. I joked to him that I was glad I was there. Otherwise, 'Mr. So and So' would have drowned. At that moment he didn't see the humor in my comment. Fortunately, he was able to dry the body before the family arrived. I didn't mention it to the family. They would have been furious.

Most funeral directors, though, have a good sense of humor. It's probably an excellent way to cope when surrounded by death. They have to keep it in check around grieving families, so pastors often are recipients. Sometimes we are able to respond with our own humor. An elderly lady once collapsed in the parking lot of our church after a memorial service while cars were lining for the procession to the cemetery. I ran and retrieved the defibrillator. The funeral director took it from me and connected it to the unconscious woman. I was grateful since I had never used it. Fortunately, it wasn't needed. Afterwards I commented to the funeral director I wasn't sure I wanted a funeral director using a defibrillator on me. It appeared to be a conflict of interest.

In my impatient and irritable moments, I try to remember the graciousness of people like Virginia, people who could complain but don't. They understand the labors of others. They understand we don't live in a perfect world. We are all imperfect people in an imperfect world, trying to do our best to get by, at least most of the time.

Russell and Virginia, as nearly everyone in the congregation, were fans of one of the state universities when it came to college athletics. They wore their school colors proudly on Sunday mornings. I attended an out-of-state school, the University of Michigan. There was no love in the congregation for the U of M. If one of the schools defeated my U of M, I had to preach facing a banner of the victorious school draped over the balcony rail or listen to their fight song during announcements. I was given a sports coat in one of the school's colors that I was to wear when the U of M was defeated. It was all in good fun and I didn't mind because, in those years, Michigan was generally winning handily. It was the least I could do to humor them.

I have a pillow on a bed in the guest room of our house, a gift from Virginia a couple of years before Russell died. The pillow reads, "It is hard to be humble when you are from the University of Michigan." I think of Virginia and her thoughtfulness whenever I see that pillow. Graciousness and thoughtfulness make the world much happier, cherished in all seasons and all places.

CHAPTER 41

You Have Come to Send Me to Hell

"What are you here for?" Thelma screamed at me. "You have come from the Holy One, the Son of God! And you have come to send me to hell! Get out! Get out!" I should have been used to Thelma's words, but they unnerved me every visit. For one or two years now, Thelma greeted me with similar invectives, spewed forth in a piercing, menacing shrill. She spoke of demons, judgment, hell and the holiness of God. I was the messenger for Jesus Christ, the Son of God, and she was going to be punished big time. She was on her way to hell.

Her older sister, Myrtle, consoled her, telling her I was the pastor and had just come to visit. Everything was okay. Thelma calmed a little, but murmurings of punishments and hell kept coming. Finally, Myrtle asked her to sit in the next room. Myrtle's quiet authority ruled in the household. She did her best to keep the little family together.

Myrtle and Thelma lived together with their sister, Blanche, and a little parakeet in the house they grew up in. I doubt if furnishings, carpets or drapes had changed since they were little girls 80+ years earlier. The house was clean, just very dated. Myrtle and Blanche lived in the house their entire lives. Thelma worked in Washington D.C. for a few years. Myrtle thought that work may be the cause of Thelma's deranged outbursts. Myrtle often said Thelma had a stressful job in Washington and came back home to recover.

At other times Myrtle thought Thelma's condition was caused by eating too much fruit when she was young. Acid in fruit was hard on her system and destroyed her equilibrium. None of the sisters ever saw a medical doctor. All doctoring was through natural, homeopathic treatments. They were the only people I knew who didn't sign up for Medicare. They were vegetarians. Sometimes when they talked about someone in derogatory terms, they concluded, "And she is a meat-eater." That was their definitive put down. I never told them I, too, was a meat-eater.

Myrtle and Thelma oversaw the church's nursery for more than 30 years. They cared for hundreds of children growing up in the church. Young mothers entrusted their little ones to them for safekeeping. They ran the nursery with a strict but loving hand. When they retired from the nursery and could finally attend worship, they never did, probably because they never had. Perhaps also the church didn't welcome them and encourage transition from Sunday morning nursery helper to worship participant. The middle sister, Blanche, rarely ventured out of the house. A predecessor of mine at the church told me Blanche was the designated 'sick child' when she was young. She was kept in bed and fussed over. She never worked as an adult. Now, in her mid-80's, she looked much healthier than her sisters.

Myrtle was now no longer able to drive. Her eyesight had deteriorated. A saint or two in the church called on the sisters on a regular basis and made sure they had groceries and other things they needed. I knew of no friends or family in town. Their only other relative was a sister three hours away. They were dependent on folks in the church for many things and Myrtle was appreciative. Sometimes her eyes teared up as she thanked me for what the church did. I rejoiced the church was able to repay her for years of work in the nursery.

Myrtle felt the burden of caring for her two sisters very keenly. She was in her 90's and she feared what would happen to them if she could no longer oversee the household. Myrtle's health was not good, but by sheer will power and help from the church she continued to persevere. She kept the sisters together.

On one visit, Myrtle gave me a publication they received in the mail and read faithfully. It appeared to be from an ultra-Fundamentalist religious group. (Perhaps this group influenced Thelma's obsession with judgment and hell?) The publication accused Billy Graham of being a communist. I didn't know anyone would ever accuse Billy Graham of being a communist. In my denomination, some leaders in the predecessor religious bodies flirted with communism in the 1920's and 1930's. We were always a church on the edge. The thought that Billy Graham was a communist was absurd to me.

When I glanced at the publication I couldn't help but smile for another reason. Earlier that day I received a book from a young man in the church extolling the virtues of the Baha'i faith. The book put forth the belief that there were few differences between Jesus and the founder of Baha'i. "Wow," I thought, "what differences of religious thought prevail in my congregation! Have I failed to impart basic Christian thinking to my parishioners?"

What kept such diverse people together in the life of our congregation? We had rich and poor, management and labor, liberal and conservative, old and young, pro-life and pro-choice, biblical literalists and biblical illiterates, a little bit of everything. Yes, we argued a lot. We also cared a lot for each other. As unlikely as it may seem, I think it was people like the three sisters who kept us together. We stayed together when we had others to care for, when we could share with others in simple, practical ways the love of God we received in Jesus Christ. Churches, especially in my tradition, are sometimes the oddest conglomeration of folks. Some may accuse us of being wishy-washy in our beliefs. I think, though, the biblical message of faith and hope, forgiveness and grace, reached people. We shared the love of Jesus caring and helping one another, and that was a good thing.

As visits with the sisters closed, I offered communion, including Thelma still muttering in the other room. Thelma might say something about communion being holy and she would be damned if she took it, but she always rejoined us. As we celebrated communion, she stopped muttering. She was quiet and respectful. Communion seemed to calm her. Maybe I should have served it earlier in the visit.

Years later as I was nearing retirement, I had lunch with a pastoral colleague who was also retiring. He was seeing his homebound parishioners for the last time, sharing communion with them. He always dreaded one visit, an elderly woman in a nursing home whose shouts, confusion and disturbances always made him uncomfortable. He heard her voice as he approached her room. "Home, home. Take me home. Somebody take me home." When he entered, she assailed him, "Take me home. Please take me home. Won't you please take me home?" He visited with her the best he knew how, and then he prepared the elements for communion. They partook, shared a prayer of thanksgiving, and then this feeble elderly woman quietly said to him, "Thank you for taking me home." Thank you for taking me home.

Through the mysterious working of God's grace, this holy meal touches us each time we come to the table. God's love, which sometimes has a hard time making its way through to us, speaks in this simple meal, and we hear. Partaking the bread and cup opens the way for us to experience the mercy of God once again. Hearing of Jesus' death upon the cross, we are reminded of the deep, deep love that gives us hope. Reminders of this love are always humbling, to know God withholds nothing from us, not even God's own Child. We know we are unworthy of such tremendous love.

In the mentally ill world of Thelma, she still experienced the love of God. I think for the brief time of the sacrament, Thelma rediscovered God's grace in her life. She was right. Yes, I came from the Holy One, the Son of God, as she said. I came, however, not to take away life but to give her life through the comfort and grace of Jesus.

CHAPTER 42

They Hanged the Black Man Right There

I walked into Sam's room as he was getting a haircut. This shouldn't take long, I thought to myself. Sam had five, maybe seven, hairs across the top of his head. Finding them would be the major challenge. Sam was 99 years old. The barber dispatched those hairs quickly and moved on to the neck, a good thing. There was an unsightly patch of coarse white hairs sprouting there. She took care of those and kept going to his eyebrows. The eyebrows were exceptionally bushy and needed to be thinned. I thought the haircut would end then, but no. Ugly, straggly hair going this way and that grew from his ears. She attacked, and got rid of them. Now must be the end, I thought, but the barber did her work well. Big, long disgusting whiskers sticking out of Sam's nostrils were next. The barber brought out a special nose hair trimmer and went to work. Finally, she was done. I don't know how much the haircut cost but Sam received his money's worth. I told Sam he looked mighty handsome. He gave me a little smile.

"You need to be looking good for your hundredth birthday," I said. His birthday was still many months away and I was encouraging Sam to hold on. "It will be a big celebration," I continued. But Sam was worn out. He was tired of living and ready to die. Life was a struggle every day. He didn't care if he made it to 100.

Many older folks, even when they reach ages much younger than Sam's, are ready to die. Their friends are all dead. Their muscles and bones ache. They are restricted to their wheelchair or bed. Their mind isn't sharp. They can't see well. They can't hear well. There is nothing they enjoy doing anymore. They are just plain tired. They have lived long enough. Life doesn't have any more to offer and they just want to have it over with, go to sleep and never wake up. They are ready

148

to see what lies ahead, even if it isn't anything.

"Sam," I said, "you have to stay alive. You have lots of stories to tell. People need to hear your stories." "No they don't," Sam retorted. "No one wants to hear my stories." "I do," I said. "Well, you are the only one," Sam shot back.

I enjoyed Sam's stories, some several times, especially how he used to sneak into the University of Illinois football games to see the great Red Grange play. I was soon moving to the city where Red Grange was raised and didn't get tired hearing the stories again and again. One story he told me only once and I never forgot it.

Sam's mother died when he was very young. His father worked long hours to provide for the family and had little time for his children. Sam said he pretty much raised himself. Sam's father found work in Pine Bluff, Arkansas. He loaded his family and moved them from central Illinois to the South. Sam was about 12 years old. Without parental supervision, he spent evenings roaming around town going just about anywhere.

One evening a crowd began to gather downtown. Some of the leading men in town talked to them. As they talked, the crowd got angrier and angrier. They left downtown and headed en masse to one of the poorer sections of the town. They stood outside a house and made a great commotion. A young white woman finally came to the door and told them to go home, but they yelled all the more. A young black man came to the door and said some words. The crowd rushed forward, caught the young black man and dragged him back into town. Someone fashioned a noose out of rope. Sam said, "They hanged the black man right there in the middle of town." If a black man fell in love with a white woman in the South he deserved to die. It didn't need to go to a court of law. He was guilty. You don't mix races, against God's natural law. That was the world Sam discovered in Pine Bluff.

Some stories need to be told and never forgotten. I doubt if any white leaders who lynched the young black man passed the story to their children. We need to tell stories of hate, cruelty and injustice to remind us of wickedness in our past. We cannot hide wrongdoing, lest we deny and repeat it. Lynching was a prominent part of our nation's history. For generations, white leaders killed black men and women to intimidate and control those they viewed as inferior. Stories like Sam's preserve the truth.

How many of us wish we had asked the generations before us to tell stories of the past, the stories that reveal what life was really like in another time and place? Stories are precious. They preserve history that molded and shaped who we are. They shouldn't be forgotten. Stories help us understand history is not dates and statistics, but lives of individual people struggling and trying to make sense of a confusing world.

I wish I had asked my grandfather more about his life when he was young, especially his experiences in World War I. He fought amidst some of the most horrific battles of the war. He said only 13 of more than 250 men in his company made it, so 13 was always his lucky number. Grandpa didn't talk about strafing machine guns and exploding bombs, running across open fields to almost certain death, the dismembered bodies of his comrades and the cries of the dying. He didn't talk about the shrapnel in his back and leg that he carried to his grave. I wish he had talked about the fears and the noise and the blood and the hunger and thirst. I wish he had talked about how he felt when he had to kill another man. I would have known my Grandpa better, but when you survive hell you probably never want to revisit. No one else could understand what it was like. I would have liked to try. I would have liked to pass his stories to my children. When our nation starts talking casually about entering war once again, they could say, "Let me tell you what war is about. Let me tell you about my great-grandfather."

As Sam and I talked after his haircut, I said, "Sam, you know, you were born in 1899. If you make it to the year 2000 you will have lived in three different centuries. Not many people have done that. How about that for a goal?" When I returned a few weeks later for my final visit with Sam, he said I made him think. "What about?" I asked. "About living to the next century, living in parts of three different centuries. I think I will do that," he said. And he did.

CHAPTER 43

No, I Can't Come Back

We were settling into our new house when Jimmie's daughter called. She, her mother, sisters and brother were gathered around Jimmie's hospital bed. His long and courageous battle with cancer was ending. His breathing was shallow. He could no longer speak. The doctor didn't think he had more than 24-48 hours. "You have been Dad's pastor, Neal," she said. "You have been there for him these last few years as he battled cancer. He loved you. He trusted you. You have been our family's pastor. You married us and baptized us and have been with us through so many hard times. You know my dad. You know our family. No one else can do Dad's funeral service. The interim pastor doesn't even arrive until tomorrow. He never met my dad. He doesn't know us. Will you do Dad's service?"

I loved Jimmie. We went through a lot together. He had a quick temper and a teddy bear heart. In a church where most men were professionals, business owners or managers, Jimmie was a die-hard union man. A former drill sergeant in the army, he had a deep bass voice that boomed when he was angry and a high-pitched spontaneous giggle when he cracked up laughing.

Jimmie had an honest, transparent faith in his Lord. One year, financial commitment time in the church came a week after he was laid off his job. Jimmie didn't know what to put down on his pledge card. He prayed and prayed. His card still wasn't completed as the offering plates started through the pews. He took a deep breath, wrote in an amount, and showed it to his wife. She gasped. He doubled his pledge. He didn't know where the money was coming from, but God was asking him to have faith. Unexpectedly, he was called back to work a month later and fulfilled his pledge. He delighted in telling the story of God's faithfulness.

Jimmie's family gathered around his death bed asking me for one final ministerial obligation. I loved Jimmie and I wanted to be there for him and his family. I knew and loved them all. In ministry, we grow very close to our parishioners. They invite us into the intimate recesses of their lives. They tell us things they have told no one. Deep bonds of trust and love develop. Over years of ministry, our lives and theirs intertwine. We call each other in times of need and come together to celebrate in rejoicing. Their faith is strengthened and so is ours.

Then, pastors make a decision to leave, usually a heart-wrenching decision to move to a new congregation. We talk about opportunities in the new church and how our gifts can be used. We say God 'called' us to the new church, shifting blame from ourselves to God. We assure our congregation God has new things in store for them, though we can't say exactly what. They will find a new pastor with gifts and graces we do not have, gifts more needed for ministry at this time in the church's life. We stay upbeat and positive as we say goodbye.

All the time I feel like a filthy traitor. I desert the very ones who trusted and supported my ministry, people who came to me for insight into God's way, people who looked to me for comfort and grace in times of deepest hurt. My own heart is breaking as I say goodbye, but I keep my chin up and my eyes dry. Stoically and obediently I move on, as if it were God's decision and not mine.

Moving on in the ministry means cutting all ties with the former church. Cutting ties with the church means cutting ties with people. We don't worship at the church and we don't associate with the parishioners. We stay out of church business and we don't interfere in the ministry of our successor. We find new friends and new ministries. Intimate relationships we built in trust and caring over many years are now gone. I say "no" when asked to officiate at a wedding of a former parishioner. I say "no" when asked to preside at a funeral.

And so, as Jimmie's family stood by his bedside, I asked how Jimmie was doing. I asked how his final days have been. I told them how much I love and respect Jimmie. I talked about all he had done for the church. Then I said, "No. I can't come back. The new interim will arrive tomorrow and he will need to do the service." The family didn't want to hear it. I didn't want to say it.

Over the next year others also called asking if I could come back to officiate at a memorial service. I only lived three hours away. I always said "no." A year after Jimmie passed, I received a call from Wilbur. I was 1,000 miles away at our church's family camp in New Hampshire. He was beside himself. His dear wife, Georgia, had passed away.

Wilbur and Georgia sat together every Sunday in the third pew. They held hands throughout the service and they held hands in Adult Sunday School. They acted like teenagers in love for the first time, except Wilbur and Georgia had been married 50+ years.

Wilbur was evangelical. He couldn't speak in church without giving testimony. He told about giving his life to Jesus in the South China Sea in World War II as he bobbed in his Mae West life vest watching the last ship disappear over the horizon. If God delivered him, he promised God he would devote his life to the Lord. God delivered him and Wilbur told the story again and again. His words often became agitated as he ended with an urgent invitation to Jesus. Georgia patted his hand and tried to calm him. Georgia's faith was quiet and personal, befitting a mainline church. Georgia was Republican, honored as the County Republican Woman of the Year. Wilbur was a Democrat, "always was, always will be." Wilbur and Georgia differed in religion and politics, but they were in love. You could see it in the way they held hands.

Wilbur could not contain his grief over losing Georgia. "Can you please come back?" he begged. "You knew Georgia so well. There is no one else who can do her service." We talked about Georgia and their love and I said, "No." Wilbur continued to beg and I had to insist I couldn't. I felt awful when I hung up the phone. I was letting a good friend down.

Not everyone is sad when I leave a church. Parishioners do not all agree on what the church should be and do. We don't agree on the budget, the color of the walls in the ladies' restroom or the type of fabric on the parlor couch. We don't agree on same sex marriages, abortion and whether an American flag belongs in the Sanctuary. I have opinions and others have different opinions. Our discussions can lead to hurt feelings. People become angry and join another church.

Sometimes people become angry but they don't join another church. They don't attend worship, don't give, and don't show their faces around the building, as long as I am the pastor. They become ill but they don't want me to call. They have a child getting married but they don't want me to do the service. They keep their names on the membership roles for when I will leave and they can return. In the meantime, they hope they don't die.

A member called one day and was angry, angry with a decision by a committee at the church and with me for supporting that decision. She told me all the reasons why I was wrong, some of them were valid, and hung up. I arranged a meeting with her and asked our Moderator to be present. I listened to her concerns. I said we were at different places but I was open to learning. I don't know that she heard anything I said. She left in a huff never to return. She was definitely through with the pastor and probably through with the church.

Sometime after the blowup, doctors found cancer in her. I knew she did not want to hear from me. She also did not have another church or another pastor. She was probably fed up enough with the church and me she didn't care for any Christian minister. Yet, I grieved she did not have someone she respected to pray for her and be with her in her time of need. Maybe with my leaving and the arrival of someone new she would have the opportunity to seek reconciliation with the church. The departure of a pastor, though sad for most, can be a blessing for some.

Pastoral departures are hard. They can be traumatic for congregation and pastor alike. A difference lies in that the pastor grieves mostly before leaving, the congregation mostly afterwards. After saying goodbye to a congregation, life changes rapidly for the pastor. In my ministry I discovered I was immersed in a new congregation very quickly. Within days, my life was crowded with new people to know, new programs to plan, and new staff to work with. Life was hectic and exciting. I had no time to think of the church and dear people I left behind, dear people with whom I travelled so intimately for several years.

The congregation is reminded of the pastor's departure every Sunday morning when someone different is leading worship. They are reminded when a new face, someone they hardly recognize, calls on them in the hospital. They are reminded especially in those significant transitions of life, birth, marriage, and death. They must trust someone new, someone they hardly know, with hidden secrets. I am not sure how we could make departures less traumatic, but churches and pastors have much more work and thinking to do to understand the goodbye process better and prepare congregations for transition.

CHAPTER 44

It's Going to Be Beautiful, Isn't It? Heaven.

"It's going to be beautiful, isn't it? Heaven," Marilyn said. "Pearly gates, streets of pure gold, priceless jewels." "More beautiful than you can ever imagine," I responded. Marilyn always immersed herself in beauty. She was a striking lady. There was nothing drab, boring or plain about Marilyn. She dressed elegantly. She walked with style. She spoke in superlatives. God blessed us with a magnificent, abundant, and marvelous world and Marilyn sought to enjoy its beauty to the fullest. Why settle for anything less?

Everything Marilyn touched turned into a thing of beauty. A simple birthday recognition at a Bible Study had festive balloons, fresh flowers, packages with more bows and ribbons than you could count, and a birthday cake heaped high with frosting and long skinny candles. It was all grand and dazzling. A simple meal to honor the choir became a luau with leis, hula skirts, orchids floating in water, tropical drinks with umbrellas and Hawaiian chicken. She served as the church's wedding coordinator and was wonderful to work with. I focused on the wedding ceremony celebrating God's love and calling forth God's blessing. She took charge of everything else, creating a sacred setting and orchestrating the holy drama.

If it couldn't be the best, why do it? I remember one Pentecost Sunday. Marilyn spent considerable time Saturday afternoon decorating the sanctuary with red balloons and tongues of fire. Festive and fitting, the decorations captured the spirit of Pentecost. By Sunday morning helium had leaked out of the festive red balloons and the Pentecost spirit was drooping. I mentioned the droop to Marilyn when she arrived for Adult Sunday School, thinking she may want to freshen things before worship. She took one brief look and just tore it all down. She wouldn't settle for anything less than the best.

Marilyn was beautiful. She was also a character. There was no other Marilyn. For her birthday one year I sent her a card. On the outside it read, "God broke the mold when he created you." On the inside it said, "Word has it he also beat the hell out of the mold maker." Of course, Marilyn loved the card.

It took a while for Marilyn to like me. She was furious with her husband, Jim, who served on the Search Committee, when he voted for me. She could barely talk to him. I was drab, boring and plain. How could he recommend me? She didn't want to be part of a drab and boring church. Jim's stability and constancy gave Marilyn permission and space to soar.

Not overnight, not in a few weeks or months, but over time, Marilyn and I bonded. Over the years, in discussions and disagreements over Bible and theology, in countless hours planning worship services, congregational retreats and celebration dinners, Marilyn and I gained a mutual respect for one another's faith and gifts. Respect grew to trust and fondness.

Marilyn invited me to have lunch with her frequently at the country club along with her soulmate and partner in beauty, Elna. Wine and dessert were musts of course, even for lunch. Conversation was never about weather or anything common or ordinary. She and Elna asked me about things deep, mysterious and spiritual, things like "Would you find Jesus in a porn shop?" I never quite knew what to say. They forced me to think about faith in new and different ways. For Marilyn, just as the beauty of the world was experienced at its fullest and deepest, so was the beauty of God. Following Jesus and knowing God was a passionate and exciting adventure.

Elna and Marilyn meandered through life together, laughing and crying, shopping and decorating, praying and searching, studying the Bible and trying to figure out this thing called faith. The bonds connecting them gave joy, hope, and an enviable strength in the valleys of life. Elna and Marilyn journeyed through some of the deepest valleys.

Marilyn was now in one of those valleys as she sat in a chair next to her hospital bed contemplating death and what it might bring. Surely heaven, with streets of gold and gates of pearls, will be even more beautiful than things of this world. Surely God, in God's goodness, saved the best for last. Marilyn had ovarian cancer and her prognosis was not good. She had always been very careful about her health, made sure to have everything checked out thoroughly as soon as she could. When health difficulties arose, she went to the gynecologist to check it out. Over a period of many months she went to more doctors. The diagnosis of cancer should have been straightforward, but time and again doctors misdiagnosed until cancer became life-threatening.

Marilyn loved to live on the mountaintops of life and experience all the goodness and beauty our world offered. Marilyn learned, of course, it is not possible to live only on the mountaintops. There are valleys between the peaks, and the greater the peaks, often the greater the valleys.

I don't know what to say when people ask me about heaven, about what it will be like. Will the golf courses be grand and lakes filled with trout and bass? Will food be exquisite and music thrilling? Will they see their loved ones? Will they see their Fido or Kitty? In a sermon, I once said Martin Luther expected to see his cats in heaven. I quipped if I died and saw my cat when I awoke I would think I went to the wrong place. I received an earful from cat lovers following the service.

The Bible doesn't talk about heaven in specific terms. Isaiah has beautiful visions about a new heaven and a new earth, about the wolf and lamb feeding together, and the lion eating straw like an ox. Isaiah gives us visions of goodness and wholeness, of justice and peace. They were written to inspire a suffering people in captivity, to assure them God had not forgotten them. God had more in store, beyond their wildest imaginations. The apostle Paul writes about being caught up to the third heaven and hearing things no mortal is permitted to repeat. Then, in beautiful words at the end of Scripture, Revelation speaks of streets of pure gold and gates fashioned of pearls to describe the New Jerusalem coming down out of heaven. God will dwell with us and wipe away every tear from our eyes.

In faith, I believe we worship a God of beauty and, if heaven is spending forever in the presence of our God, then I think heaven will be a beautiful place. It will be more beautiful than we can begin to imagine. God's goodness and grace would have it no other way.

With help from chemotherapy, prayers and faith, Marilyn beat the initial attack of cancer. When I accepted a call to serve another church, Carolyn and I stopped unannounced at the home of Marilyn and Jim. When I leave a church I tell few persons outside the established hierarchy of the church in advance, but I wanted to deliver news of my leaving to Jim and Marilyn personally. Marilyn, her usual passionate and spontaneous self, burst into tears, "Who will do my funeral service?" I couldn't answer that question. I could just give her a hug.

Marilyn battled cancer a few more years, undergoing stem cell treatments and enduring all the indignities cancer inflicts. I rarely attend the memorial service of a former parishioner but when I received news of her death, I drove three hours to sit in the congregation. Her friend and soulmate, Elna, offered the eulogy. She captured the essence and spirit of Marilyn perfectly and powerfully. The message and service was beautiful, befitting a beautiful lady, and I pray Marilyn was not disappointed when she opened her eyes after death and met her God face to face in heaven. I suspect she was overwhelmed beyond her imagination.

CHAPTER 45

Can You Do My Funeral the Last Week in January?

My old friend and funeral director Bill greeted me at the door of my former church, "I guess if anyone was going to tell the Almighty when they were going to go, it would have been Joyce." I came to attend the memorial service for the Choir Director/Organist who served the church for more than twenty years. Joyce was an accomplished musician, an excellent organist, and she reigned over the choir in the balcony. If Joyce had an opinion I was sure to hear it, and I better be well prepared to defend my opinion if it differed from hers. Music in the worship service was her domain and she delivered quality music Sunday after Sunday, not pretentious, not saccharine, but music that strengthened the worship experience and supported my message. She corralled our unruly choir and coaxed an excellent performance from them every week, beyond their capabilities.

Joyce retired from the organ bench at age 75. She always said she would retire before anyone suggested it was time, and she did. She provided quality music to the end. Her musical ability never diminished. Her hearing did though. On several occasions her whispers to choir members in the balcony at the back of the sanctuary reached my ears in the chancel. Judging by the number of heads turning to the balcony, many in the congregation also heard.

Joyce was proudly independent. She didn't want to rely on anyone for anything. She took care of things herself. She did for others, but she was never comfortable about someone doing for her. She liked to plan. Music was chosen as far in advance as reasonably practical. Joyce endeavored to control the things for which she was responsible. She was a strong personality and few in the church dared to question or criticize her. Years before I knew her, when her husband became an alcoholic and could no longer control his drinking, she placed a bottle of booze and a photo of herself on the kitchen table. The accompanying note said simply, "Choose which of us you want." She left. When she returned, her husband made his choice and never drank again.

Every Monday morning at 9:00, Joyce came into my office. The purported task was to choose hymns for the following Sunday's worship. Of course it was much more. We talked about the service the day before. Joyce kept me informed about thoughts and opinions in the congregation. Sometimes it was simple feedback on the sermon, but usually it had more to do with those unhappy and disgruntled. She gave me the unadulterated skinny, as in one case when she said, "So and so said the rich people in the church have you by the balls." I found the statement curious because the woman who said it was richer than the people I think she was referring to. I regret not calling this lady and saying, "Joyce says you told her the rich people in the church have me by the balls. What do you mean by that?"

Joyce always enjoyed excellent health, but time works on all of us. I don't know Joyce's thought processes as she aged. After we turn 80, death becomes a more frequent visitor in our mind. We wonder how death might come. We wonder what indignities we might endure, what pain we might suffer. We wonder if we will be able to care for ourselves. We don't want to inconvenience our children or be a hardship for anyone. We fear spending our final years babbling incoherently up and down hallways of a nursing home in a wheelchair. Joyce talked about a friend of hers whose biggest worry was how she was going to leave this earth. When she was diagnosed with cancer at the age of 55, Joyce thought she was almost relieved. Her fretting was over. She knew how she would die.

One October, when Joyce learned she had a serious illness that would require surgery, she began to plan her memorial service. The doctor assured her though the surgery was serious, it was not life-threatening. After rehabilitation and therapy, she could expect a full recovery. But Joyce was determined her time to die was now.

Joyce didn't care for my successor, the present pastor of the church. Being in the church all her life, she also understood pastoral ethics. She couldn't bring in a pastor of her preference to do a memorial service at the church. However, Joyce knew the present pastor would be out of the country on vacation the last week in January. She called a predecessor of mine, a dear friend of hers who served the church for 16 years but now lived in Arizona during the winter. She asked him, "Are you available to come back and do my funeral the last week of January?" He laughed and said sure. She told him to reserve that week on his calendar.

Joyce had surgery. The doctor assured her again of a complete recovery. Joyce told him her own plans to die the last week in January. Sure enough, after surgery, Joyce continued to decline. She grew worse and worse and finally died just in time to have the service the last week in January while the pastor was away on vacation. So, my old friend and funeral director greeted me at the door of my former church, "I guess if anyone was going to tell the Almighty when they were going to go, it would have been Joyce."

I have known many people who wanted to die, but couldn't. They were tired of living or living with disease, pain and suffering. They longed to escape their body, but try as they might, they couldn't die. Joyce made arranging for one's death look so easy.

I think my grandmother Ethel perhaps arranged her death also, but she didn't have to plan so far in advance as Joyce. Grandma was failing. For the last year she had lost weight, now a mere hint of the large person she used to be. After much urging by her family, she finally agreed to see a physician, the first time since her youngest son was born 61 years earlier. My grandmother was three weeks shy of her ninetieth birthday. She didn't trust doctors. She didn't want people messing with her body. In those 61 years, the only medication she took was an occasional Tums for indigestion. Grandma took care of herself. I never remember her being sick.

The doctor examined her and said he couldn't diagnose her in the office. He would have to admit her to the hospital for tests. Grandma asked if it could wait until tomorrow. The doctor said fine. My parents took Grandma back to her home. She lay down on the couch and asked my mother for a clean pillow case. Grandma was always neat. Within ten minutes she passed away.

Grandma did not want to go to the hospital. She didn't want to be poked and prodded by physicians. Besides, she knew all her grandchildren were in town or close by. Now, she thought, was a good time to die, and she did.

I don't know why Joyce and my grandmother could die when they wanted and others cannot. Perhaps some have stronger wills, or have no fear of death. Perhaps more likely, they simply discern the time and know their bodies are giving out. Such deaths, seemingly planned and peaceful, make it easier on loved ones remaining. It is easier to say goodbye. It is easier to celebrate life and move ahead. Maybe there are a few who plan their deaths as Joyce and Ethel did, but I believe most of us aren't able to order the Almighty around quite so easily. We receive our fate as the Almighty, nature, happenstance, or whatever has orchestrated. I pray we do so with grace, faith and dignity.

Joyce's advanced planning worked well. It spared the present pastor of the church the discomfort of planning a service for someone who did not like him. Joyce's good friend, her former pastor who returned to perform the service, painted Joyce's personality and essence with humor and grace. I think Joyce was pleased.

CHAPTER 46

No, No. I Want to Dig It

"Can I help?" I asked Dave. "I am happy to dig the hole." We were in the pretty little Memorial Garden the church created to inter ashes for members and friends of the church. Dave had staked the measuring chains, and removed and set aside the layer of sod. He was leaning on the posthole digger. I dug holes in the past when Dave was on vacation and I knew this might be a difficult one for him to dig.

"No, no," Dave responded, as I knew he would. "I want to dig it. I want to do it for Keith. Keith was the brother I never had."

People poured into the church the night before for Keith's memorial service. Sound technician saints ran wires and set up TV screens in the Fellowship Hall and elsewhere to accommodate the expected crowds. And the crowds came. They overflowed the sanctuary and narthex, spilled into Fellowship Hall and beyond. More than 600-700 people came to remember and celebrate Keith's life and grieve their collective loss. Chicago TV channels gave much time to the story. Their broadcasting trucks were outside the building.

Keith died in a flying accident. He retired the previous year after a long career as an airline pilot. He gave himself a wonderful retirement party and said he didn't plan to fly anymore. But flying was in Keith's blood. He was a fighter pilot in the Air Force. He also had friends who participated in a formation aerobatic flight team. The team flew in air shows across the country and occasionally for special events. Keith began helping with ground support but the flight bug bit. He bought a plane and began rehearsing with the team. He loved it. Keith was particular (some called him 'bull-headed', others called him 'anal') and he immersed himself in the details and mechanics of formation aerobatic flying.

In preparation for a show along the Chicago lakefront, the team practiced routines above the countryside west of the city. Something went tragically wrong.

Keith's plane touched wings with another plane in the formation and spun downward out of control. Keith was killed instantly when the plane crashed in a cornfield.

The flying community is tight-knit. Members know well the dangers of their profession, how quickly their life or a loved one may be taken away. The death of a colleague reminds them that accidents happen, even to the best. Life is fragile. Many attending the memorial service knew Keith only casually, if at all. They gathered to share their common grief with those who understood their profession best.

Dave didn't know anything about flying, but he knew Keith. Dave and Keith got together frequently for lunch and outings, often with their wives. They travelled overseas together. Like brothers, they sometimes fought. There were many things they did not see eye to eye on. Dave teased Keith unmercifully and Keith did his best to fire back. And like brothers, they loved one another.

They both loved the church and provided good leadership for years. Ironically, though he was only 60 years old, Keith met with me a couple of times over lunch in the past months to talk about end-of-life financial planning. Keith was a planner. Keith and Dave loved mentoring young people and helping those in need. Dave and I were supposed to be away on a church mission trip in Mississippi rehabbing homes of the poor, but Keith's crash changed our plans.

Now, Dave was digging the hole for Keith's final resting place. Dave was the church's part-time volunteer custodian, or 'Interim Facilities Engineer,' as he called himself with a playful glimmer in his eye. When Dave retired at age 62, his wife graciously volunteered him for this new position in the church. It would keep him busy and out of her hair. Dave embraced the position with perpetual humor, dry wit, heart of service, and love for the church. When his young granddaughter wrote a theme for school about her grandfather, the church custodian, Dave loved it. I think Dave's wife wanted her to mention Dave's success in his career. Dave's career was a corporate attorney. He earned undergraduate and law degrees from a prestigious Ivy League school. Dave and his wife, Diane, were true saints of the church.

Digging holes for the interment of ashes was one of many tasks about the church Dave put in his job description. The church contracted with a cleaning service for basic, weekly routine work, but there are abundant repair and property concerns around a church beyond cleaning. Dave didn't know how to fix a thing, but he knew who to call. He was always willing to do the simplest, humblest tasks with humility, even cleaning human feces off the doorstep when someone from the bicycling/hiking trail alongside the church experienced an emergency.

Digging the hole was one final act of devotion Dave could do for his 'brother' Keith, similar to the women who came with spices on the first Easter morning to anoint Jesus's body. Their Teacher and Lord was dead, cruelly nailed to a cross. There was nothing they could do as they watched his agony on the cross. They felt so helpless. Now, anointing his body, they could do something. They could show Jesus they still loved him dearly. Dave couldn't stop Keith's plane from crashing, but he could dig a hole for his cremains to show his love.

Sometimes, the pain of grief is numbing. The loss is so profound and the hurt so deep we are overwhelmed with heartache and agony. We can do nothing but weep. Sometimes expressing grief in visible or active ways though, ways that honor the memory of the deceased and perpetuate their spirit in the world, can begin to heal the hurt and pain. Maybe it is lighting a candle for our loved one. Maybe it is embracing a cause they embraced, or carrying on a legacy important to them. Maybe it is anointing the body and maybe it is digging a hole for burial.

There are times and places for public grief and different ones for private grief. The hundreds who gathered the night before to remember Keith needed the support of one another. The public memorial service ministered to their common sadness, questions and fears. Together they were stronger. Their faith was strengthened. Dave's grief was personal. He assuaged his grief alone in the privacy of the Memorial Garden, digging a hole for his friend, remembering and grieving 'the brother he never had.'

One month later Dave would dig another hole in the Memorial Garden, this time for his son. His son was killed in an automobile accident 20 years earlier. Dave and Diane could not decide what to do with the ashes. Their son's urn sat on the shelf in their closet all those years. They often thought they might return to their roots on the East Coast and would want their son's cremains with them there. They realized now this community and church was their home and it was time to commit their son's cremains to this place that was dear, to the place where their cremains would also rest. Once again, I asked Dave if I could dig the hole and, of course, Dave said, "No. This is something I want to do." When the time comes to dig a hole for Dave, I will be honored to do it.

CHAPTER 47

The Most Beautiful Music I Ever Heard

Lee was the most unhappy, saddest man I ever met. I can't begin to guess at the demons lurking within him. He showed up at my office one day, as he would many times over the next couple of years, desperate, bent over, and nearly in tears. Physical pain racked his body. Emotional anguish disturbed his psyche. Evil spirits tormented his soul.

The substantial inheritance he received from his mother 25 years earlier was nearly depleted. He relied on these funds to cover his living expenses. He went to the funeral home to pay for his final arrangements while he still had something. The funeral director sent him next door to an attorney to write a will. The attorney, a friend of mine, sent him to me. Lee told me about his life, how he was totally and completely alone. He was frightened because his money was about to run out and he had no idea what would happen.

Lee never really had a home after his mother died. He rented small apartments but kept his things in boxes so he could move at a moment's notice. When Lee tried to reach out or someone tried to reach out to him, it always seemed to go awry. He told me a church defrauded him of $100,000. Lee was a sensitive person, a gentle person in a cruel world, a world that simply did not have a place for him. He was caring and compassionate, wanting someone to love, someone to love him, and he never found it. Whether it was the circumstances of his life, his mental instability or something else, I don't really know.

Christine, my attorney friend, and I tried to help, but there didn't seem much we could do. Lee was in his fifties and too young to qualify for services for the elderly.

He still had too much money to qualify for Medicaid and assistance programs. When we spoke about going to a physician or a counselor so he could qualify for disability and receive Social Security benefits, he became enraged. Doctors, he said, had done indescribably evil things to him. He would never go back.

Lee had absolutely no one in his life – no family, no friends, not even enemies. He existed 'alone among the living.' I was the only person he spoke with on a regular basis. I listened to Lee a lot. My heart ached to see his torment. I didn't know how to help. Lee and I prayed a lot, that the demons would leave him, that he would have strength to get a job, that God would take care of him. Prayer seemed to help Lee. He seemed more calm and hopeful when he left my office.

Lee was always gentle and kind with me. Another side of Lee appeared in emails. Emails were sent to the White House, a Senator or Congressman and I was copied. They began reasonably, addressing a particular concern, but quickly plunged into baseness. They weren't just angry emails. They were vile. They spewed forth hatred and venom toward the President, Senator or whomever. They were irrational and tailed off in nothing but gibberish. I often wondered what FBI lists those emails put me on. I wondered also what was stored in Lee's head all those years to produce such tormented writing.

Christine, the attorney, received a call from police one day telling her Lee was found dead. His neighbors reported a smell from his apartment. We feared suicide but it was a heart attack. In his will he left the little bit of money remaining to a young violinist by the name of Rachel Barton. The one thing in Lee's life that brought relief from pain was beautiful classical music. He especially loved Rachel's music. Rachel's violin gifts were renowned, known as a virtuoso not just in Chicago but throughout the country and beyond. She, like Lee, had suffered. She had an accident on a Chicago Metra train and lost her leg. Because of her accident and his own suffering, Lee felt a close kinship to her. He attended a couple of her concerts and had his picture taken with her once.

Burial was 2-3 hours downstate in a little country cemetery surrounded by cornfields. Lee was being buried next to his mother, the mother he always loved. I picked up Christine and we drove together. The funeral director was there when we arrived. I helped the funeral director place the casket on the vault supports. Rachel Barton and her manager soon arrived. There were just the five of us.

I said a few words by Lee's grave. I talked about his sweetness and pain, his living as a stranger in this world. I quoted Jonathan Kozol, the educator who spent years studying schooling in America's worst neighborhoods and wrote the book *Savage Inequalities*. He once said something to the effect: I am not a religious man. But I do hope there is a heaven. It would seem so cruel if all these children ever knew was the violence and abuse of the streets in their few short years here on earth.

I felt the same way about Lee. Life would seem terribly cruel if all the happiness Lee ever knew was contained in his 59 years on earth. I don't think there was much joy here. I quoted II Corinthians as I often do at memorial services, "So we do not lose heart. Even though our outer nature is wasting away, our inner nature is being renewed day by day. This slight momentary affliction is preparing us for an eternal weight of glory beyond all measure, because we look not at what can be seen but at what cannot be seen; for what can be seen is temporary, but what cannot be seen is eternal."

Life does not end at the grave. Our final breath does not signal the end, but a new beginning. That beginning is an eternity with the Lord. Life oftentimes on earth is unkind, even cruel. Human beings have never learned to treat each other with love, respect and dignity. But there's more to life than can be seen, and heard, and touched, and smelled. What can be seen and heard lasts only for a brief time. What cannot be seen and heard lasts forever.

After these few words, Rachel played for Lee, offering him his own personal concert. I don't remember names of her selections but it was the most beautiful music I ever heard, the most enchanting music ever played in a little country cemetery anywhere or anytime. Music floated over old headstones, into surrounding cornfields and maybe all the way to the gates of heaven, music to bring solace and comfort to a life that never experienced it, music that I think accompanied Lee's soul on its journey upward.

I talked about Lee in an Easter sermon a few years later. After telling of his life and death, I then went on:

"I believe in the resurrection of Jesus because I believe the God who created this most beautiful world in which we live, the God who created the stars and moon and sun above, the God who created mountains and valleys, oceans and rivers, birds of the air and fish of the sea, the God who created lions and tigers and bears, the God who created you and me, the God who created Lee, this God would not just leave this world and everything in it, you and me and Lee, leave us all to die a slow painful death, to let it all one day, whenever that day is, be null and void and empty and forgotten, to exist no more, not even a memory. That's the end of the world as put forth by the theories of physics that govern the universe. I don't think the God who created this world would do that.

"I believe the resurrection of Jesus Christ from the dead tells us God has more in store for us. God does not let his creatures weep forever. God does not let his children die empty, meaningless, vile and violent deaths with nothing better in store for them. I believe Lee has a place in God's heaven. Lee's miserable life did not end on the floor of his apartment, poor, alone and frightened. The resurrection of Jesus from the grave tells us there is more to life for people like Lee, more to life for children living on garbage heaps on the outskirts of Sao Paulo, Brazil, or sold as sex slaves in Thailand, or conscripted into armed militias of the Congo, more to life for children starving in Darfur or enslaved in sweat shops on Manhattan's lower east side. I believe in the resurrection of Jesus because I believe all of them are God's children and God didn't bring them into the world to know nothing but pain and sorrow. God brought them into the world that they might have life and have it abundantly, and they aren't receiving it on this earth now, but because of the resurrection they will someday receive what they were born to receive as God's children. They will know life as good and precious and wonderful. And some of us (all of us at times) may not know life as very good and precious right now, but because of the resurrection we, too, you and me, will receive what we have been born to receive as God's children, life and life abundantly."

CHAPTER 48

What's with All the Betty Boop Jackets?

"What's with all the Betty Boop leather jackets?" I kept saying as more and more people, mostly women, came into the church building and hung their coats in the narthex. Betty Boop is the cartoon caricature of a 1920's flapper with big round eyes. She is overtly sexy but also inherently naïve. She originated in the 1930's, became very popular, and has enjoyed a string of revivals in the decades since. I didn't know at the time but she is a favorite of the gay community. I am not sure of the reasons why.

Lisa, whose life we gathered to remember, was gay. I did not know Lisa well. Her mother attended our church and I became acquainted with Lisa primarily through hospital visits. She was smart, good-looking, fun, and athletic. She seemed to have a great group of friends and a devoted partner. She was also an alcoholic, and alcoholism was destroying her body. Cirrhosis of her liver was severe. She was warned repeatedly by physicians if she continued to drink her veins would hemorrhage and she would bleed to death. Health crises led to hospital stays giving notice of the seriousness of her disease. Lisa continued to drink, despite pleas from family and friends. One day she hemorrhaged to death, just as physicians predicted. She was only 38 years old.

Our church was filled with mostly young women, mostly gay guessing by the Betty Boop jackets, grieving the loss of one of their friends and peers. Perhaps some had pleaded with Lisa to give up her drinking and didn't understand why she could not. Perhaps others had been drinking partners. Lisa's death was a sober reminder of the risks of excessive drinking. I guessed many friends experienced guilt. Some feeling guilty because they had not tried hard enough to persuade her to give up drinking. Perhaps others feeling guilty because they offered her a drink knowing only too well her inability to control alcohol consumption and the seriousness of her disease. They were all there to grieve, to mourn the death of someone bright and beautiful who should not have died so young.

I don't know how many possessed a religious faith or belief in God. The church, by and large, has not been accepting of the gay community. But they came to our sanctuary that evening to support each other in their grief. They came to hear words of comfort and hope, to know Lisa's life had meaning and purpose, despite its tragic ending.

The irony for me was Lisa's memorial service coincided with the weekend of our conference's Annual Meeting. I served on a task force studying whether our conference should become Open and Affirming. An affirmative vote would declare the conference welcomed all persons regardless of sexual orientation. It would mean same-sex sexual orientation was innate and good, not something to be ashamed of or changed. Same-sex marriages were to be celebrated and embraced. I wasn't sure how I would vote. I knew the outcome was a foregone conclusion. The conference would follow the denomination's guidance and vote to be Open and Affirming. So here I was, instead of attending the Annual Meeting where I would be one of only a few having reservations with the motion, ministering to a sanctuary full of gay women.

I tried to understand my reservations about voting to be Open and Affirming. I wanted to affirm my gay sisters and brothers. They, too, stood under God's grace, as I did. They were people of faith, who loved and served the Lord Jesus Christ, as I did. I wanted to, but could I? It had been planted in me for so long that the Bible condemned same-sex relationships and I wanted to be faithful to Scripture. But did the Bible really condemn loving, life-giving, same-sex relationships? To be honest with myself, I knew the biblical references to homosexuality were few and ingrained in the cultural context of the time. Nearly all contemporary Christians, no matter how conservative, recognize the cultural context of the passages surrounding homosexual prohibitions, and do not adhere to these other laws. We eat pork, we charge interest, we get tattoos, women wear makeup, we don't kill our incorrigible children and we don't marry raped daughters to their rapists.

Quoting only those verses of Scriptures supporting our positions while ignoring other verses is inconsistent. It does an injustice to the Bible and reveals our hypocrisy. All readers and interpreters of the Bible see the Bible through their own interpretative lens, formed by childhood teachings, life experiences and much more. Reading the Bible and letting God's Spirit guide us into deeper understandings of God's mysteries is difficult. God's Word can never be infallible to us because we are very fallible people interpreting it.

I heard many advocates supporting same sex relationships use the theological argument: "God is good. God created me. I must be good. God created me with a gay sexual orientation. My gay sexual orientation must be good." I felt this argument was too simplistic. It didn't take into account the fallenness of the world. Children are born blind. They are born with physical and mental disabilities that prevent them from experiencing many of the beautiful things in life that the rest of us may enjoy. These disabilities wouldn't be called good. To be born with a same sex orientation didn't automatically mean that this sexual orientation is good.

The good news of the gospel, though, is that we live in a world of redemption. Grace has the final word in God's realm. Judgment does not. God's redeeming power in Jesus Christ makes all things new. The Christian faith doesn't celebrate our goodness or perfection, but celebrates God's love for us despite our failings and flaws. Our faith looks to the redeeming power in God's grace to remake us in God's image. Persons born with disabilities receive grace to know joy and beauty in ways that the rest of us may never know, and so experience fullness of life. Whether straight or gay, our sexuality is marred by the fallenness of the world, but the good news is that God's grace can redeem our sexuality, whether straight or gay. It does so in the same way. God gives us persons with whom we can live in beautiful relationships of loving and being loved. God's grace enables us to move beyond self-centered ways to self-giving ways and to begin to share the kind of love that Christ Jesus shared with us.

Jesus said the greatest commandments are to love God and to love your neighbor. We read the Scriptures through this lens of love. When we do so, we discover we support and care for our gay sisters and brothers. Sexuality is a beautiful gift from God. A whole book in the Bible, Song of Songs, celebrates the gift, often with erotic symbolism. The gift of sexuality is best experienced in monogamous relationships of faithfulness, commitment and love. At first, I had doubts that gays could enter into such relationships. I had heard reports of their rampant promiscuity. But then I began meeting many gay couples whose commitment and faithfulness to one another was deeply rooted. The love in their relationships matched those who are heterosexual. To deny the beauty of the love of same sex couples revealed a prejudice within myself. I was condemning what I did not understand.

In my message to Lisa's family and friends, I lifted up many of the same themes I would in a suicide. Everyone there knew of Lisa's struggles with alcohol and her drive to continue drinking despite the warnings of doctors and pleas from her friends. Her continual drinking almost seemed like a death wish. I said that we don't understand the struggles, the pains, and the anguishes of another. We have a hard enough time trying to understand our own struggles. We don't always know why we say and do the things we say and do. And I said we shouldn't be angry with Lisa for hurting us as she did by leaving us. And we shouldn't be angry with ourselves for thinking maybe we didn't do all that we could have done to save her. Let us leave any judgment to God, knowing that we worship a gracious and forgiving God. Let us instead celebrate and remember the beautiful person that Lisa was and give thanks that she is now in the presence of her Creator. All torment is over for Lisa. In Jesus Christ, God has broken the bonds of death and has brought life and immortality to light. Lisa is at rest with her God.

I think it was the message we needed to hear whether we were gay or straight, whether we wore a Betty Boop jacket or not.

CHAPTER 49

I Never Heard Our Organ Sound like That Before

"Wow!" I said to my next door neighbor Dan as we stood at the back of our sanctuary listening to the preservice music for Pete's memorial service, "I never heard our organ sound like that before." The electronic organ was giving up tunes such as "Camp Meeting Blues" by King Oliver, "Mr. Jelly Lord" by Jelly Roll Morton, and "Nobody's Blues but Mine" by Bessie Smith.

Our neighbor Pete died after a ten-year battle with cancer. I talked to him occasionally, when I saw him on one of his twice daily walks around the neighborhood. I knew he was quite a jazz musician before cancer settled in. He talked about flying to California on weekends, playing Friday, Saturday and Sunday evenings, catching the red-eye back, and going straight from the airport to his job at the insurance company downtown Chicago Monday morning.

Pete grew up at a crossroads in the country near where I previously served a church. I knew the area well -- cornfields dotted with farmhouses, barns and silos, sporadic woods and tree-lined creeks. Not much to look at in the way of scenery, but I thought good, wholesome values grew along with the corn. Pete went to the nearby university, immersed himself in the jazz greats, and then left for the big city to play in nightclubs. He also found a real job at the insurance company to pay the bills.

In the ministry, our parish is larger than those on our membership role or attend worship on Sunday morning. We meet folks in the community and around the neighborhood who ask for help in difficult times. Some share the values and perhaps even the faith of the church, but for some reason are not connected.

Perhaps they were burned by past involvement and are reluctant to enter the fray of church life again. Perhaps they haven't had an invitation. Perhaps they are wary of new groups. More often, their lives have simply been directed elsewhere. They look for a connection to God within the church mostly in times of crises.

I knew Pete and his wife, Shirley, didn't attend church and didn't have a pastor. When Pete's life was nearing its end, Carolyn offered my services to Shirley. Not having other options, they were thankful for my willingness to help out. Pete was receptive to prayers I offered. He honestly sought God and wanted to be connected to God. He talked openly about his faith and lack of faith. I visited Pete in the nursing home and baptized him five days before he died.

Music fed Pete's soul in ways I could never fully appreciate. I enjoy music, but I do not begin to have the depth of music knowledge and intimacy that lay within Pete. Music was a spiritual experience for him.

Music, in evoking memories and character of the deceased, can touch us deeply in a memorial service, in ways words may never do. Music connects us to the spirit of the one who died. Music connects us to the grace and promises of God. I can think of many songs in memorial services through the years that moved the hearts of the congregation. The songs unite us with our deceased loved ones and open our souls to receive the love of God.

Secular music can become sacred at a memorial service. I remember another man, also named Pete, who loved to sail. I am not sure he was a great sailor but he loved to wear his captain's hat and entertain folks on his sail boat talking about the wind, waves and adventures. Sailing gave him joy and satisfaction in life he often failed to find elsewhere. I was blessed with an Associate Pastor with a gorgeous voice. She sang the Styx's "Come, Sail Away" for his service. She altered the lyrics where it refers to the starship. The song captured well the dreams, longings, spirit and hopes of Pete. Every head was nodding, every face smiling, as she sang. Pete was sailing away.

Shirley and her sons knew many of Pete's former band members and other music friends wanted to come to the memorial service, but were scattered around the country. We set a date a few weeks out so they could arrange schedules. In those intervening weeks, I received calls from Pete's friends. Could they play something in tribute to Pete at the service? I checked with Shirley to see if it were someone Pete would want, and it always was. So, I added them to the Order of Worship. Also, they wondered, could they say a few words about Pete? There was much about Pete I didn't know. I was thankful for those who could recount stories and bring to light his personality. The service kept growing.

The service kept growing, but it also captured Pete's character. I chose Psalms of praise to read. I chose Scriptures that spoke to Pete's outlook on life, like Ecclesiastes 3, "For everything there is a season and a time for every matter under heaven." Others represented his character, like the Beatitudes, "Blessed are the poor in spirit, for theirs is the kingdom of heaven." We had Scriptures of hope, like Revelation 21, "Then I saw a new heaven and a new earth."

The service became a joyful proclamation of the goodness of God as seen in all of creation, especially expressed through music. We listened to tunes of jazz greats, like "Skid-dat-de-dat" by Louis Armstrong and "Bay City" by Turk Murphy. We joined in singing "Amazing Grace" and "Just a Closer Walk with Thee." Of course, they were played with a swing and swagger we didn't typically have Sunday morning.

Fellow musicians talked about their time with Pete, his music-making, his humble spirit and gentle ways. The service lasted more than two hours, but the energy and joy made it a very quick two hours. In music, Scriptures, prayers, remembrances and tributes, Pete's family and friends celebrated Pete's life and mourned their loss in words and ways that spoke to them.

I didn't know the faith of musicians who spoke and worshipped. Some spoke with familiarity about God and things of God. Some did not. I doubt if many worshipped in church on Sunday morning. I think, though, they all had a longing for God, to know God was alive and looked over us, God's grace would protect us and God's love would cover us both in life and death. They needed to hear that death is not the end. Death does not win the battle. Our lives do not end with our final breath. God has more in store.

I was reluctant to call on the women of the church to provide a reception following the service. They work hard. Neighbors, though, were quick to help. They provided refreshments, hospitality and space for Pete's friends and family to continue the celebrations and remembrances.

Of course, grieving for Pete was not over. Those who knew Pete well would continue to mourn their loss in the months and years ahead. But I believe the memorial service celebrating his life was an important first step inviting God's healing presence to comfort us and replace our sorrow with hope. Church-goers and non-church-goers both long for the grace of God offered in Jesus Christ. I rejoice the church offers ministry and hope even to those who are not part of our immediate church family.

CHAPTER 50

Never Give Up

"Do I see a little passion in the way Edwin grasped the hand of Juanita?" I said to myself as I stood in the rear of the sanctuary. At the conclusion of worship the pastor invites the congregation to join hands as we sing a simple chorus. During humming in the midst of the chorus, the pastor offers the Benediction. As I stood singing the words to the chorus, I thought it sure looked like Edwin grasped Juanita's hand with a little extra squeeze. It seemed to suggest, 'I care about you more than just someone standing next to me in worship.'

Edwin's wife of 60+ years, Loretta, had died a little more than a year earlier. Edwin gave her compassionate care during their final years together. Her death broke his heart. He continued to be lonely and despondent. In a brief instant I was sure I saw a little of the old sparkle glimmering in his eye as he took Juanita's hand. I was a little taken aback. Edwin was in his late 80s and Juanita nearly 20 years younger. A couple of weeks later my suspicions proved correct. Edwin asked Juanita out on a date. Edwin was not giving up on life after all. I should have known. Edwin never gave up. A friend of his wrote a book about his life. She titled it *Never Give Up*. It was the way Edwin always lived.

Edwin's father died when he was a young boy. His mother felt overwhelmed caring for Edwin and his siblings. One Sunday afternoon she took them for a drive. They stopped at an orphanage/old folks home run by churches in my tradition. His mother simply said, "Goodbye." No suitcases, no advanced warning, not even a hug, just "Goodbye. Here is your new home." Edwin never forgot the seeming betrayal by his mother, but he adjusted to his new home. It was a remarkable place where old folks, mostly of German descent, cared for young boys and girls who lived there. Together, across generations, they found hope in one another.

Like other young men of his generation, Edwin served his country in World

War II. He enlisted in the Air Force and worked as a navigator on B-29's. On a bombing run his plane was attacked over German-occupied territory. Bullets burst through the fuselage. One bullet passed through his arm. Another bullet grazed his chest. It cut in two the photo he carried of his beloved Loretta in a leather case next to his heart, but left him unharmed. As the plane went down, he and the other surviving crew members bailed, landing in German-occupied territory. Instructions from their commander were to surrender to the German Army if downed in enemy territory. If German civilians found them first, they would most likely kill them.

Edwin surrendered as ordered. German soldiers took him to an old hospital. The architecture of the hospital reminded him of the dormitory at the orphanage. German surgeons conferred and quickly decided to amputate his arm. It would be easier than trying to fix it. Unbeknownst to the surgeons, Edwin understood German. He learned it from the old German men and women at the old folks home. He protested to the doctors in German. They would not cut off his arm. They would patch it up and save it. They listened to him. The arm was repaired. It healed and served him well the rest of his life. Edwin was always grateful for the upbringing that taught him German and saved his arm.

Edwin's prison camp was popularized in the movie The Great Escape. Escapees caught by the Germans were executed about a month before Edwin's arrival. The POW's were not disheartened by the failed escape. They continued to dig tunnels in the dangerous sandy soil beneath the walls. Rations were slim and life in the camp was not easy. Edwin, along with other POW's, persevered with the hope of liberation one day, if they endured. As the Russian army approached, the POW's were marched through a January blizzard to a new camp hundreds of miles away. Many died along the way, but Edwin kept going. Eventually he was liberated and returned home to Loretta, whose photo perhaps saved his life.

After the war Edwin completed his education and began a career as an engineer. He bought a small bungalow in a quaint suburb. He and Loretta enjoyed the good life of his generation. They were unexpectedly blessed by Edwin, Jr. Edwin was told he would never be able to have children because of injuries and malnutrition during the war, but Edwin, Jr. came anyway. Edwin eventually retired, and he and Loretta enjoyed yearly trips to Europe, this time as a vacationer and not a soldier.

I rejoice Edwin's story was captured in Never Give Up. Not everyone is so blessed. Herbert and Grace were a Chinese couple, members of another parish I served. Herbert came to the United States to study long before it was common for persons in Asian countries to do so. He received a PhD and went to work as a researcher at an American university. His Chinese friends told him he was foolish to stay in America. He would never have the respect of American scientists and always be considered a second-class citizen. So, Herbert returned to China to continue his research.

But Mao and the communist revolution arrived. Scholars came under suspicion and Herbert was relegated to menial work. He was not allowed to conduct the high level research he enjoyed. He longed to return to the U.S. Herbert and Grace raised their five children in communist China, all the time dreaming of life in America. Finally, Herbert and Grace found a way to flee the country, and in the ensuing years were able to bring all their children to the U.S. as well.

Herbert went to work doing research at a local university. Grace opened four Chinese restaurants. Once or twice per year they invited Carolyn, me and our children to join them at one of their restaurants. The food was outstanding and abundant. Grace boxed up leftovers and sent them home with us. We ate off them for days.

Herbert began to suffer with Alzheimer's. I visited them at their home one day. Their house was filled with beautiful Chinese furnishings and artwork. On Herbert's desk I saw an unfinished manuscript, his autobiography. I was snoopy. I picked it up and browsed through it. The beginning chapters were well-written. As chapters progressed, though, I could see the quality of writing decline rapidly. The last chapters were mostly incoherent. The effects of Alzheimer's had progressed too far and too fast for him to continue writing. I felt sad he did not begin to write his life's story earlier so it could be complete before the onset of dementia. I pray his children were able to continue his writing. His story was a remarkable one of persistence and courage.

Now Edwin, in his late 80s, was beginning a new adventure as he squeezed Juanita's hand during the singing of "Alleluia" at the conclusion of worship. He could offer Juanita the financial stability she lacked. She could offer him the companionship he craved. Edwin would continue to employ home health aides who cooked meals, washed clothes and cleaned house so Juanita would not have to do those chores. I performed the marriage ceremony for Edwin and Juanita less than a year later.

Life with Juanita did not go as Edwin planned. Juanita didn't want to move out of her condominium and Edwin didn't want to sell his home. They kept both properties. They usually met for dinner each evening, but slept in their own home at night. It was not the original plan but seemed to work well for them.

Life took another unexpected twist. Juanita got early dementia. She became more and more forgetful. Instead of Juanita caring for Edwin in his old age, he was caring for Juanita. Edwin had to cling to his motto "Never Give Up" once again. Life wasn't getting any easier over the age of 90.

I said goodbye to Edwin and moved to another congregation. I heard through friends that Edwin, Jr. had gone through a divorce and moved in with Edwin. Edwin, Jr. always lived far away but now they had time to enjoy one another's company. Edwin finally had someone to be with him in his final years.

I received a call from Edwin a couple of years after I started at the new church. He was in tears. Edwin, Jr. had died. Edwin came home and found him lying on the floor, dead of an apparent heart attack. On the phone Edwin just kept saying, "This is the worst thing ever. I don't know how I will ever make it through this one."

I don't know how you keep going when life gives you unexpected heartbreak after another. Many older folks discover there really are no golden years in life. Our challenges and struggles just change. Life never becomes easy.

Since I was no longer his pastor, I don't know how Edwin survived this blow. I prayed he found the resolve to carry on despite the death of this son. As he always said, "Never give up."

CHAPTER 51

Getting a Little Green?

Our mission team arrived in Mexico early afternoon. We were just seated at our host's favorite taco place when I received a call. Carolyn told me Ted just died. Ted was one of the few remaining charter members of the church, a pillar who had faithfully supported the congregation for many years. Ted's family knew my commitment to mission work and was not asking me to return. The Associate Pastor knew the family well and could preside over the memorial service. It was not necessary for me to return but it was something I wanted very much to do. Ted's daughter-in-law was on the mission trip also. She and I arranged our flights and were soon headed home.

Usually on mission trips, I would not feel guilty leaving a mission team on its own as I headed home to be with the family of a deceased and officiate at the memorial service. Our mission teams were experienced and worked well together. I offered no significant construction skills, just sweat and grunt labor. This trip, however, was different.

We normally partnered with familiar mission organizations. We knew the people and the work. On this trip, though, we partnered with an organization for the first time. We came prepared to paint the interior of a brand new school. The church-related school took a large leap forward in faith to expand. Members of the church offered their personal houses as collateral to purchase land for the large beautiful new building. We were told when we arrived the building would be mostly finished. We would complete painting in classrooms and hallways. When we arrived, we encountered just a few walls standing in a muddy field. There was no roof, no floor, no doors or windows – just some freestanding walls. We didn't even have paint. In addition, the construction foreman to guide our work was in the hospital with what they believed was a heart attack.

I felt guilty leaving the mission team to confront this mess without me. Our host was an amazing person with endless optimism and contagious energy. I was sensing, though, his spirits were sagging. Construction of the new school was presenting colossal challenges, even for his unbounded enthusiasm. What would our team do? Painting walls exposed to the sun and rain above and mud below seemed ludicrous. They would need to be painted again. That is what we came to do and what they were still asking us to complete. The team ribbed me a little for deserting them in their hour of need, but they knew I should be home with Ted's family.

By every measure one could think of, Ted was a success in life. The son of an Albanian immigrant, he was a man of high integrity, honesty and courage. He built his business not on words and promises, but deeds and action; not what you say, but what you do. He was respected and admired not because he was successful, but because he was someone to be trusted and counted on. He expected a lot from himself, but was gracious toward others. His wife of 60+ years, four children and numerous grandchildren and great-grandchildren adored him.

I appreciated Ted's servant heart. He offered to do whatever necessary in the life of the church, no matter how humble. When the church was young and couldn't afford a custodian, he volunteered himself and his family to clean the church building for Sunday morning. He took the dreaded late night shift when we worked with the homeless. The closest Ted came to complaining about the church was when he expressed disappointment a sermon was cut short because too many other things were happening in the worship service. He came to church especially to hear a good sermon, he said, and didn't think sermon time should be sacrificed. I don't hear too many people say my sermons are too short, so I appreciate those complaints. I also liked Ted because he sat in the front pew. Preachers always love folks with the courage to sit up front.

Ted was a pillar of the church. He exhibited many characteristics of people in what Tom Brokaw called "The Greatest Generation." He possessed deep loyalties to family, church and community. He was generous with money and time. Ted was different also. He didn't just accept cultural norms. He questioned them. He questioned tenets of the Christian faith. Ted had a sharp, inquisitive mind. He asked good questions not only about business, but about faith. Faith, for Ted, had to be thought about and wrestled with. Faith wasn't just about accepting certain doctrines of the church, but understanding them, living with them, and eventually trusting God with them.

Ted was a fighter pilot during World War II and continued his love for flying. With other flying enthusiasts, he founded an aerobatic formation flight team and flew with them for many years. He gave up formation flying after open heart surgery but continued to fly for the joy of it. One morning he poked his head into my office. He was flying that afternoon and asked if I wanted to join him. Of course I said, "Sure." He had an old navy two-seater trainer plane. I sat behind Ted underneath a glass canopy. The views were spectacular. We flew along the Chicago skyline and out to the countryside west of the city, not far from the area where Keith had his accident. Ted asked if I was up for some loops and rolls. Of course I said, "Sure." Ted began to put the little plane through its motions, doing a variety of stunts, each with a name I don't remember. Flying upside down with a glass canopy gave me incredible panoramas and thrills. It also started my stomach to churn. Upchucking while upside down in a glass canopy plane was not something I wanted to do. As calmly as I possibly could, I said to Ted I thought we should land soon. He looked back at me and smiled, "Getting a little green, huh? I could do this all day." I was very happy to be back on the ground with everything still in my stomach. A few days later I wondered whether flying upside down with a man with a weak heart approaching 80 years old was a good idea, but knew I would say, "Sure" if he asked me again.

Ted shared something at one of our first Men's Retreats that really opened me up to his courage and honesty. We were a small group, perhaps ten men, talking about significant events in our lives where we felt, or did not feel, God's presence. Ted chose to share about his depression. Depression quickly set in after he retired from his business and turned the company over to others. In my ministry I have spoken with many men, mostly successful men, who encounter depression on retiring. Ted could do nothing to shake it. This successful man, who accomplished so much during his lifetime, whom others looked up to and admired, was paralyzed by depression, and finally hospitalized. He spent several days on a psychiatric floor.

Most men of Ted's generation would not talk about depression. They would not admit they suffered with it, now or any time in the past. Depression was considered a weakness. Ted's strength was he was honest with himself and others. He understood his weakness. He could talk about it. He was not ashamed of it, nor did he dramatize it. He spoke about it plainly and simply, recognizing it was part of who he was. I think because he was so honest with himself he was able to manage his depression well.

Back in Mexico, our mission team painted and painted. They did as they were told. They painted everything they could see. It seemed ludicrous but they did it. They didn't need me, except to keep them from too many margaritas in the evening. Miracles happen and construction on the school accelerated that summer. Work went on around the clock. Local volunteers signed up and, of course, re-painted the walls our team painted. The round-the-clock effort enabled the school to open as scheduled.

Our host in Mexico came to our worship service one Sunday morning the following winter, and thanked our congregation. He said the week our team helped was the turning point in the progress of the school. Local people felt if Americans were contributing labor, the school must be viable. Soon, enrollment increased rapidly. They also felt humbled the Americans were willing to donate vacation time for painting. They, too, could donate time to help. They didn't say anything about the absurdity of painting interior walls with no roof or floor. The attitude on the school project changed after that week of mission work from panic and doubt to one of hope and belief. When we returned the following year to help at the school, we saw a beautiful building with classrooms full of noisy children. They didn't need our help anymore.

Life is not always as it seems. Seemingly pointless work gave hope to a school. A businessman whom everyone admired for starting and growing a company perhaps found greater success in a more personal challenge of life. God works in ways that often surprise us. We know in life there are twists and turns, even barrel rolls in airplanes, we don't see coming.

CHAPTER 52

God Will Take Care of Us

Cathy and Niels sat in my office filled with faith Cathy would be cured. They came to tell me she was just diagnosed with melanoma. She would begin treatments soon. It sounded scary but they were confident of God's healing touch for Cathy. "We have faith," they said. "God will take care of us."

Cathy and Niels were a cute young couple in their 30s, sharing an innocent and honest love. They exuded a simple faith in Christ, quietly radiating joy and trust in God. Common faith brought them together and united them in their marriage. They were best friends in love forever. You could not help but like them. Cathy was sweet and sincere, Niels funny and warm. They made friends easily. Cathy worked as a cover artist for a nearby Christian publishing house. Born and raised in Scandinavia, Niels was fluent in several languages. He worked in customer relations for a major airline. They had three beautiful young daughters. A more delightful family could not be found, positive and gracious, cheerful and kind.

Cathy began treatments, lost her hair and continued her optimistic outlook for healing. The treatments worked and she entered remission. The family continued with joy and thankfulness, confident of answered prayer.

Cancer is not always easily disposed of. Cathy and Niels sat in my office a second time sharing news the melanoma returned. They remained confident of God's healing in Cathy's life. She would undergo treatments once again. God would continue to watch over them.

This time cancer was not to be denied. It spread through her body popping up as small lumps under her skin. Family, friends, community, and even the world surrounded them. Niels' parents came across the ocean for weeks and months at a time. Cathy's parents dropped in and out on a regular basis. Church and community friends took care of their daughters, lining up transportation to their activities and providing day care when grandparents were not available. Meals were delivered on a regular basis. Cards poured in. Cathy's employer promised to keep her job open. Niels' co-workers donated scores of PTO (paid time off) days so he could stay home and attend to Cathy's needs. Cathy was on every church prayer list in our community. Across the country and the ocean, people prayed for Cathy's healing.

Cathy and Niels kept the faith. They believed God would give them a miracle. They remained hopeful and positive, always gracious for the love and prayers surrounding them. But the bumps kept growing. From marble size to golf ball size to baseball size they grew, on her back, her shoulders, her neck and even her skull. Beautiful Cathy was becoming difficult to look at.

The disease tried to strip away her dignity, self-respect, and joy. It disfigured her body and caused pain and discomfort. It tried to make her less a person than she was. There her cancer failed. Cathy met each progressive stage of her disease with hope and courage. She would not give in to despair and gloom cancer sought to inflict. She could have given up and waited for death, but she didn't. She gained strength from God and embraced life. She refused to surrender and accepted the gift of life God offered each day.

The dignity and radiance of Cathy's spirit continued to shine. It overcame the indignities her physical body endured. She would not let bumps growing over her body, the loss of hair from chemotherapy, or any other debilitating effects of her disease devalue her character or her being. She could have easily evoked pity or made others feel self-conscious or uneasy, but just the opposite happened. She didn't let cancer define who she was. She continued to live a full life, a giving life, using gifts God gave to her, and fully hoping and praying for the miracle of healing.

As she began to realize death was inevitable, Cathy wrote letters to her family to be read after her passing. Niels promised her the girls would always know their mom. The final days were hard for everyone. Cathy's pain and discomfort were difficult for her to bear, difficult for her girls to see. We prayed Cathy might be released from her body soon. Death came mercifully on Thanksgiving Day. I was thankful, rather than journeying to see family that year, extended family came to visit us. I visited with Cathy and her family in the morning knowing the end was near. A few hours later Niels called with news Cathy had gone to be with her God. I returned to their house. I was thankful I was able to be with them those first few minutes to remember and honor the faith that sustained them during Cathy's battle with cancer.

If faith alone can save, faith would have saved Cathy. She would not have died. Cathy and Niels had faith in their Savior and Lord, and faith in God's power to heal. They were surrounded by people of faith. But Cathy died.

If love and kindness alone can save, love and kindness would have saved Cathy. She would not have died. Cathy and Niels shared a profound love. Their family and friends embraced them in love. But Cathy died.

If prayers alone can save, prayers would have saved Cathy. Prayers went to heaven from our church and all the churches in our community, from churches across the country and the world. Cathy and Niels prayed, as did family and friends. They were bathed in prayers, prayers for healing and prayers for wholeness. But Cathy died.

If justice alone can save, justice would have prevented Cathy from dying. Here was a young mother of three beautiful girls. She and her husband were good, generous and thoughtful. They gave and served. Justice should save someone like Cathy. It would spare her daughters growing up without the loving presence of their mother. But Cathy died.

Cathy had it all on her side, faith, love, prayers and justice, and still she died. If a miracle ever needed a reason, it had it in Cathy. If a miracle could ever be coaxed out of God, it would have happened for Cathy. Despite what some preachers proclaim, faith, love, and prayers cannot demand miracles.

I don't know why miracles of healing seem to happen for some but not others. Does God really intervene in areas of sickness or death? Or, is it just forces of nature giving us a reprieve that seems like a miracle? Can prayers really bring healing? Can faith disrupt the world's design?

At Cathy's service, I spoke about the miracle of Cathy's faith that inspired us amidst the misery and heartache of melanoma. I spoke about the miracle of love around Cathy. I spoke about the miracle of all who surrounded Cathy becoming stronger and kinder as we journeyed with her. I could not speak about the miracle of liberating Cathy's body from cancer, which was the miracle we all prayed for.

We worship and serve God because of faith, because deep within us we believe we are profoundly connected to a loving Creator who cares about us intimately and compassionately. We don't worship God because God answers prayers and makes life grand. Worship comes from a longing deep within, a longing to know the God who fashioned the universe and breathed life into our souls. I believe through our grief, prayers, searching and questions, we come to know our God more and more. I have no physical proof of that, only what I believe lies within my spirit. So, I continue to pray, have faith, love and strive for justice because I believe that is what the God of heaven and earth calls us to do.

I said words at Cathy's service that might seem trite and ridiculous to those outside the faith, but words giving hope and purpose to those embracing the faith. Cathy was experiencing a greater miracle than the one we prayed for. She was experiencing the miracle of eternal life in Jesus Christ, an eternity in the presence of a loving Savior. All sickness and pain were finished. Death was a thing of the past. She had a new body and a new home. I quoted words of the apostle Paul I often say, "For I am convinced that neither death nor life, nor angels, nor rulers, nor things present, nor things to come, nor powers, nor height, nor depth, nor anything else in all creation, will be able to separate us from the love of God in Christ Jesus our Lord."

Faith is a mystery, I said. Life and death are also mysteries. The apostle Paul says we see only dimly now. We know only in part. There will come a time when we know fully. In the meantime, Paul writes, "And now faith, hope, and love abide, these three; and the greatest of these is love."

CHAPTER 53

April Fools

I was running late. Traffic around Chicago was heavier than anticipated, as usual, and the three hour drive became quite a bit longer. I ducked into the last pew in the sanctuary just as the minister was beginning the memorial service for my cousin Roger.

I was able to attend Roger's service because I failed in ministry. A memorial service for a member of my congregation was being held that afternoon. The pastor who preceded me in the church presided over the service. In times of serious illness, the family called upon him to offer pastoral care. I made calls, but probably not enough. I never sensed my ministry was received or desired by the family, so I became lax in what I offered. The family was close to the previous pastor and I couldn't remember them attending worship more than once or twice since I arrived. They were still on our membership rolls and I felt badly I didn't connect with them. So now the previous pastor conducted the memorial service.

I try very carefully not to overstep boundaries in churches where I have served. I do not want to interfere with the ministry of my successors. I turn down requests to preside over funerals and weddings. Pastoral ethics ask this protocol of pastors and I follow it. However, it did not bother me if previous pastors provide care to my parishioners. If parishioners are not receiving pastoral care they desire from me, I rejoice they have someone who can offer God's grace and comfort in difficult times. The focus should be on the needs of the family and not the ego of the pastor. The previous pastor stayed close to many in my parish, which was okay with me. Sometimes it caused problems with his own congregation and brought about questions from the Association. I rejoiced, however, he was able to help in those situations where I faltered.

Pastors fail. Sometimes we blame it on too much to do with too little time.

We simply do not follow up as we should. Sometimes we blame it on distractions or unreasonable demands of the family in need. Sometimes we just don't connect with a grieving family or a family in crisis despite our best efforts. Words we offer may not resonate nor bring healing and hope we desire. A family's ties to another pastor may be so strong they cannot easily transfer. For whatever reason, we may not gain a family's trust and they may look elsewhere in times of need.

Because I failed to connect with the family of the deceased in my home parish, I was free to attend my cousin Roger's funeral. It seemed like the only time I connected with my extended family was at funerals.

I hadn't seen Roger in years. One drawback in being a pastor is being busy most Saturdays and Sundays when family gatherings happen. We may live hours away from relatives and busy weekend schedules prevent us from connecting with our families. I remember one year when a cousin was planning a family reunion. He knew my summers were busy with mission trips, family camps, VBS and weddings. I wasn't able to make previous get-togethers. He called me specifically to find dates I was available. I could only give him two weekend dates for the summer. He set the reunion for one of those dates to accommodate my schedule. What happened? A parishioner died. I presided over the memorial service and missed another family reunion. My cousin teased me about that absence several times.

I hadn't seen Roger, but my parents were wonderful keeping connections to their nieces and nephews and updating me on what was going on. Roger had not had an easy life growing up. He had a brother two years older who was good-looking, smart and athletic. Roger was scrawny, struggled in school and had serious eye problems. Trying to live up to his perfect brother had something to do with his scrappiness.

Roger met a good-looking gal, Diane, taller than what he was. People were impressed Roger found such a looker. They married and had two children. But Diane had a wandering eye, and her adulterous affairs led to a volatile end to their marriage.

Later, Roger was blessed. He met Janice. Janice loved Roger just as he was. Roger settled down, worked a good job in the RV industry, and they were married. They built a house in the country, raised a few chickens and were quite content. In his 50s, Roger discovered he had cancer. He accepted it with grace and good humor, and felt he was blessed to live the life he did. Cancer didn't progress quite as rapidly as he and Janice were led to believe. On April 1st, Roger woke up and said to Janice, "April Fools." "April Fools what?" Janice asked. "April Fools, I bet you didn't think I would still be alive by now," Roger responded.

I enjoyed the memorial service for Roger, then went to the cemetery with the rest of the family for the committal. Family was milling about afterwards, getting ready to leave, when I saw a familiar figure tentatively coming to Roger's grave. I hadn't seen her in years but realized it was his first wife Diane. I hadn't heard anything about her except she remarried and moved to another town. I wasn't sure what had happened within the family in intervening years and didn't know how the family would receive her. I sensed Diane didn't either by the tentative way she approached.

I remember my dad, who never carries a grudge and welcomes all, seeing Diane, smiling, and saying, "Well look who's here?" Everyone greeted Diane, welcomed her warmly, even Roger's widow, Janice. The rocky breakup of their marriage was a long time ago. Diane was forgiven and accepted as part of the family. Life moves on.

I pray families I disappoint or fail to reach in my ministry forgive me for my failures, absences or lame attempts trying to bring comfort and hope. I also pray I can forgive those who slight and demean me. I pray we can all gather around the banquet table of the Lord and accept each other as part of God's family. Life moves on into eternity.

Roger could joke about life and death on his final April Fools Day. He lived longer than doctors expected. He surprised everyone. Perhaps the resurrection can be understood as the biggest April Fools joke of all time. God surprised everyone by raising Christ from the dead that first Easter morning. The power of death was defeated, the gift of eternal life given. God continues to surprise us today. "April Fools!"

CHAPTER 54

I Will Be Forced to Arrest You

"Do they really need all the yellow crime tape?" I said to myself as I approached Rebecca's house. Three or four police cars were parked in the street. Several police officers milled around. I stepped over the crime tape to approach one. "Sir," he yelled with a voice of authority. "Step back across the tape! Now!" "I am Rebecca's pastor," I replied. "May I talk with her?" "Sir, if you do not step back over the tape, I will be forced to arrest you." I stepped back over the crime tape. "Is it possible for me to speak with Rebecca?" "No, sir, it is not. She is being interrogated." "How long do you think it will last?" "As long as it needs to." "Can you tell Rebecca I am here?" "No, sir, I cannot." I waited on the street for an awkward 15 or so minutes, then drove to the hospital.

The night before we celebrated the life of Douglas, Rebecca's husband. Douglas succumbed to cancer at the age of 53. The sanctuary was full of family, friends and co-workers. We shared stories. We sang songs Douglas loved. We played "Take Me Out to the Ballgame" and rooted for Douglas' beloved and beleaguered Cubbies, the Chicago Cubs. At times we even got a little rowdy. Foremost, we heard God's promises for eternal life. It was a good celebration. We sent Douglas off to the Lord in the style he would have desired.

I was at the church waiting for the family to arrive to inter Douglas' cremains in the church's little Memorial Garden when brothers of Rebecca's son-in-law arrived to tell me there would be no interment this morning. There had been another death in the family, the 18-year-old niece of Rebecca.

After the memorial service, families of Douglas and Rebecca returned to their home to continue the celebration of Douglas' life. The adults were drinking, probably a little too much, and paying no attention to those who were underage. Rebecca was tired and wanted to go to bed. Rebecca's niece, her sister's daughter, had stayed at their house since Douglas' death. She was a good friend of her cousin, Rebecca's daughter, and was keeping her company during this difficult time. As her sister went to leave, Rebecca asked her to take her daughter home with them. Rebecca said she needed rest and didn't want the responsibility of caring for her. Her sister insisted her daughter stay. She and her cousin were such good friends. Being together would be good for both of them. Her sister and husband left the house and Rebecca went to bed. The adults continued to drink.

So did the underage girls. The girls also found OxyContin Douglas took for pain. Perhaps, too, they found other prescription drugs. A couple of years earlier, Rebecca's daughter struggled with addiction issues. Her parents sought treatment for her. She seemed to be doing much better. Her cousin was also struggling with addiction, unbeknownst to her parents.

When the adults awoke in the morning, Rebecca's niece lay on the couch. The adults left her alone as they had morning coffee. Finally, one of them looked at her a little more closely and realized she was not breathing. They called 911, but it was too late. She had been dead too long.

I left the 'crime scene' to be with family members as they gathered in a waiting room in the emergency department at the hospital. It was a quiet room. The hospital chaplain sat with them offering spiritual comfort. But what comfort is there for parents living through the worst nightmare imaginable? What can you say to parents when the daughter whom they loved and nurtured dies suddenly of a drug overdose? The niece's parents were in shock, not believing this nightmare was unfolding.

So we sat, mostly in quiet. Just one question was asked, "Why?" "Why did it happen?" "Why? Why?" How do you answer that question? Oh, I could say their daughter is with Jesus now and everything was okay. I believed that. I believe in the amazing grace of our God. But aching grief doesn't respond to simple platitudes. Grief must be felt. All the hurt and pain must thrash inside us in all its penetrating rawness. All I could say was "I'm sorry. I don't know why your daughter had to die." Then, I dared to add, "I believe God loves your daughter very, very much and there is nothing that can ever get in the way of that love. God, too, aches now and grieves your loss. God never wants young girls to die."

As we sat longer, the "How?" questions started. "How could it happen? How could she die?" The "How?" questions led to questions of responsibility. "Wasn't anyone paying attention?" "What kind of drugs did she have?" "Where did she get them?" Mostly it was just numbing pain. It was too early for questions to be asked in earnest.

The family of the deceased girl prepared to leave. I offered my help in any way possible. They lived in another city, however, and I suggested a clergy person there might be better support. They said they knew a priest in their hometown who could help. He knew the community and they trusted him. We said goodbye. I knew their heartache, and questions, were just beginning. The pain of their grief would hurt for a long time, even forever. The emptiness of their missing daughter would never go away.

I returned to Rebecca's house. I stayed carefully behind the crime scene tape. Another police officer guarded the perimeter. I introduced myself to him and asked if it was okay to talk with Rebecca. He thought they were about through and I would be able to speak with her in a few minutes. He went inside, checked on what was happening, returned, and told me it was okay to go in.

Rebecca was wrung out. She had been questioned for nearly two hours. No one should have to go through what she endured. All she wanted was to come home after Douglas' service and go to bed. She was exhausted. She didn't want to entertain guests. She didn't want the responsibility of caring for her niece. She just wanted to grieve her dead husband, and sleep.

A teenage girl was dead of an overdose. It could have been avoided. It could have been avoided if the girl's mother heeded Rebecca's request to take her home. It could have been avoided if the adults supervised the minors' drinking. It could have been avoided if Douglas' unused drugs had been disposed. It could have been avoided if many things happened differently. But it wasn't avoided. The girl died.

I know in succeeding weeks, family relationships strained as blame shifted from one person to another. Guilt is an odd thing. We don't want to admit it. We don't want to get to the root cause of guilt if it is our own lack of judgment, misdeeds, forgetfulness or whatever. We find it difficult to accept responsibility for our failures or decisions. We find it difficult to say we were wrong, confess our mistake, receive forgiveness, and invite healing to begin. Instead, guilt causes us to lash out in anger toward others, shift blame and responsibility to someone else. We can never heal when that happens. Grief is difficult to process when we remain angry. Grief is difficult to process when we remain in denial, also.

Everyone, I am sure, wanted to turn the clock back and re-live that night. They would make different decisions. They would behave differently. But that was not possible. Death is irreversible, except in God's realm. Each person at the house that evening would have to process their feelings, remorse and anger their own way. They would have to live with what they did or didn't do. Somehow, they would have to discover forgiveness and grace from God and from one another. If they did, perhaps they could move forward, experience healing and reconciliation. It is possible, even with scars as deep as those from the wound of that night.

CHAPTER 55

Ashes to Ashes, Dust to Dust

I kept telling myself it was better than doing nothing. "Ashes to ashes, dust to dust." I was interring ashes in our church's Memorial Garden. I wished I could say something personal about each one, their dreams and delights, people who loved them, people they loved, things they did or places they went. But I knew nothing about any of them. I never met the folks whose ashes I interred. I knew only their name and date of death. So, with Scripture and prayer, we committed their ashes to the ground. We gave their cremains a permanent home next to the deceased in our church family.

I received a call from a local funeral home a few months earlier. They were aware of our Memorial Garden. In their closets they kept black plastic boxes of unclaimed ashes. No one wanted the ashes. In some cases the person died alone without living relatives and close friends. In other cases, the family told the funeral director they had no intention of ever picking up the ashes. Some funeral homes, in other parts of the country, received negative publicity when thieves broke into storage sheds and stole or vandalized ashes. The local funeral home did not want to keep unclaimed cremains in perpetuity. Thus they made the call asking if our church's Memorial Garden would be willing to serve as a final resting place for the ashes on their shelves.

Pastors have frequent contact with the homeless and transient, the forgotten, neglected and deserted, those cast out or those who walked away in defiance and anger. They stop at our churches, usually asking for a handout but sometimes asking for counsel or prayer. Sometimes we get annoyed because they may come back again and again, as long as we are willing to give financial assistance. Sometimes we get angry because we feel they can be too impertinent. We receive calls in the middle of the night, demanding help and cursing if we don't help. Once a couple of brothers stole my tool box after I purchased a new starter for their car and gave them my tools to install it. Their stories may also break our hearts, especially when there are families with little children. We weep with them as we buy tickets at bus stations or nights at a local motel. We wish we could do more to help, and pray God will take care of them. Often we wonder if we would have their persistence and courage amidst so much adversity.

The homeless drift in and out of our lives, sometimes over a period of years. We refer them to food pantries or homeless shelters. We give them $10 for a meal at a local diner or go with them to a local unsavory motel and buy them a night or two of lodging. We help obtain a government ID or a needed prescription. We give them a gas card or a bus ticket to help them on their way. When they quit coming we rarely know whether they found a place to settle and call home, moved on, or perhaps died.

When the local funeral director called I wanted to help. The homeless and wanderer, rejected and friendless, need a permanent home for their cremains. For their ashes to sit unclaimed in the closet of a funeral home for decades or even longer seemed like a continuing injustice. The people suffered enough in their lives. Perhaps by giving their ashes a simple committal and burial in our Memorial Garden, we could offer a little respect and dignity to those who endured a life of wandering. Maybe we could provide a home in death for those who never had a home in life. Most people long for a home, for a place where they belong, a place where they are loved and cared for.

I explained this to our Church Council and they agreed our Memorial Garden should be a home for all persons. The church staffed a homeless site once a month providing breakfast, lunch and dinner to 50 or so folks who slept on pads on the floor. Caring for the homeless was a meaningful part of the church's ministry and our Memorial Garden could be a part of that ministry also.

Not all my churches have been so mission-minded. In my first parish, our church building was located on a busy federal highway. Many people stopped asking for assistance. Many came to town looking for work at a local egg farm. The work paid poorly and the environment unhealthy, but it was a paycheck. They arrived in town with nothing and came asking for a little assistance until the first payday.

That community lacked assistance ministries. In my early days of ministry, most communities, especially smaller ones, lacked adequate social agencies. One day a young family arrived at the church. They had been living in their car for weeks with two little children, travelling from town to town looking for work when they heard of the egg farm in our town. The family broke my heart. At the next Church Council meeting I asked for $25 for assistance to travelers. One older man spoke up, "If they want to eat, let them work." The discussion ended. Fortunately, others in the church were willing to help when needs arose.

Most homeless who drop by the church tend to be younger. Senior citizens can no longer endure the grueling regimen of life on the streets. Also, many of the homeless simply do not make it to old age. A man in his late 70's stopped by our church one day asking for a meal and a ride to a truck stop. He walked slowly and with pain. His breathing was labored. As I drove him to the truck stop, he told me his story. His social security check was minimal. He could not afford monthly rent on an apartment. He could afford two weeks rent each month in a rooming house. For the other two weeks, he travelled the interstates sleeping in truck stops. He said truck stops were nice and would let him stay one night. Each day he would hitchhike to the next one. He wanted to settle down but the waiting list to obtain government subsidized housing (Section 8 housing) was several years long. On this trip he travelled through three states unsuccessfully searching for a place with available Section 8 housing. He figured he would keep staying in truck stops. I bought him a room in a cheap motel for the night so he wouldn't have to sleep at the truck stop.

I may have been wrong about the homeless wanting a home for their ashes. Perhaps they preferred their ashes spread along highways and byways where they travelled, in some special park where they camped, or a roadside rest stop they frequented. Some folks, for whatever reason, do not prefer a permanent home for their earthly remains. They want their ashes spread amidst places special to them – a lake where they sailed, a woods where they walked, a camp that touched their lives in their youth.

When I was backpacking recently in the Weminuche Wilderness of southwest Colorado, my friend and pastoral colleague brought along ashes of a friend. His friend's wife asked if he could spread some ashes of her husband amidst the grandeur of the Rockies. The man died young, of cancer. He loved the outdoors and was never able to fulfill many of his dreams of adventure. Perhaps in death he could go places he never went in life. Atop a beautiful high mountain pass, surrounded by fields of colorful wildflowers offering stunning vistas of soaring peaks and deep valleys, alpine lakes and plunging waterfalls, we paused on the trail. My friend opened the zip lock bag containing the cremains and let the wind take the ashes of his friend through the stunning natural beauty of the San Juan Mountains.

So, a few homeless or friendless folks found their home in our church's Memorial Garden. Interment sites are not marked in the garden, although a brass plaque gives the names of those interred. Adding names to the plaque was expensive and we never added names of the homeless. I always felt a little bad about that. I felt it would have been a nice gesture. It probably didn't matter to those whose ashes we interred.

More importantly, I pray those whose ashes we buried found a permanent home with their Creator and God. Scriptures tell us we are all sojourners in this life. We are all just passing through. Though we like to have markers and monuments to give us an illusion of permanence, our permanent home is the place our God prepares for us. Then, we will be "no longer strangers and aliens, but citizens with the saints and members of the household of God."

CHAPTER 56

Floating By

I sat toward the back of the sanctuary attending the memorial service for the mother of a good friend. The sanctuary was nearly full, perhaps 250 people. It was quite a tribute for a woman more than 90 years old. My friend's mother was a dear saint of her church. Friends and family came to honor her remarkable life. She was not well-known or wealthy. She did not hold positions of leadership or power in the community. She lived a simple life dedicated to serving others and making the world a better place for all. She did so treating each person special. She touched many lives.

An American citizen of Japanese descent, she spent World War II years interred in detention camps along with other Japanese-Americans living on the west coast of the United States. Racism in America has shown its ugly head again and again through the years, including the Japanese detention camps. This remarkable woman, like many Japanese-Americans held in the camps, harbored no bitterness or malice from time spent behind barbed wire. She used her time wisely for learning and teaching, culture and community. Instead of nursing the memory of injustice, she remembered the blessing to her and her family when a church sponsored them to relocate in the Midwest. As a result, she was a lifelong and devoted member of our church tradition. She spent her life working for justice and fairness for all people, building bridges to understanding and peace.

This old saint was generally patient. For some unknown reason she lost her patience one day sitting in her car at a railroad crossing. Delays at the crossing sometimes seemed intolerably long as unending coal trains headed through town to points further east. Trains carrying empty cars returned west. When the eastbound train passed and the crossing arm had not lifted, she decided to drive around the lowered arm and cross the tracks. She did not see the westbound train on the second track. She was killed instantly. Impatience was not typical of her character but this one exception cost her her life.

The memorial service was beautiful, honoring her generous life and lifting up her pursuit of justice for all, especially the oppressed and forgotten. It was a celebration of a life well lived. One of her children, however, was not able to attend. Her son was an astronaut serving on the space station. He would not return to earth for a few months. Sending a space shuttle to retrieve him for his mother's service was, of course, out of the question. Being away from family at significant times is one of the sacrifices made by astronauts, armed service personnel, and others deployed a long way from home.

Technology enabled her son to create a video and send it to earth to play at the memorial service. In the video he gave a wonderful tribute to his mother's persevering and kindhearted ways. What struck me most about the video were other astronauts floating in the background while her son talked. In the zero-gravity world of outer space, astronauts gently passed by in mid-air, freely and effortlessly. The space station existed in a very different reality from here on earth. Here, gravity rules and defines everything about our physical existence. We can't imagine a world without gravity. There, gravity was absent. You move differently, eat differently and go to the bathroom differently.

Reality is not always as we envision it. Physicists see a world defined by laws of thermodynamics, behavior of sub-atomic particles, and long, complicated mathematical equations. Chemists examine a world through molecular structures and reactions. Biologists see a world determined by an evolutionary process of natural selection, survival of the fittest, and genetic mutation. The creation of suns and planets, the creation of life and human beings have resulted from the steady forward movement of the universe as determined by laws of physics, chemistry and biology. To many scientists, the world is a closed, impersonal system, explained through scientific study and natural laws. Values and morals, love and grace, kindness and compassion, are creations of human beings and not embedded into the fabric of the universe.

Christians value the contributions of science. The discoveries scientists make to understand how this incredible world is put together and functions are astounding. Science reveals the handiwork of God. As a Christian, though, I don't think science tells the whole story of our universe. There is more to this world than what the most brilliant scientist can fathom. A deeper reality to the universe lies within a living, loving God who has created and continues to create. At the center of this living, loving God are principles as enduring, true and unchanging as the laws of physics. They create a deeper reality than that which can be measured scientifically.

The deeper reality of the universe, which finds its expression in the teachings of Jesus, defies the natural laws of selection just as astronauts appear to defy the natural law of gravity. All human beings have value because they are created in God's image, not because of their strength, wisdom or ability to procreate. We love our enemies and do good to those who persecute us. We reach out with compassion to the blind, lame, leper, and others the world chooses to exclude. Others may see them as stumbling blocks to a more prosperous society. Christians see them as children of God. Forgiveness and grace, kindness and compassion, goodness and honesty, are building blocks of our universe just as much as laws of thermodynamics. When Jesus taught and lived among us, he sought to open us to these truths at the heart of our world.

The large numbers who gathered for the memorial service of my friend's mother came because their lives were touched by her kindness and caring. In their connections with this dear saint, they experienced an encounter of a deeper reality in the universe. They were bound together in mutual caring and concern. Their love and compassion made the world a better place. It was how the world was meant to be. They came seeking to re-connect with the true reality and celebrate the love that bound them together.

In the scientific world, we are born, live, die and that is all. In the Christian perspective, there is resurrection. There is new life, eternal life. God breaks into our history and shows us a different reality. The resurrection of Jesus tells us there is a reality more profound than anything we see with our eyes, hear with our ears or touch with our fingers. There is life, death, then life again. Not life as we know it in flesh and blood, mass and energy, air, water and fire, but something much deeper. Life defined by love and grace. Death is not the end of life as science might lead us to believe. Death and oblivion is not the final destiny of the world. The reality of the resurrection tells us of a reality of life beyond life.

In this deeper reality, death is defeated and evil vanquished forever. Love and forgiveness reigns. There is no injustice. Blessings abound.

CHAPTER 57

Losing This Finger Was a Lot Easier than the Last One

"So, what did you do to your finger?" I asked Leo's son Benny. The memorial service for Leo was delayed a couple of days as Benny recovered from losing part of a finger. Benny and his wife Mattie were consummate Alaskans. In the early 1970's, they drove their pickup up the ALCAN Highway to vacation in Alaska and quickly fell in love with our 49th state. Benny stayed. Mattie drove the pickup down the ALCAN Highway, loaded essentials in the back, sold everything else and drove back to join Benny. The ALCAN Highway was not paved in those days and was quite an adventure to drive. Benny and Mattie prospected for gold. They did okay until the price of gold dropped. They left the pursuit of gold and used their machinery for road repair and other construction jobs.

Construction is mostly during summer months and summers are short in Alaska. To love Alaska you must embrace the long, cold, dark winters, which Benny and Mattie did. They fell in love with dogsledding. Benny became known for building the best dogsleds anywhere. Champion mushers sought his advice and workmanship. He also became known for training sled dogs. His reputation within the mushing world earned him the honor of Marshal of the Yukon Quest, a 1000-mile race between Fairbanks, Alaska and Whitehorse, Yukon Territory. It is perhaps the most grueling of all dogsled races.

I met Benny the first time at the funeral of his mother Ida. Ida had severe Parkinson's. Leo cared for her at home with the assistance of live-in help. When I knew his mother she simply slumped in her wheelchair, head sagging close to the tray. I detected no sign she heard me or was aware of my presence. Leo spoke to her as if she were fully aware of her surroundings. The conversation was always three-way, not two-way, although Ida did not participate. I admired Leo's gentleness with her and the dignity with which he cared for her. Communion was always difficult since eating and drinking were hard for Ida, but the difficulty made it even more special. When Ida died Leo put her ashes in an urn and set the urn on the railing of their loft. He felt like she was always looking over him.

I saw Benny only the one time before, but it seemed like I knew him. Leo talked fondly of him and kept me up to date on happenings in his life. I felt a connection since Alaskan fever flowed through the blood of Carolyn's family. Carolyn's sister Linda built a cabin in the Alaskan wilderness far from any roads. Her brother Steve mushed dogs weeks on end across frozen tundra and rivers. He knew Benny. Also, Steve completed the grueling Yukon Quest one year.

"Losing this finger was a lot easier than the last one," Benny replied to my question about his finger. "Why? What happened with that one?" I asked. "Well," Benny began, and I was treated to a story that belongs in the annals of Alaskan folklore.

Benny was working in his shop repairing machinery in the midst of the cold, dark winter when something slipped. The end of his middle finger was cut off. He went into the cabin and showed it to Mattie. Mattie wrapped Benny's finger in gauze and hooked the trailer to the snowmobile. Benny and Mattie lived about six miles from the main road. In winter they parked a truck at the road and used the snowmobile to shuttle back and forth. Mattie drove while Benny sat in the trailer, his middle finger extended in the air.

When they arrived at the road the truck wouldn't start. Temperatures had been flirting with 50 degrees below zero and it was just too cold. Mattie would have to take care of Benny's finger herself. They headed back on the snowmobile trail to their cabin, Mattie driving, Benny on the trailer.

It was a snowy winter with snow stacked high on either side of the snowmobile route. Mattie and Benny came face to face with a mother moose and her calf. The snowmobile couldn't leave the snowmobile track and the mother moose refused to. Moose and snowmobile squared off. Neither gave an inch. Mattie tried to nudge the moose away, but a mother moose protecting her calf is not easily scared. She attacked the snowmobile destroying the windshield and hood. Mattie and Benny retreated to the safety of willows. Finally, the moose moved away from the snowmobile. Mattie warily repaired the machine well enough to drive. She started it once again. Benny ran to the trailer and they took off.

Unfortunately, the baby calf was now in front of the snowmobile and the mother behind. Mother moose chased the snowmobile trying to dislodge Benny from the trailer. Mattie was able to nick the heels of the calf and clip it off the trail. Bad luck once again caused the calf to land in the trailer on top of Benny. Now, mother moose was furious as Benny desperately unloaded the calf behind the snowmobile. The calf disposed of, Mattie continued toward their cabin, with Benny sitting on the trailer holding high his extended middle finger.

Soon, Benny and Mattie could see in the distance over the tundra their neighbor and good friend, Susan Butcher. Susan was a great American dog musher and four-time winner of the Iditarod race. Her sled was upended and her dogs scattered. (Benny would later discover the moose that attacked them also attacked her dog team, killing one of them.) She motioned for Benny and Mattie to come and help. Benny and Mattie continued on their way, Benny still with his middle finger extended and held high. Susan shouted a few words and returned the gesture.

Benny and Mattie returned home. Mattie removed bone fragments and sewed up Eddie's finger. Three weeks later the weather warmed and they were able to start their truck once again. They drove to Fairbanks to see the doctor. The doctor x-rayed and examined the finger. He said he couldn't have fixed it any better.

I tell this story not because it relates to coping with or understanding grief and death. It does not. I tell it because it is a great story and should be told again and again. It captures the indomitable spirit of Alaskan pioneers. I tell it also because I have the privilege of hearing many wonderful stories as I sit with the grieving. Stories capture the spirit and passions of the dying and their families. They preserve cherished memories and pass on values and family history. They bring forth surprising connections and relationships. Our culture absorbs stories on television and at the cinema. We read novels and attend the theatre. We forget we have many beautiful stories in our own families and communities.

Benny and Mattie represent the present-day spirit of homesteaders in Alaska. Carolyn's ancestors symbolized that spirit on the Great Plains 130 years ago. Her grandfather, Ora, was born in a sod house in southwest Kansas in 1889. His parents moved west in answer to the 1862 Homestead Act. The Act promised 160 acres to those able to settle and plant crops for five years. That was not easy in southwest Kansas in the late 19th century. Like many homesteaders, Ora's family was not able to make it. The hardships were simply too much. After the second locust plague destroyed their crops, tools, livestock and about everything else, Ora's parents packed up their 11 children to head back east.

Carolyn's family is blessed because Ora, at the urging of his children, wrote about the daily challenges of life on the Kansas prairie. He described building a sod house, digging a well, breaking soil, planting crops, caring for livestock, making contact with Indians and outlaws, enjoying pastimes and amusements and deciding to pack up and leave. His story is a source of wonder to his grandchildren, great-grandchildren and now great-great grandchildren. The strength, perseverance and ingenuity of those who have gone before us continue to inspire us today.

We have many stories in our families to pass on. We may not think future generations will be interested in the seemingly routine lives we live, but times change and we easily forget where we come from. Our stories preserve our roots.

CHAPTER 58

The Best Years of Our Marriage

"These last few years were the best years of our marriage," Rita said as we sat in her living room planning the memorial service for her husband Bernard. I heard her say these words before while Bernard was alive. I have heard other couples say similar things. As their days on earth lengthen beyond the biblical "seventy years, or perhaps eighty, if we are strong," they know their time together on earth grows to a close. Their passion for one another continues strong and time is precious. They reap the blessings of a lifetime of faithfulness. Despite aches and pains, indignities and infirmities, they find comfort in one another. Life is not easy and the golden years are not always so golden, but love still abounds.

But that is not why Rita said the final years were the best years of their marriage. Her marriage of over 60 years was difficult at best. She endured it, but didn't enjoy it. Bernard was controlling, emotionally distant, and sometimes just plain mean. He demanded obedience and respect from Bernard and the children. He didn't earn it.

I knew a dear Christian lady, sweet, pious, articulate, funny and strikingly beautiful, who would say, "I don't like my husband, but I love him." Her husband was unfaithful on numerous occasions. He broke her heart again and again. I asked about leaving him. Wouldn't she be happier? But she did not believe in divorce and refused to file for dissolution of her marriage. She prayed her husband would change and become the loving man she knew he could be. Perhaps Rita was similar. She kept hoping and praying for a sweet man to emerge.

Once the children moved away, Rita found work as hostess at a nearby country club. It kept her out of the house in the evenings when Bernard was home. That was okay with Bernard. He liked quiet at home. He spent evenings putting together beautiful, elaborate wooden models of ships. They were incredible. When church carolers journeyed to their condominium to sing, everyone was awe-struck by the craftsmanship of the models. Intricate and beautiful, each model took thousands of hours to complete. They reflected the work of a man who was meticulous and a perfectionist, who demanded the very best from himself and everyone around him.

Rita found joy at the country club. I find some country club members can be condescending and demeaning toward their workers. They put on airs in front of fellow members and arrogantly make unfair demands on serving staff, cooks or whomever. Rita never found that true. She was there to serve, make guests happy and comfortable. She knew each one by name and their friends and families. She knew what each one wanted and did her best to make it happen. She had years of experience at home serving her husband this way. He never thanked her. He only commented when things were wrong. She made members of the country club feel special and they responded with graciousness and appreciation. She was loved by all. She commented when a new member arrived the first time she was able to greet them by name even though they had never met. She knew everyone and the unfamiliar face must be the new member. The new member was stunned by such hospitality.

I thought how wonderful if church hospitality equaled Rita's. We greet everyone by name and make them feel special and welcome. We don't do it to impress or get them to join but because we care. What a wonderful way to build the community of Christ! What a joy to gather as the Body of Christ if we serve one another like that!

The final years Bernard and Rita shared were happy not because they reaped the fruit of a close, loving, giving relationship. They were happy because Bernard had Alzheimer's. His personality changed completely. He was no longer a demanding, controlling husband, but sweet, gentle and kind. His daughter commented that Alzheimer's broke down the wall around his heart and released the gentle, loving heart within. Underneath the gruff and rough words of her father was a sweet man longing to be let out. Perhaps Bernard is the only one I have known whose Alzheimer's was a blessing for the family.

As Bernard suffered from Alzheimer's, the father of a woman in our congregation also suffered. He was a pastor all his life. His daughter said he was a wonderful pastor, sweet and gentle, respected and admired by all, including his children. Alzheimer's released a different man within. He became vile and violent. He swore and cursed. His words were filthy, nothing like the beautiful person he had been. He struck out at caregivers with fists. They tried to restrain him. He moved from facility to facility because none could handle him. The children no longer recognized their father.

Why did Alzheimer's release an inner person in each of these two men opposite the character they displayed throughout their lives? Do we all have a good and gentle side? Do we all also have a mean and nasty side? What determines which side is revealed in life?

The apostle Paul writes about the conflict between flesh and spirit. Flesh represents evil and opposes the will of God. Spirit represents good, God's heart within enabling us to walk in the way of Jesus. We want to do what is right and just, but try as we might, we cannot. We do the very things we do not want to do. Both evil and good lies within each of us. They are at war. Each one battles for expression. But which will win? The apostle Paul cries out, "Wretched man that I am! Who will rescue me from this body of death? Thanks be to God through Jesus Christ our Lord!" As we read the apostle Paul, the struggle is not easy. Victory comes only through Christ.

Robert Louis Stevenson's classic novel, *Dr. Jekyll and Mr. Hyde,* portrays this inner struggle between good and evil. Spencer Tracy, in the 1941 film adaptation of the novel, re-creates Jekyll in all his goodness and Hyde in all his grotesqueness. It is a film expressing horror without the weird and strange characters of today's movies. Is there such good and evil in each of us?

Rita told me Bernard knew no love as a child. His parents were mean and abusive. They were more emotionally distant and critical than Bernard. What had he endured? What emotions and feelings were suppressed? Was he bruised so much by their maliciousness he could never learn to express love with sensitivity and tenderness? Bernard had a good job as an engineer. He provided his family a comfortable home, food to eat, and all the other necessities of life. Maybe that was the only kind of love he could express. Maybe Alzheimer's allowed his heart to release an inner person locked up for years, as his daughter said.

Maybe it wasn't just the Alzheimer's freeing his heart. Perhaps it was 60 years of marriage to a woman who loved and cared for him despite his meanness. Oh, and that woman who 'loved her husband but didn't like him?' I received an invitation to her Golden Anniversary celebration. Inside was a handwritten note in her beautiful script telling me how wonderful her marriage had become. It gave her much joy. She wrote she now not only loved her husband, but liked him also.

CHAPTER 59

We Have to Help

Everyone loved Ann. You couldn't help but love Ann. She was kindhearted and compassionate, easy-going and nonjudgmental, positive, never critical, and always giving to others. A member of the church said Ann was 'someone who quietly went around doing good.' Raised in the mountains of Tennessee, she never lost her accent, nor the downhome hospitality of the hills. Giving to others made Ann happy and endeared her to all.

Ann came on a church mission trip to Honduras. We built concrete block homes for the poor. It was hard physical labor, mixing mortar and concrete by hand, hauling the blocks in the hot sun. Food and water were sometimes not safe and some of us occasionally ate or drank something to upset our stomachs. After lunch one day my stomach began to churn. I knew what was going to happen and I walked over to the side of the road to the ditch carrying waste away from the small village. I bent my head, and began to empty my stomach. One of the men on the team narrated to others what I ate for lunch, then what I had for breakfast, then what I ate at dinner the night before. Everyone kept their distance, everyone but Ann. Ann wet a paper napkin with cool water and held it on my forehead while I finished emptying my stomach. That's the kind of person she was.

Ann also volunteered to chaperone a youth trip to the Boundary Waters Wilderness Area. I was surprised. Ann was a large woman. Getting in and out of canoes on rocky shorelines and sleeping on the ground in a tent didn't seem like things she would be comfortable doing. But Ann had that Tennessee mountain spirit and would attempt anything. She maintained her grace and good humor even when tipping the canoe and getting dunked. Ann was on my team. Each evening she took charge of dinner. Seeing all that Ann did, the other male adult chaperone on our team accused me of self-interest putting Ann on our team. But he was very thankful for her help.

When Ann was diagnosed with cancer, people in the church said, "We have to help." They were right. Our Caring Committee joyfully accepted the task. We put together a team to coordinate services the church could offer. The team leader checked with Ann each week to go over needs and schedules. For two years church members brought meals to her family 2-3 times per week. Often a meal would last two nights. Rides were arranged to drive Ann to her frequent chemotherapy and radiation treatments. One woman volunteered to clean her house on a regular basis and did so for many months.

Assistance the church provided enabled Ann's husband to return to school for training in a new field of work. Her adult children continued their schooling. Ann was able to work part-time to continue the family's health insurance. The meals eased the pinch on the family budget and lightened the burden of the many disruptions of Ann's illness and treatments. I was proud of the church. Finding volunteers never seemed difficult. People were happy and honored to help. The team assisting Ann stayed faithful through the many months of her illness.

Most families in the church going through serious illness do not receive the help Ann received. Many families simply decline the offer. They view their homes as private, personal space and are uncomfortable with folks, sometimes strangers, popping in and out. They would rather accept the full burden of care. Other families feel awkward accepting help from anyone. They are used to giving and not receiving. They may have fixed many meals for others in need but can't accept help when they need it. They do not want to infringe or burden anyone. Every family has its comfort zone. Caring assistance is always personalized.

Assisting parishioners in need does not always go as well as it did with Ann. On rare occasions, a recipient family grows accustomed to the help and a sense of entitlement develops. They complain the meals arrive cold or they receive too much chicken or pasta. They put in too many special requests to the Caring Team and those who provide meals wear down more quickly. Most persons who deliver meals put much thought, time and expense into planning and preparation. When the gift is not received gratefully, they grow weary of doing good. Ann was always appreciative and people wanted to help.

Sometimes people don't receive help because the pastor forgets to pass on needs to the caring teams, or teams already are stretched thin. Usually friends and neighbors step in and provide assistance. It is never a perfect system. Overall I have been humbled by the graciousness of those providing meals, transportation and other assistance and the sincere appreciation of those receiving.

Providing meals and other services is a wonderful way to form relationships and build bridges within the church community. We deepen friendships and become more faithful in our prayers. Our bonds of love are strengthened, even during adversity. I remember one woman in a congregation with strong beliefs on a variety of matters. She was often sharp and critical of those who disagreed. She added a lot of tension to the life of the church. But whenever anyone was ill, she was quick to appear with a pot of soup, whether friend or foe. It is easier to work out differences in the church if we have given or received a meal from our adversary.

Death and serious illnesses within a congregation do much to bring people together. There might be undercurrents of bickering about worship time, type of music, night of the youth meeting or something. When we see life and death struggles of friends in the church, bickering seems petty. Struggles of another inspire us to be less selfish and more giving. The love of Jesus grows in the life of the church. In the pain of those who suffer, we strive to be better people.

Sometimes in my pastoral work, I begin to burn out because of squabbling and wrangling. I think this is not what ministry is about. I become discouraged. Then someone dear in the life of the congregation becomes seriously ill or dies suddenly. Ministering to the grieving family, I re-discover my sense of call and commitment to the pastorate. Caring for another can revive sagging spirits. I consider myself blessed to be a pastor.

Receiving gifts from the congregation graciously, Ann strengthened the love of our church. Receiving my visits graciously, she strengthened God's love within me. When Ann passed away we all grieved deeply. We also celebrated the spirit of grateful giving and receiving she engendered. The church is never perfect but sometimes it can be very beautiful.

CHAPTER 60

I Want the Church to Have Our Property

John and Jan lived across the road from the church on five beautiful acres of woods and lawn. The city was gentrifying. Aging, smaller homes were torn down and McMansions built in their place. Open land was rare and expensive. The property John and Jan owned was the envy of local builders, who stopped on a regular basis with offers. A popular bicycle trail connecting the suburbs ran along one side and a stream flowed across the back. It was the perfect setting for a row of million dollar homes.

John and Jan had no interest in selling their property. For more than 35 years they lived in the small older Cape Cod house at the front of the property. They loved it. Jan raised vegetables in their large garden. John felled dead trees and split wood for their fireplace. They carved paths in the woods. They watched song birds by their patio during morning coffee. Deer, fox, skunk, beaver and woodchuck visited during dinner. Though in the heart of the city, coyotes raised pups in their back yard. John and Jan enjoyed their slice of heaven.

John was a retired airline pilot, Jan a former flight attendant. They met on the job. At first, they kept their marriage a secret. In those days flight attendants were not permitted to marry. John was in his mid-80's now. Jan was 20 years younger. John's knees were giving out and he relied on his garden tractor to get around the property. We hung a sign by a door to the church reading "John Deere Parking Only." John rode his tractor across the road to worship and always knew he had a place to park.

John and Jan's property was dear to the church. We had an outdoor worship service and congregational picnic there in the summer and a Blessing of the

Animals in the spring. Youth gathered in the back for bonfires and hot dog roasts. The Youth Pastor hooked a wagon to the garden tractor and took children on 'jungle cruises' through the trails. The property was also the only possible place for the church to expand. Our building was used to capacity. Additional space and parking was desirable.

John said to me every now and then, "I want the church to have our property." I assured John the church was very interested. When he was ready to discuss it further just let me know. John called one day and asked me to come over. He reiterated he wanted the church to have their property. John hoped he would live for several more years but he was ready to make a plan to transfer the property. We arranged an evening when we could meet with the Church Moderator, attorney, and a member who specialized in bequests and large gifts.

At the meeting John expressed his concern that his pension had no survivor benefits. When he died Jan would not have a pension. He wanted to ensure sufficient income for her as long as she lived. John's only daughter was the beneficiary of trust funds providing generously for her needs. They did not need to consider her in the agreement.

The property was divided into two relatively equally-sized plots, front and back. We arranged for the church to purchase the rear plot immediately through a joint life annuity payable by the church. The annuity would provide Jan with needed income after John's death. Once John passed away, Jan stated her intention to move to her hometown to be closer to family. At that time the church would purchase the front portion of the property with the house. We assured John and Jan as long as they lived on the property we would make no improvements or changes to the rear plot so they could continue to enjoy the beauty. Purchase through the life annuity provided John and Jan with more charitable tax deductions than they could use.

A few months after the agreement John's heart condition deteriorated. He checked into the hospital on a Friday and the cardiologist gave him the difficult news he would never go home. John was ready. His body had weakened considerably. He could no longer work his chain saw or split wood. John slipped away peacefully 48 hours later.

Jan continued to live in the little Cape Cod but began making arrangements to move out of state to her old hometown. She considered her finances and figured how much she would need to buy her new home. She arrived at an appropriate amount she thought adequate to meet her expected expenses and offered the front plot to the church for that amount. It was less than half the property appraisal. Jan received more charitable deductions for her taxes. Again, more than she would ever be able to use. The church quickly raised funds to purchase the property through Notes Payable to the congregation.

Through their thoughtfulness and generosity, John and Jan blessed the church. The church now had land for expansion, and additional valuable land to sell for a considerable profit. When the excess land was sold a few years later, proceeds paid off the Notes Payable and church mortgage and still provided nearly $1 million to finance overdue capital projects and future building expansion. The church was able to do things not dreamed of otherwise. John and Jan always loved the church. Through their financial planning they converted that love into tangible blessings for future generations to enjoy.

As a pastor I have seen churches blessed through estate planning and bequests. Sometimes I have been aware of gifts and sometimes they are a complete surprise. In one church, we received a large gift from someone away from the community for more than 30 years. No one could remember her actually being a member or attending church. Volunteers would see her name on the mailing list, ask who she was, and wonder why we spent postage to mail an out-of-state non-member a newsletter every week. I said keep her on the list and she will tell us if she doesn't want the newsletter anymore. The church received an enormous return on that postage.

Advanced financial planning by generous members enabled churches I served to undertake new projects and missions. The gifts preserved historic structures and added new facilities. They provided funds for new ministries in Christian Education and Evangelism. They blessed community organizations and cared for the poor and forgotten. As people use their income to bless the church during their active years, they use their accumulated wealth to bless the church at the end of their lives. I suggest to faithful members, just as they tithe their income, they should consider tithing their wealth when they pass.

When it came time for Jan to move to her new home, she had a large regret. She befriended a feral cat roaming her property. She named him Spook because of his skittishness around people. Every morning the cat came inside and sat on her lap as she drank her morning coffee. Every evening the cat returned and sat on her lap as she read or watched television by the roaring fire. Spook and Jan bonded deeply. Jan wanted to take Spook to her new home. Though affectionate to Jan, he remained a wild cat. He (or maybe she) did not remain indoors overnight or long periods of time. He did not trust anyone besides Jan. His home was the woods and fields behind Jan's house. Disastrous, unsuccessful, tries to put Spook into a kitty carrier convinced us Jan could not take Spook away from his home. Leaving Spook behind stressed Jan more than anything else in her move.

I promised Jan I would feed Spook as long as I served the church. So, after Jan moved away, the first thing I did upon arriving at the church every morning of the week, 7 days per week, was to trudge over to the little Cape Cod. Spook waited in the distance. I went inside, retrieved cat food, and filled Spook's dish. He watched me closely but never approached the food until I disappeared around the corner of the house. When I first started feeding him, I tried sitting at a distance to see if I could perhaps make friends. He never approached and, if I approached him, he took off running. A few times I doubled back and watched him silently while he ate. If I was unavailable to feed him, our Church Secretary Evelyn filled his dish. Neither of us, try as we might, were able to establish a bond with him. Feeding Spook gave me a brief glimpse each morning of the peaceful scene John and Jan enjoyed for over 35 years.

One morning three years later, I found Spook lying on the picnic table bench as he often did. However, this morning he didn't jump down and run to the corner of the house as usual. Instead, he cowered on the bench hissing at me. After filling his dish, Spook finally hopped down and hobbled to the food. He was in a lot of pain, his front paw red and swollen. He couldn't put weight upon it. I visited frequently the next couple of days but Spook was not around again. I called Jan's next door neighbor and told him of Spook's condition. Most of my contact with him had been negative, fielding complaints about members parking on his grass and concerns that we would sell Jan's property for development. He, like John and Jan, enjoyed the quiet retreat in the city. He didn't want to see their land developed. I was relieved to find him sympathetic to our concerns about Spook. He quickly found him hiding under one of his old cars. He put a humane trap with some food in it next to Spook. Spook took the bait and was captured.

I took Spook to the vet. Spook's injuries were severe. He was in much pain and it was unlikely a feral cat could recover. We made the decision to have Spook put to sleep. After the procedure, I dug a hole in Jan's backyard. Evelyn and I had a little memorial service to say goodbye to Spook, then I covered him up. Spook would remain in the beautiful surroundings where he lived his life, not far from the house where he spent mornings and evenings on Jan's lap.

CHAPTER 61

I Would Have Taken It Outside

Evelyn, the Church Secretary, and I were talking in her office when I spotted a spider climbing the wall toward the ceiling. I was at my new church less than a week and in the very early stages of learning the peculiarities of the people. I pulled a tissue from the box on Evelyn's desk, stood on a chair, caught the spider, squished it between my fingers, and threw the tissue in the wastebasket. I thought nothing of it. That is how I deal with spiders invading my space indoors.

Evelyn said to me very softly, though, "I would have taken it outside." Taking the spider outside never crossed my mind. Squishing a spider never crossed Evelyn's mind. Evelyn loved all living things and would never willingly take the life of another. From then on, I took spiders, crickets, ladybugs, beetles, ants or any other flying or crawling creature invading our office outside.

Evelyn loved animals. She loved her pet dog and cats. She loved all the dogs that came to visit in the office. Again, she wouldn't willingly hurt any living thing. One day she returned to her house after taking her cat to the vet. The cat was loose in the car. As Evelyn pulled into her driveway, the cat slithered between the brake pedal and the floor. Evelyn was terrified of harming it. She refused to put on the brake and drove through the closed garage door. She told her husband, Milt, the brakes gave out. He would never understand not applying the brake pedal and crashing into the door. Try as he might, he could never find anything wrong with the brakes.

Evelyn was not young when I arrived at the church. I guessed she was approaching 80 years old. She was the only secretary the church had known. She was skilled in dictation, shorthand and things that made for excellent secretaries

40 years earlier. She was the only person, besides Carolyn, able to decipher my handwriting. The computer was not her friend. They quarreled constantly. She worked hard to learn each new update or program. She stuck with it and, with a little help, was able to do what she needed. But she was never happy with it.

Evelyn wasn't fond of anything new or technological. She loved the simple, traditional, good old-fashioned ways of the past. She fought change tooth and nail. When her silver Volvo finally ran out of steam and had to be retired, she wanted one exactly like it, nearly 20 years old. She had to settle for a newer model, though silver once again. She loved nature and her garden. When the city widened her road she was prepared to chain herself to the old maple tree in front of her house if they threatened to take it down.

Evelyn had her own unique filing system. Necessary papers for church business were kept properly filed in the filing cabinet. Everything else was under her desk in piles without files. Each grouping was perpendicular to the one below. Evelyn almost never took a vacation so I didn't worry too much about her system. As she aged, though, she was in the hospital on occasion. If I needed a letter or document, I went to her hospital room and told her what I was looking for. She would say something like "the third stack from the left, the fifth horizontal group from the top." Sure enough, back at the office I would find it exactly where she said. She was very organized. The rest of us just couldn't figure out her system.

Other pastors might have asked for a new secretary, one skilled in computers, internet, copy machines and filing systems. But I liked Evelyn as our secretary. We didn't have the most efficient office in the world, but perhaps the most caring. Evelyn greeted everyone with a smile and managed to keep the M&M dispenser filled despite my chocolate addiction. You couldn't help but love Evelyn. She was simple, kind and generous, a constant reminder to me, and the congregation, that the Body of Christ isn't about efficiency and slick marketing programs. It is about mutual love, caring and acceptance. Her presence in the office gave our church a heart and soul, more important than speed on a computer.

Evelyn said she wanted to die at her desk in the church office. She never wanted to retire. In part, it was because she loved her job and the people who came into the office or called on the phone. Of course, she enjoyed the phone much more than email. She was not possessive or controlling of the office or church affairs. She didn't seek power in the least. Besides her vegetable garden, the church office was where she felt most at home.

Evelyn's husband, Milt, was another reason she didn't want to retire. As he aged, Milt changed. In his best mood he was cranky. In his worse he was verbally abusive. Coming to work every day was a wonderful respite from Milt. It was a place where she was loved and accepted, not derided and ridiculed. Milt suffered from depression. Anti-depressant drugs seemed to help his mood, but Milt didn't want to stay on the medication. Evelyn slipped an anti-depressant into his coffee in the morning. Both Evelyn and Milt were happier when she did.

No one knew for sure how old Evelyn really was. She did her best to keep it a secret. Milt drove off one day without telling Evelyn and didn't come back. Evelyn and I both knew he was just being ornery but we thought we should report his disappearance to the police in case something unfortunate happened to him. At the police station the officer asked Evelyn the question I never had the courage to ask, "What is your date of birth?" I could tell Evelyn was reluctant to answer but she did. And I learned her real age.

Evelyn was sad when I announced I had taken a call to another church and would be leaving in three months. We had grown very close over the years. My leaving also caused a dilemma. Was it now time to retire? Evelyn and I got along fine but that may not be the case for the next pastor. I could tell she struggled with the decision. She didn't want to retire but she also wanted what was best for the church. One morning she announced to me it was time. She would be almost 90 years old when a new pastor began. That was too old. A new pastor deserved a younger secretary. Also, due to his declining health, Milt had moved into an assisted living facility. That living arrangement made the decision a little easier.

After her retirement Evelyn continued to work in the church office on Friday morning. It kept her connected. Her knowledge of church history and families was valuable. A couple of years after retirement she and her daughter, who lived with her, were observing an hour of no electricity. The 'dark' hour was a nationwide blackout supported by friends of the earth. Evelyn and her daughter, both committed environmentalists, willingly joined the observance. Unfortunately, Evelyn was walking down stairs in the dark, missed the final step, took a tumble, and broke her hip. Evelyn eventually recovered from the fracture, but I think the broken hip took its toll. Broken hips often seem to accelerate decline in older folks. Evelyn passed away a couple of years later.

Evelyn reminds me the latest, fastest and most innovative is not always the best way to convey the good news of Jesus Christ. The gospel is best communicated not through artful, slick, and deceptive marketing campaigns, but through the genuine love of people expressed in simple deeds of kindness and respect.

CHAPTER 62

Salmon and Budweiser by the Lake

A handful of Steve's friends gathered with us on a hill just above Healy, Alaska. We were 11 members of Steve's family who flew from 'the lower 48.' It was a sunlit August day and the view was gorgeous. Alaskan mountains and tundra stretched for miles in all directions. Mount Healy rose just to our west, Denali National Park visible beyond. It was a beautiful, fitting spot to gather.

Alaska was Steve's home for more than 30 years. He built his one-room cabin just a few miles from this hill. He, of course, built it himself. In Alaska you do everything yourself or, if too big to do alone, you buy beer and call together a few friends to help. You don't hire things out. Steve put large picture windows in the front of the cabin. Big windows are un-Alaskan, not practical and a waste of energy, but the view of Mt. Healy was too beautiful to cover. Steve staked his two dozen sled dogs in back of the cabin.

He added a garage twice the size of the living area. With heated coils in the floor and an I-beam and hoist overhead, it was a place he could build his dream ocean-going sailboat. So what if he lived hundreds of miles from the ocean? Alaskans follow their dreams. That is why they live in Alaska. The 39 foot keel stretched the length of the garage, but the boat never progressed beyond the keel. Other dreams had to be followed first. Many Alaskans aren't born there. They are drawn there because their dreams could not be realized anywhere else. That is why Steve settled in Alaska. There was no other place in the world where he wanted to live, except, after he grew older and gave away his sled dogs, on a sailboat off the Mexican coast during long, cold Alaskan winters.

The hill above town was a small cemetery. We came to remember, grieve, give thanks, and celebrate Steve's life. Steve passed away six months earlier at the age of 52. He was Carolyn's younger brother. We received news of Steve's passing from Carolyn's sister the evening of my farewell celebration at my previous church. It had been an emotional, tearful, and joyful celebration of ten years of mutual ministry. We were drained from the day's festivities when the terrible news came.

Steve died alone in the cabin surrounded by over-the-counter flu and cold remedies. He was found by a friend perhaps three days after his death. His family often feared for his death in other ways. He could have perished in a spring thaw mushing his dogsled team across the Alaskan wilderness, or fallen off a mountain precipice he was climbing, or attacked by a grizzly wandering into his camp. His death came in a less dramatic way, perhaps pneumonia, or a heart attack. We don't know for sure.

Steve's friends seemed uneasy. Perhaps they weren't used to death by natural means at a young age. It reminded them of their own mortality. Alaskans are independent, self-reliant, hardy and self-confident. They chase dreams and embrace each day as it comes. They are not worried about what may be coming down the road. They deal with life here and now. In this beautiful cemetery on top of the hill above Healy maybe they were thinking about the length of their days.

Perhaps another reason they seemed uneasy is that we were having a quasi-religious memorial service. Pastors sometimes serve as 'family chaplains.' We offer prayers at holiday meals. We marry nieces and nephews. We bury our grandparents and sometimes we have to bury a brother-in-law. I offered prayers and they probably weren't used to spoken prayers. I read Scriptures and they weren't sure about the Bible. Organized religion wasn't part of their lives since they arrived in Alaska. They knew, though, it was important to remember Steve and to share stories of Steve's life.

We moved down the hill and went to the little park by Otto Lake, just a couple of hundred yards from Steve's cabin. The family set up a picnic and put out a spread of food. More of Steve's friends arrived. A friend of Steve's, owner of a salmon restaurant in the tourist center of the canyon outside the Denali Park entrance, brought loads of fresh salmon. Other dishes appeared. And there was plenty of beer, Budweiser, Steve's favorite.

Most of the family knew few details of Steve's life in Alaska. He came to the lower 48 only for special family gatherings. Few letters or emails came in between. Communication with his family was not Steve's strong point and probably isn't with many Alaskans. He told us of some of his adventures and work. We had occasional 'sightings' when Carolyn's sister or a friend of the family visited Alaska. We didn't know his friends. We didn't know how his life unfolded in the small community around Healy. Steve's friends began opening up and sharing stories, many of which we had never heard. It was good for us to see and experience the community where Steve lived.

Two years prior to his death we had a siblings' get-together with Steve. For some of us the trip was our first venture to Alaska. Steve enjoyed showing us his world, at least the world he could show us accessible by road. We could see Steve's love for the land and the people. Steve belonged in Alaska. He dreamed of living there since he was a young boy in Connecticut with a malamute, Maxwell, for a pet dog. Alaska permitted him to follow his heart in a way no other land could.

Though independent and adventurous souls, I sensed Alaskans connected with each other in times of need. The human family generally rallies to help and support one other. Deep down we know we need each other. We draw strength from our relationships. I think Steve's death hit his buddies pretty hard. Most were single men of his age. They spent the last 30 years seeking adventure, into the wilderness or wherever else life led. As they grieved the loss of Steve, perhaps they wondered how long their adventures might continue. Perhaps in their grief, their connections with one another grew stronger.

I have been blessed to spend my life in the community of the Christian church and see people come together and care for one another in times of grief and illness. I know that strong communities of faith give us strength and hope in the difficult journeys of our lives. But many people find their support and strength in communities other than the church.

Nancy was a quiet worker in the life of my church. She was a precious soul who ministered beneath the radar. She never fussed and would never want recognition for her work, but her ministry strengthened the church. She received joy and purpose in giving herself to others through simple acts of service. Her husband, Mark, did not attend the church. Much of their community life centered in the Harley-Davidson club with which they rode. When Nancy died of cancer at the age of 55 the H.O.G.'s (Harley's Owner Group) in their club surrounded Mark. Forty or so beautiful, shining Harley's escorted Nancy from the church to the cemetery and the H.O.G.'s continued to minister to Mark in the ensuing months.

As a Christian pastor, I wish everyone could find support and comfort in a grace-filled fellowship within the church. However, I am glad there are other communities to fill in where the church fails or is unable to reach. I have spoken with persons who find a supportive community in diverse groups from the Masons to AA to alternative rock music crowds.

We all seek community, even the most independent and adventurous of us, even the most introverted and socially backward among us. I give thanks that, even though it was brief, we were able to experience the Alaskan community of my brother-in-law. I pray in some way they were strengthened also by our presence. The death of Steve was able to unite his diverse worlds. Together, we were all blessed to experience fellowship and support through mutual love of a dear friend and loved one.

CHAPTER 63

Are You Willing to Do the Service for My Disabled Son?

Wanda arrived at the church the same Sunday I began my ministry. She worshipped in the contemporary praise service in our Fellowship Hall. The service was informal and lay-guided. People sat around tables, drinking coffee and eating goodies during the service. Lay preachers spoke most Sundays. Music came from songs popular on Christian radio stations. A friend of hers, Ellie, attended the service. She invited Wanda, and then drove 20 miles out of the way to pick Wanda up at her trailer court in another community. Wanda could not afford a car.

Wanda came from a Pentecostal tradition, much different from ours. She struggled with our style and theology. We didn't talk a lot about the blood of Jesus. We didn't offer impassioned altar calls to receive Jesus into your life. We certainly didn't speak in tongues. Wanda, though, was searching for acceptance and I think she was finding it with us.

Wanda approached me after worship my second Sunday at the church. Her 43-year-old disabled son died on Tuesday. Would I be willing to do a memorial service for him? "Sure," I said. "Give me a call and we will get together." It was Easter Sunday and I was leaving one worship service to begin another. Life was a bit of a blur at the moment. I didn't have time to talk right then.

Wanda didn't call. I had no contact information for her so we didn't connect that week. She approached me after worship the following Sunday. "Are you willing to do the service for my son?" she asked again. "Of course," I said. She said her pastor refused to do a memorial service for a disabled man. I couldn't believe a pastor would refuse a memorial service for a person simply because of disabilities. I assumed there was much more to the story than what Wanda told me. I learned with Wanda that was often the case.

I never met her son, Barry. He was born with cerebral palsy and other illnesses. In Wanda's words, "On the day of his birth God sent a broken boy angel from heaven to start his mission on earth." According to Wanda, Barry fought hard to survive. He endured a lifetime of physical, occupational and speech therapies and corrective surgeries. He never gave up. He learned how to walk with the aid of crutches and braces. He learned sign language. He loved swimming and won trophies in Special Olympics. He worked at the Achievement Center. Wanda was proud of him. Often the case for a person with cerebral palsy, he did not enjoy a long life.

We celebrated Barry's life in a simple memorial service held in our Fellowship Hall. A friend of Wanda's read a poem entitled "And God said, 'No.'" The poem talked about God saying "no" to our various prayer requests. One line in the poem read,

"I asked God to make my handicapped child whole and God said, 'No.'
He said his spirit is whole. His body is only temporary."

That line meant a lot to Wanda. I had trouble theologically with a loving, gracious God saying 'no.' For Wanda, however, it answered her question as to how children are born misshapen, disabled and afflicted in a world where God reigns.

During my reflections, I said, "God loves all of us. We are all children of God, created in God's image, persons for whom Christ died. But I think persons such as Barry have a special place in God's heart, persons for whom life is so fragile, who are not blessed with strong, healthy bodies, but endure each day by determination and faith. God reaches out and gives these persons God's special grace. God embraces them a little tighter and walks by their side a little closer."

I continued, "I believe God grieved over the illnesses of Barry. We live in a broken world. Some like Barry endure the brokenness more than others. The world is broken but I believe God is redeeming it. Someday there will be a new heaven and new earth. All the nastiness of the world will be gone. God will bring forth a new world without tears and pain. In the meantime, we strive with God's help to love one another and to bind one another's wounds and support one another. Amidst our own brokenness we try, with God's help, leading and power, to touch the world with God's peace."

Although our church was much different from anything she was used to, Wanda continued to attend our contemporary worship. She was a baker. Every week she baked coffee cakes, cookies or pumpkin bread to share at the service. It was her way of saying 'thank you' to the church and people who surrounded her during the time of her son's death.

Sometimes funerals are a means of evangelism, a way of welcoming newcomers into the fellowship of those who believe, or would like to believe. Death confronts people with questions of eternal meaning and the church is where we talk about those questions. If they find a caring, loving community of faith, they might stick around for a while. They might rekindle or rediscover a faith of their own. Wanda journeyed with us for several years although she always had trouble reconciling our ways of worshipping, serving and believing with the ways of her Pentecostal tradition.

Wanda came every Sunday, too, because of Ellie. Ellie drove an extra 40 miles each Sunday so Wanda could attend. When I thanked Ellie for such faithfulness, she said when she was young she relied on others for rides. She always said when she had a car and money for gas she would never deny another person a ride. She kept her word. Those who embrace a ministry of transportation to worship are a great blessing to churches.

Eventually, the relationship between Wanda and the church became strained. Ellie's health deteriorated and she was no longer able to offer rides. Mostly, it was because relationships always became strained for Wanda. She had a lifetime of strained and severed relationships. When I called and talked with her she said she needed to find a church close by her home. I said that would probably be best. I visited her at her trailer once but she declined future visits. I wish I had just gone. I later discovered Wanda was in the early stages of dementia and could have used some spiritual support.

Although it was never designed for that purpose, the contemporary worship service Wanda attended provided a space where persons with disabilities found a spiritual home. People with physical and mental disabilities felt welcomed and included. Some in the community who lived on the margins with respect to financial or emotional stability also came. Some in the worship service didn't care for the intrusion of special needs folks. I always considered it a blessing, though their attendance made my life more complicated. They called far more frequently than typical parishioners with financial or transportation needs or just wanting to talk. However, I think my relationships with them made my life fuller and richer.

Melvin was one of those with special needs. Melvin was a big man, probably in his late 40's. He made a growling sound as he walked. You heard Melvin before you saw him. He arrived late every Sunday. He was frightening in appearance but gentle as a teddy bear. He loved to eat and loaded a plate as high as he could with coffee cake and cookies. He carried his plate and cup of coffee to a table down front. As he went he greeted everyone by name. Melvin knew everyone in town it seemed and greeted them all. Many times Melvin would see me across the town square and cry out, "'Lo, Pastor Neal." I would yell back, "Hello, Melvin!" I always enjoyed his greetings. Needless to say, when Melvin entered worship, the service was disrupted.

Melvin had a paper fetish. He couldn't resist collecting anything of paper. To encourage him not to walk away with reading material others might find useful or valuable, our church secretary put together a packet of papers with bulletins, newsletters, etc. for Melvin each week. When I arrived at 7:00 am Saturday morning to make coffee for our Men's Study, Melvin was outside the church, even in zero degree weather. I would ask if he were staying warm. He always said, "Yes, Pastor Neal." He was there early in the morning looking for his papers and a cup of hot coffee.

Melvin was late to our worship service because he already attended an earlier service at the Methodist Church. After our worship he would mosey over to the Catholic Church. Melvin was very ecumenical. Melvin was present at nearly every community event, especially if there was free food. I was glad Melvin was a part of our church and community. His presence was a reminder for us to be gentle, giving, welcoming and maybe a little childlike ourselves.

One great joy for me arising out of that worship service was officiating at the wedding of a young couple with mild developmental disabilities. The whole community shared in the joy of the young couple. Guests filled the entire sanctuary for the ceremony. Celebrating their love, seeing it sealed as they made vows to become husband and wife, was a beautiful thing. The simplicity, naturalness, honesty and genuineness of their love was the envy of many. The glow in their faces, broadness of their smiles and innocence in holding one another's hands were reminders to all of the preciousness of marriage.

Sometimes we spend countless hours strategizing, formulating visions and setting forth plans for ministry, which may never come to fruition. Instead, God has other designs for us. God leads us in new directions. Sometimes we see the way most clearly in the lives of those with disabilities. God surprises us. And God's surprises are always better than those tediously created and overly detailed plans envisioned by church committees and pastors.

CHAPTER 64

Easter Dinners

When Deb invited Carolyn and me for Easter dinner, I was grateful but also reluctant. I was grateful because I arrived at my new parish the Monday before Palm Sunday. In less than two weeks I had nine worship services to plan. I knew I would be ready for a breather after four services Easter morning. Also, I was living in temporary quarters and Carolyn was travelling from our old home six hours away to join me on weekends until our house sold. Carolyn and I did not have kitchenware, groceries or time to prepare a meal. Dinner at a restaurant on Easter Sunday by ourselves didn't seem right. Easter dinner is meant to be shared.

I was reluctant to accept the invitation because I knew Deb had been battling cancer for seven years. She was undergoing chemotherapy. She kept an active schedule but tired easily. I didn't want to impose on her generous hospitality. Deb, however, was insistent about the invitation and insistent we not bring a thing. We accepted the invitation to join her family for dinner on this joyful Sunday when we celebrate the resurrection of our Lord Jesus Christ. A dear older couple from the congregation, close friends of Deb, Hope and Don, also joined us. The dinner was relaxed, food delicious, and conversation easy. It was wonderful for me to get to know Deb and her family as well as the sweet spirit of Hope and dry wit of Don.

Deb's cancer soon returned with ferocity. It became apparent her struggle with cancer could not continue long. Deb was ready for her final battle. She had cultivated a wide group of friends. They called regularly and gave comfort and joy. She drew from a deep reservoir of faith nurtured through a lifetime of worship and service to God. She was positive and optimistic. Her strength and hope gave strength and hope to others. She didn't just succumb to the ravages and indignities of the disease. She took charge and planned her death the way she desired, surrounded by friends, full of faith, joyful and positive. I called or stopped on occasion but sensed she really didn't need my ministry much. She drew on the many resources of courage and faith she had developed. Her family probably needed more support than I provided. So often pastors focus on the needs of the dying and forget needs of those left behind. Deb died at age 53, six months after that Easter dinner. Her battle with cancer ended victoriously for her. Through her joyful, giving spirit, cancer was defeated, no matter what it accomplished with her body.

When I spoke with Deb about her memorial service, I discovered she had already given it much thought. She asked four dear friends to give Words of Remembrance. She chose music for our Sanctuary Choir to sing and our Praise Band to perform. She arranged for vocal and instrumental solos. The service was a beautiful celebration of her life and faith. She gave me all the pieces. I just had to choreograph it. Her son, who has a beautiful voice, sang the lovely song popularized by Josh Groban, "To Where You Are." There was not a dry eye in the sanctuary.

In the latter half of my ministry, I tried to write a paragraph for the funeral bulletin to capture the life and spirit of the deceased. These are the words I composed for Deb:

> "Deb opened her home and her heart to all. Her simple spirit of caring provided the center of warmth and affection in her family, and her gentle embrace and genuine kindness endeared her to countless many. Her numerous friends were blessed by her ministry of hospitality, the depth of her love and the perseverance of her faith. Her passions for music and service met and found expression in the life of the church. For eight years, Deb revealed remarkable courage and faith in her battle with cancer. In that battle she showed us all how to live and how to die. She has gone now to be with her God, receiving the crown of glory that God offers to all who love and serve the Lord. Let us celebrate Deb's life among us as we celebrate the eternity she will spend with her Savior."

I pray this paragraph in the bulletin captures the spirit of the deceased. Sometimes I wonder if we were to write our own paragraph, what would we say? How would we describe the essence of our journey? What would we lift up as most dear and meaningful? Does our perception of our lives conform to the perceptions of others?

One of many joys in ministry is journeying with dear saints who in their final days unveil the power of the resurrection in their lives. Faith overcomes fear, hope dispels despair and love is stronger than death. When I journey with these folks, I often feel my ministry is not essential. They have built a storehouse of faith throughout their life. Facing their final days on earth, they draw on that storehouse of strength and pass it to others. I go to give the grace I receive in Christ and leave filled with grace they bestow on me. Apostle Paul writes at the beginning of his Second Letter to the Corinthians, "Blessed be the God and Father of our Lord Jesus Christ, the Father of mercies and the God of all consolation, who consoles us in all our affliction, so that we may be able to console those who are in any affliction with the consolation with which we ourselves are consoled by God." Those who have been consoled and strengthened by God have the means to console and strengthen others.

Sometimes, folks look to pastors and draw from our faith and words of comfort. We are mediators of the grace and love of Jesus Christ. They need our prayers of hope and words of assurance. They draw power from our reading of the Scriptures. They look forward to our visits. Their hope is strengthened through our hope. We are needed in their journey to the resurrection. Other times it is good to feel non-essential in ministry. Some folks have the gift of faith to journey without professionals.

I believe those who experience a good journey in their final days share common qualities. Nearly always they have faith which elicits hope. Usually, faith is rooted in promises of God in Jesus Christ but not a rigid set of beliefs. It is not afraid of doubt, yet reveals a confident trust in the grace and mercy of God to work things according to God's good and perfect will. These folks have an expansive faith, not a narrow one, a positive expression which invites mercy, welcomes compassion, and feels comfortable amidst mystery. Faith enables them to look outward toward others. They rarely engage in self-pity or regrets. Their faith enables them to express and share their love with all people. So, they are usually surrounded by dear friends. They receive the blessings of true, intimate community.

I received the following email from a pastoral colleague following the passing of his wife:

"Shirley was finally able to go home at 3:35 AM on Monday. She slept away peacefully at the end, with just the two of us bathed in hymns quietly playing, gospel words and prayers. It was a special holy time for the ending of 55 years together in this life. Whatever the ravages of the ALS we had no complaints against the Management of the universe. The love and support we experienced through the whole ordeal, from all of you, was special beyond words. I washed and anointed her body, brushed her hair, covered her with clean bedclothes, talking to her the whole time about our beginnings in high school, our deep caring for each other, our wonderful kids, our store of memories. It was a very holy time for me and gave a sort of closure feeling. I rejoiced with her that she could finally take leave of a body that had become a total burden on her spirit. Now she's walking again, or soaring, and will soon be haunting me if I forget a grandchild's birthday."

This email reminds me death is a holy time and our journey to death is a holy journey. I rejoice as a pastor I can share in this holy journey with so many, those who need my ministry and those who find my ministry simply reinforcing their own steadfast faith.

Carolyn and I settled into our new home and invited Hope, Don and another couple for Easter dinner the following year. We remembered the gracious hospitality of Deb one year earlier. We rejoiced Deb was enjoying Easter dinner this year seeing her Savior face to face and knowing the fullness of the power of the resurrection. We felt blessed to have shared a resurrection meal with Deb before we gather together at the banquet table in heaven.

CHAPTER 65

A Nursing Home Next to a Car Dealership

The photo on the nightstand showed a handsome couple in their early 50's, dressed in fancy western wear, standing next to their handsome horses. The rolling hills of the Arizona desert were in the background. The couple was happy. Life was good, maybe just about perfect.

The woman lying in the bed before me, however, was in the advanced stages of Alzheimer's, strapped into her chair, her body sagging, her head drooping above the hospital tray in front of her. Drool dripped from the corner of her mouth. I spoke and called her by name, Vivian, but there was no response. I couldn't tell if she were aware of my presence. She had given up so much – her beauty and poise, but also her ability to walk and feed herself, her hearing and sight, and, most importantly, her memory and mind. Try as I might I couldn't see the beautiful woman of the photo in the elderly woman slumped before me.

We give up so much as we age and it is so difficult.

We give up possessions. I have journeyed with many couples through progressive stages of downsizing. The first move is from a large house where they have lived for 40+ years raising a family and enjoying fruits of an active, healthy life. That is perhaps the most difficult move, knowing their ages have advanced and years ahead of them are becoming few in number. They give up furniture, clothing, pictures, knick-knacks, and grieve each one. They are not giving up 'things,' but part of their life. Each item has memories contained within – of children and grandchildren, pets and friends, hobbies and accomplishments, a life slipping away. They grieve because they understand they can never go back. They know additional moves will come in the future. They will move from the apartment to assisted living, then to skilled nursing care, and finally to hospice.

I speak with many elderly folks who grieve because they have no one to pass on prized china, crystal and silver. These items represent hard work over many years. To acquire such beautiful things was the dream of their generation, but their children and grandchildren want nothing to do with them. They are outdated. They are impractical. They are ugly. You can't put them in a dishwasher.

We were talking about this phenomenon at a pastor's meeting once when a gay pastor spoke. "That is why," he said, "every family needs a gay son. Everyone in my family passes their prized china and crystal to me and I love it. I eat off of it breakfast, lunch and dinner."

Giving up things is difficult but giving up one's health is even more difficult. Arthritis arrives and we can no longer walk or run as we used to. We discover heart or lung disease or another debilitating illness and must curtail activities and pace ourselves throughout the day. The afternoon nap is no longer a luxury but a necessity. Our hearing fails and hearing aids seem to help so little. The world goes on but we can't join the conversation because we can't hear what others are saying. Our eyesight begins to fail and driving privileges, vital to independence in America, are taken away.

The most heart-wrenching and hurtful comes when we discover we are giving up our mind. Dementia becomes real for us. We forget names and faces, places and people. We begin to forget our history and who we are. We cry and pray dementia is not happening to us, but it is and there is nothing we can do. We wish we could end our lives before it happens but we can't. Giving up our minds means giving up our past and future. It means giving up our self-awareness and self-understanding. Giving up our minds is the final giving up in preparation for death.

When I mentioned my visit to Vivian to her husband Gordon he indicated he visits her every day around 5:00 pm to feed her dinner. If possible, I tried to time my visits to Vivian when Gordon was present. Gordon told of the wonderful life he and Vivian enjoyed. Gordon was very successful in business. They semi-retired early in life and purchased a sprawling ranch in the gorgeous hill country of Arizona. They had many friends and travelled to wonderful places. They rode horses and enjoyed the good life until Vivian's dementia forced a return to their hometown and a senior retirement community.

Vivian soon passed away. Shortly thereafter Gordon discovered he had Parkinson's disease. Gordon tried to remain as active as possible. He lived a full life and wanted to maintain his independence as long as he could. Just as we cannot stop the advances of Alzheimer's, we cannot stop the advances of Parkinson's. Gordon's physician suggested he no longer drive. His children dutifully took away his keys. Gordon was not yet ready to throw in the keys with respect to driving.

Somehow Gordon found the strength to walk the half mile to a car dealership near his retirement community, bought a new Cadillac, and drove it home. His kids and doctor weren't going to tell him what to do. When I mentioned this little incident about Gordon at a church staff meeting, a member of my staff piped up, "Well, I guess the lesson in that is if our children put us in a nursing home, make sure it's next to a car dealership."

Gordon gave up his keys on his own a couple of years later. Even then Gordon would not be corralled. He drove his motorized scooter onto the narrow busy road near his community. After a couple of encounters with police, staff at the retirement community moved Gordon into the locked memory care unit. It is so hard to give up things we have treasured in life, things that gave us joy, things that gave us independence.

At the time Gordon was living in the retirement community, another member of my congregation, Willard, moved in. Unfortunately his wife had a heart attack and died instantly while unpacking their things. Willard was a salesman most of his life. He had a big expense allowance and was expected to entertain customers in style. Willard loved it. He was raised in the coal mines of West Virginia and joked he never had a pair of shoes until he enlisted in the army. That was untrue but Willard was quite happy to leave the poverty of the West Virginia hills behind. He loved fancy suits and monogrammed shirts. He loved upscale restaurants. Most of all he loved telling stories over cocktails. Willard said he never worked a day in his life. He just did what he loved to do.

When Willard retired his wife went to a local motel (at least the way Willard told it) and said she would pay Willard's salary if they hired him as greeter at their breakfast buffet. They hired Willard and he loved it, regaling guests with stories (mostly of the coal mines of West Virginia) as they ate scrambled eggs, sausages and hot cakes. When Carolyn and I stayed at the motel for my candidating weekend at the church, Willard quickly figured out who we were and began telling his stories. Working the motel's breakfast buffet, he learned what was going on in the community, weddings and funerals, soccer and lacrosse tournaments, conventions and fairs. He loved that 'job' in his retirement.

Single men are few in senior living facilities. Activities for single men are even fewer, perhaps an occasional poker or card game. Willard missed storytelling over a couple of drinks. He still had evening cocktails, but he drank alone. Men often don't make friends easily. He asked if I would share a beer. I told him I couldn't drink with him and then go on another visit with alcohol on my breath. Old ladies in the congregation would start to talk. Well, Willard said, make me your last visit of the afternoon. I agreed and called on Willard about 4:30 in the afternoon. Willard was happy to see me and offered a Coors Light. I looked at the beer and said, "Willard, if you invite me for a beer, you need something better than a Coors

Light. That would have been fine 30 years ago, but not anymore." It was the only time I saw Willard flustered and at a loss for words. He then said, "My son-in-law says the same thing. Next time I will have a better beer for you." After that, when his daughter made his beer runs, she always made sure he had a good beer for the pastor.

We give up so many things as we grow older. It is hard. We grieve their loss. Some folks though are blessed as they age, blessed with a good mind, decent health, caring friends and loving family members. Life is good despite aches and pains. They find joy in new pursuits. Memories give them comfort, not grief, and they find life can still be happy and fulfilling as they anticipate what God has around the next corner. It is too bad we all can't have those blessings in our final years.

CHAPTER 66

I Had an Affair with His Mother for 25 Years

Francis was up in years when I met him, in his mid-90s. He still lived alone in his own house, even tried to mow his lawn on a riding mower. His broken hip, though, slowed him down. He was frustrated. He could not do things he used to. He apologized for the way his gardens looked. Flower beds lay mostly barren, trellises and arches empty and unpainted. He showed me photos of the gardens in their prime. They were beautiful and extensive, featured in *Better Homes and Gardens.* When the gardens flourished, brides in the community stopped for photographs.

Most men have a barebones style of decorating, simple and useful, an absence of clutter. Not Francis' house. It was a feast for the eyes – lots of baubles, glass and mirrors; frills, antiques and fancy lamp shades; ornate picture frames, bowls, statues, and knickknacks everywhere. Walls were covered in flocked wallpaper with a proliferation of decorative hangings. There was an over-abundance of furniture, some with leopard skin upholstery, not comfortable lounge chairs, but uncomfortable Victorian style. And movie memorabilia and movie posters. Francis had hundreds of old movie posters, everywhere you looked.

On our first visit Francis spoke of wandering in Hollywood. He journeyed there in the 1930's when Hollywood was at the height of its glory. Francis was charismatic and good-looking. He could sing, dance, act and play the piano. He took his gifts to Hollywood to see what fate might have in store. For a few years, he worked around the sets, got a bit part or two, and met some of the beautiful people. Francis never made it big, but he loved it. He returned home to care for his ailing mother.

I assumed Francis never married and was probably gay. I was wrong. On my second visit he talked about Bea. I wasn't sure who Bea was and asked. Bea was his wife. They married after courting more than 40 years. They each cared for an elderly mother and did not marry until after both mothers passed away. I think I only got a taste of Francis' life. If I had more visits with Francis and time to develop more rapport, I think more stories would have come, probably shattering more stereotypes.

Francis had no children. He talked affectionately about a nephew who stopped regularly and was attentive to his needs. Whenever I asked if the church could help with something, he said his nephew would take care of it.

I met Francis' nephew, Anthony, the first time when we met to plan Francis' memorial service. Anthony spoke with a lilt in his voice and used dramatic gestures and flowery language. Flamboyance seemed to be part of who he was. He spent his life as a floral arranger for a local flower shop. On the day of Francis' memorial service he wore a red velour sports jacket and ascot. A man, perhaps ten years younger, sat next to him. There were a couple of photos around the funeral parlor of Francis, Anthony, and this younger man with arms around each other.

I minister in a denomination that has affirmed gays in ministry for decades and was the first to endorse same-sex relationships and marriage. By this time in my ministry, I viewed myself at least a little open-minded. After the service, I approached Anthony and asked if the man sitting next to him was his partner. He gave me a rather puzzled look, then burst out laughing. "Oh no," he said, "no, no, no! I had an affair with his mother for 25 years."

Life is always more interesting than our stereotypes. Stereotypes blind us to the fascinating and engaging people we meet every day. First impressions are not only usually wrong, but they prevent us from encountering the depth of character and personality in others. I didn't ask Francis' nephew about the 25-year affair. Those things are best not discussed following a memorial service. I don't condone affairs but his admission blew away my caricature of this man.

Often, in our arrogance, we think we have people figured out. We think we know what they believe, what they will say, how they will act. We take a few cues from their mannerisms, way of dress, or word choice, and think we can fill out the rest. We hear where they are from, the school they attended, or the profession they followed and, again, we tend to fill in the rest. With nearly everyone, the more we engage them and the deeper we listen to their stories, the more surprised we are. We discover, because of our prejudgments, we are the shallower people, not they. When we listen to stories of others, we discover complexities and inconsistencies within all of us.

I try to be sensitive to stereotypes because in my ministry, parishioners and colleagues tried to put me in a box. I went to an Evangelical seminary so I must be narrow-minded. I stammer a little when I talk so I must lack confidence in what

I say. I tend to be quiet so I must not have leadership qualities. I am from Indiana so I must be a Hoosier hick. I can't sing on key so I must not know anything about music. I find myself fighting stereotypes others pin on me all the time.

I try to be sensitive to stereotypes because I know I misjudged a lot of people through the years and it hurt my ministry. I remember a visit during my CPE days in seminary. I called on a lady in the Cardiac Care Unit in her late 50's. She seemed to be a fussbudget, worrying about every little thing. When she mentioned she was worried about her daughter being home alone, I asked how old her daughter was. Twenty-six, she responded. I dismissed her concern responding, "I think she is probably old enough to take care of herself."

The lady left the hospital only to return a couple of weeks later. I was catching up with her concerns and remembered her daughter. I asked how her daughter had done home alone while she was in the hospital last time. She said her daughter threw a party in their house. Drugs were bought and sold, and a drug dealer took much of their furniture in payment. I was wrong stereotyping her as a fussbudget and dismissing the concern about her daughter.

I still have much to learn, but sometimes I say the right thing. When Josh, a young gay man, called the church and asked if we welcomed gays, I responded, "I hope so." He came the next Sunday and nearly every Sunday for the next few years. We offered him God's grace and reconnected him to the church. He sang in our Praise Band. Josh was also bi-polar. His presence and participation was a reminder of the saying in our denomination, "No matter who you or where you are in the journey of faith you are welcome here." He also reminded us that each part of the Body of Christ is unique and vital to the health of the whole body.

I visited Josh's grandfather in a nursing home. I heard many stories from Josh about his grandfather. Josh loved him dearly, but portrayed him as old, narrow-minded, dogmatic, bigoted and Pentecostal. Life was black and white to his grandfather. In the visit his grandfather expressed how appreciative he was of our ministry with Josh. Our church was a wonderful blessing for his grandson. We gave Josh a place where he was accepted. He could worship and grow in his faith and use his gift of music for the Lord. Wow, I thought, our church had been a blessing?! I never dreamed I would hear a Pentecostal say our liberal church was a blessing. With Josh's grandfather I made the mistake I disliked so much in others. I stereotyped him and once again I was wrong. His grandfather was more accepting and grace-filled than I imagined.

I know I will always have more stereotypes to resist. Marlene, a down-to-earth, transparently honest, loveable parishioner, called. Her son Jason had just taken his life. I went to Marlene's apartment right away. Of course, the suicide was unexpected. The family was in shock. He left a loving wife and teenage children. No one could understand.

I was always confused whether Marlene had two daughters and a son or two sons and a daughter. I found out why. Marlene's daughter transitioned as an adult. Marlene sometimes referred to her son as 'he' and sometimes as 'she.' She didn't disapprove of the change in sexual identity. Old speaking habits were hard to break. Marlene was just glad her son was happier now than ever before. In previous years she was fearful her daughter/son might take her/his life. Instead, it was her straight son with the family, fitting the cultural norm, who took his life in a moment of depression.

Marlene's transgendered son was an ordained pastor in another denomination. I invited him to assist in the memorial service as he desired. I enjoyed meeting and working with him in the memorial service. I must confess transgendered sexual identities confuse me, just as gay orientations used to. I try to understand, however. We are always learning, trying to move past stereotypes and discover what lies at the heart of each person.

CHAPTER 67

Pastor to
the Unchurched

A parishioner invited Jeff and me to join him for lunch so he could introduce the two of us. He thought we would enjoy getting to know each other. Jeff used to lead Bible studies in our congregation. Folks loved them. The studies were very popular, filling our little chapel. Bible study wasn't a big thing in our church so I knew Jeff must have been a captivating Bible teacher to draw a crowd.

Jeff gave a bit of his history over lunch. He was ordained a Lutheran pastor as a young man. He was called to a parish and served for 10 years. After 10 years in the church, though, he discovered he no longer believed in its doctrines. To him it was not a crisis of faith. He just no longer believed what he was called to preach. He felt he could not stay in ministry. That would be hypocritical. He left the church and never looked back, as far as I could tell. He found jobs in county government and then banking, serving in those positions the rest of his working life. He was retired when I met him. He also had a bout with cancer. Jeff was positive and upbeat, funny and entertaining. I sensed he would connect well with parishioners, if he had the faith they expected.

I occasionally speak to other pastors who no longer believe in the central tenets of the Christian faith. Most continue in ministry, some because they have no idea what else to do. Others see their lack of belief in the basics of the faith as irrelevant to effective ministry. They can still minister to persons in times of need, counsel the troubled, teach the Scriptures, strive for social justice, lead worship, and administer the business of the church without belief in Jesus as the Son of God, the Trinity, redemption of sins on the cross, or something else considered essential to orthodox

Christianity. The Christian faith, they say, is wide enough to accommodate a broad field of beliefs and practices. Jeff left the ministry. He couldn't preach what he no longer believed.

Jeff still loved the Scriptures and taught them with insight. He made stories of the Bible come alive and people of my congregation were drawn to his classes. Both skeptics and faithful came to learn from him. One church member referred to Jeff as "Pastor to the Unchurched."

After lunch that day I had little contact with Jeff, until Elnor died. Elnor, a lifelong member of our congregation, had advanced dementia when I arrived at the church. I never got to know her. Elnor was the aunt of Jeff's wife. He offered to assist with the service and give the eulogy. I was thankful. We planned the service together. I chose traditional funeral Scriptures. He chose poems by John Updike and Jane Kenyon and a reading from Tao. Jeff brought Elnor's character alive. His engaging manner of speaking connected with the congregation. If he stayed in ministry, Jeff probably would have served a large church in his tradition.

Working with Jeff, I began to understand what my parishioner meant when he referred to Jeff as "Pastor of the Unchurched." The unchurched, as well as the churched, have spiritual longings and needs. The images, symbols and message of the Christian tradition bring comfort, hope, and faith to those in the church. We are raised with Christian Scriptures and embrace their message. The images and messages do not touch everyone, however. In the church we tend to dismiss these folks as unbelievers or heathens. Our task, we say, is to evangelize and bring them to a true faith. We proclaim the good news of Jesus Christ and invite all to join in the journey. We want all people to embrace the Christian faith. I know they won't and I am learning to accept that. Their search for God may take them other places.

Pastors to the unchurched, like Jeff, understand the role of doubt in people's lives. They understand some cannot accept by faith things those of us in the church accept. They know just believing something doesn't make it true. Believing a dead man, Jesus, was raised to new life doesn't make him alive. Some people trust their rational, sane mind rather than believe in something stretching the bounds of reality we experience. The English poet, Alfred Lord Tennyson, wrote, "There lives more faith in honest doubt, believe me, than in half the creeds." I think God respects an honest doubter, in search of truth with honesty and sincerity.

Our Confirmation class and their mentors listened to a rabbi answer our questions about Judaism. We had just attended a Friday evening Shabbat service. The rabbi was articulate and funny, interpreting Jewish traditions and beliefs with lively stories and illustrations the young people could understand. A mentor asked him the simple question, 'What happens after you die?' The rabbi paused and was silent for several seconds. He then said slowly, 'Christianity is a faith. Judaism is not a faith. Some Jews, in the more orthodox expressions, believe that God will create a New Jerusalem here on this earth. One day, faithful Jewish people who have died will be raised up and live in this new city on earth.' He continued, 'But not all Jews believe this. I believe that after I die, my good works will live on and I will live on in the legacy of my children and grandchildren. But I will not live forever as Christians believe.' I appreciated the rabbi's honesty. Not everyone shares the hope of eternal life that lies in Christians. The eternal life we Christians foresee is understood only in faith.

Phil, a parishioner of mine, frequently referred to himself as a doubter. He attended an adult Sunday School class regularly but never stayed for worship. When I asked, his reason was simple. He didn't like anyone talking to him when he couldn't talk back. So I told him, "Phil, if you have a question about what I'm saying when I'm preaching, go ahead, stand up, and interrupt my sermon. Maybe others have the same question." But he said, "No, the congregation wouldn't like it."

Nevertheless Phil, who loved to question and doubt, stopped in my study from time to time, plopped himself on my couch, and told me something happening in his life or his family's life that seemed a little miraculous. Then he would say, "Almost makes you want to believe, doesn't it?" An old Polish proverb says, "To believe with certainty, we must begin with doubting." Perhaps there is some truth there.

By the time I left the congregation Phil was in worship nearly every Sunday. He never interrupted my sermons. On Monday mornings though, he would stop in and have a question about something I said. God was honoring his doubt.

Doubt lies within all, even the faithful among us. Bob, a dear member of our church, gave his life to Jesus when he was young. He was never the same. He went to a Christian college and did his best to make Jesus the focus of his life. Devotion to his Lord continued his whole life. He attended a Baptist church until joining the congregation I served when he was 70.

Bob became ill with pancreatic cancer and was approaching death. I visited with him. We knew death was only days away. I said to Bob, "When you are ready, God is ready. God is ready to welcome you home with the words, 'Well done, good and faithful servant!'" Bob was silent for a moment and then said in his weak voice, "That is one question I always asked myself. Have I been a faithful servant? Have I been a faithful servant?" I thought for a second and replied, "The fact you have always asked that question tells me your heart is in the right place. Your heart is where God wants it to be. I think you tried to be that faithful servant and that has pleased God. God honors the desire of your heart." I think God is pleased most when we don't demand entrance to God's realm, but humbly accept the gift God offers.

A couple of weeks after Elnor's funeral, Jeff's cancer returned. I visited him in the Intensive Care Unit at the local hospital and asked how he was. Jeff said, "It hurts. It hurts." I asked, "Where? Where does it hurt?" Jeff replied, "The soul. My body is okay but my soul hurts." Jeff knew he was very, very sick, not likely to beat the odds. Cancer came aggressively. Although he prepared himself for this moment since diagnosed a few years earlier, saying good-bye to this world he embraced with a passion, saying goodbye to people he loved dearly, was not easy. His soul hurt. Frequently, when we talked later, I didn't ask about the body. I said, "How is the soul today?"

As I visited with Jeff I discovered this "Pastor to the Unchurched" had no pastor of his own. I tried to fill that role in his final days. I was blessed to journey with him. Jeff died less than 2 ½ months after Elnor's funeral. At his memorial service I read traditional Christian Scriptures of assurance of God's love. We also listened to songs Jeff enjoyed, "Don't Worry, Be Happy", "May the Circle Be Unbroken," and "Teach Your Children Well."

In my message I tried to honor his search for God. I said, "Jeff was transparently honest, about himself, and others, what he knew, but more importantly what he didn't know. He was a pursuer of truth, truth about the world and truth about people, truth about himself, but especially truth about God. He didn't accept simple formulated answers but always searched deeply. He knew that in discovering truth, it is not just about the answers but also about the questions. He pursued truth with this gentle humility, always knowing that the more he discovered, the more there was to know, that the final answers would always, always, lie just a little beyond where he could reach.

"No one theology or way of life was sufficient for Jeff. His search for God took him not just through the Bible, but into a whole variety of religious writings. Through that search he continually found a God of grace and love, a welcoming God, a God reaching out and inviting us all to be God's children. We commit Jeff now to the God he has sought so earnestly all these years, believing that God has opened for Jeff the door of eternal life, life forever in the presence of our Creator and Redeemer."

CHAPTER 68

I Baptize You in the Name of the Father, Son and Holy Spirit

Little Sahara lay on her bed in the crowded living room of her paternal great-grandmother. Her father was nowhere to be seen, which was good. Sahara was clearly delighting in the attention and gifts. Moving about was difficult for her. She looked uncomfortable lying on her pillows. Tumors from neuroblastoma had grown large. She seemed like she must be in pain, but she was smiling, laughing and enjoying her special day. Friends and family gathered for Sahara's baptism. Her fifth birthday was just 2 months away, but she would not live long enough to celebrate.

Baptism is about God. It is about God's grace, love and the gift of God's Spirit. When I baptize an infant during Sunday morning worship, I talk a great deal about God's love and what that love means. Baptism is also about us. God's love is personal and focused. God's love has an object. That object is us. I think God forgave us that day if, at times, we seemed caught up directing our attention and love on little Sahara and maybe not as much on God. The baptism was an opportunity to celebrate Sahara's life among us before she was taken away at such a young age.

I could still see in Sahara that day the spark and little mischievous smile that endeared her to everyone. My favorite memory of Sahara is of her and her little sister, Maxine, giggling and on the move in our church lounge – Sahara running and laughing, Maxine crawling and trying her best to keep up with big sister. I got on my knees and crawled with Maxine in the chase after Sahara. Sahara seemed a happy child, animated and full of life.

Sahara spent a lot of time at the church when she was young. Her father was absent for the most part and, as I said, that was a good thing. He was extremely immature and self-centered, also unpredictable and menacing. Life was more ordered and safe when he was absent. Sahara's mother was well-meaning but had difficulty coping with life. Perhaps it was ADHD, but she had difficulty with focus, decisions and commitment. Maternal grandparents, active participants in the life of our church, were often primary caregivers for Sahara and Maxine. It was not a role they anticipated or sought, but they loved their granddaughters and wanted the best for them. They willingly and graciously stepped in to provide their granddaughters with a secure and nurturing home.

Neuroblastoma is a tricky cancer to diagnose in its early stages. It is rare and, I would guess, not often on the initial radar of family physicians. If it is not diagnosed early, while still localized, it is almost impossible to treat effectively. A family, in a previous parish I served, also had a daughter with neuroblastoma. However, her disease was discovered early while surgery was still an option. The tumor was removed and their daughter grew to be a healthy young adult. Thankful for the new life for their daughter, the family organized and sponsored a biennial gala raising hundreds of thousands of dollars for research into neuroblastoma.

Sahara was not so lucky. By the time the disease was diagnosed surgery was no longer an option. The family was told, in clear terms, though treatment might slow the progress of the disease temporarily and she might have one or perhaps two good years, little Sahara would succumb to the cancer and never enjoy a normal childhood.

Sahara was admitted to a nearby nationally-renowned hospital and began the regimen of chemotherapy and radiation. She was connected to tubes and wires and poked with needles of all sorts. She learned to endure pain and indignities with grace. For much of her conscious life needles, tubes and wires were simply a part of living. Long weeks were spent in the hospital. Sahara lost her hair and, to keep her safe from infection, was confined mostly to her own room. Her dad returned and entered her life once more. Sahara's mom and dad stayed at the Ronald McDonald house near the hospital campus so they could visit Sahara more easily. Grandparents, great-grandmother, aunts and uncles also visited offering support and overseeing care.

On one visit, I met Sahara's mother in the hallway outside of Sahara's room. I casually mentioned her father was keeping me up to date on Sahara's progress. "Oh," Sahara's mother responded sadly, "you've talked to my dad. So you know the news." "The news?" I asked, afraid Sahara had taken a turn for the worse. "The news that I am pregnant," she said somewhat embarrassed. "No," I told her, "I did not know that news." She told her dad the day before and he was not very happy. Between hospital stays, Sahara and her mother usually stayed at the home of the paternal great-grandmother. The parents of Sahara's mother provided fulltime care for Sahara's little sister, Maxine. Sahara's grandfather knew he now would have another child to care for.

Sahara responded to treatments. Her hair grew back and she became the fun, active, mischievous little girl she was intended to be. Sahara's little brother, Hayden, was born and the grandparents welcomed him into their home with the same love they showered on his older sisters. Despite the disruptions of Sahara's illness and the dysfunctionalities of his parents, Hayden enjoyed a safe and loving home as his older sisters did, thanks to his grandparents.

Now, as we gathered with Sahara in the little living room for the baptism, we all knew Sahara would not be with us for long. Her disease was progressing rapidly. Everyone wanted to celebrate her short life while she was still among us. The apostle Paul writes that all of us who were baptized into Christ were baptized into his death. One of the symbols of baptism is dying as we are united with Christ. Death was on our minds as we baptized Sahara.

Yes, we are buried with Christ by baptism into Jesus' death, but through baptism we are also united with Christ in his resurrection. As we have died with Christ, we will also live with him. Baptism is a celebration of life, the gift of life here on earth and eternally in God's presence. We celebrated Sahara's life the best we could that day. In baptism we declared Sahara to be a unique and precious child of God. God's love and grace would never leave her. In baptism God embraced her with love and surrounded her with God's Spirit always. I think God's love for Sahara permitted us to indulge in our love for her.

Baptism is about family, too. Family members make vows to love and support the little child. We acknowledge the baptized child is part of the family of God and will never be alone. They will always have a community of faith to surround them and offer hope. Sahara was blessed with a community of faith. Her parents could not offer the stability she needed, but Sahara, Maxine and Hayden were surrounded by love through an extended family and a community of faith caring for them deeply. Through the care and affection of so many, love, not cancer, won the day in Sahara's short life.

The first time I baptized someone near death was much different. There were no smiles, no celebration, no family, just an elderly man living by himself in a small motel renting a room by the week. Arthur's health was failing, his hip broken, emphysema destroying his lungs. He got by only through the thoughtful concern of the motel manager and a pastoral colleague of mine. Arthur wished to be baptized but my pastor friend served in a tradition where baptism was permitted only by immersion. The old man's health precluded a trip to a baptistery for dunking. My friend asked if I would baptize Arthur through sprinkling.

I called on Arthur in his motel room. He was expecting me. We talked for a while. He was agitated, knew he was dying. He also knew he had not lived the best life and was worried about his eternity. He invited Jesus into his heart many times but wasn't sure whether it ever stuck. I talked to Arthur about God's love and forgiveness. Salvation wasn't about us. It was about what God did for us. That was what baptism was about, accepting what God has done for us. I asked if he wanted to be baptized and he said yes. I asked if he professed Jesus as Savior and Lord and again he said yes. I asked if he wanted to walk in the way of Jesus as his follower. Again, he said yes. I sprinkled water on his head baptizing him in the name of the Father, Son and Holy Spirit. I did my best to assure him God had a place for him in God's reign.

I wish I could say Arthur calmed down and experienced the assurance of God's grace in his life. If he did, I couldn't see it. He still seemed agitated. In part, I don't think he viewed a few drops of water as real baptism. Real baptism meant being dunked. I ran into my friend the pastor the following week and asked about Arthur. Arthur died alone in his motel room. I prayed he was receiving the peace he longed for and was never able to find.

Angels came and escorted Sahara to her new home less than a month after her baptism. Her grandfather gave beautiful words of remembrance celebrating the spirit of Sahara eloquently and poignantly. We celebrated the few short years Sahara blessed us with her twinkle and mischievous smile. We know the kingdom of heaven belongs to children like Sahara.

CHAPTER 69

Do You Really Want to Send This Letter?

"Do you really want to send this letter?" I asked Dolores. "Yes, I do," she said. "How do you think he will respond?" I asked. "He will get mad," she replied. "Is that what you want?" I asked. "He deserves it," she said. "Pray about it for a couple of days before you send it," I suggested. "Maybe," she said.

Dolores was a volunteer in our church on Wednesday morning. Usually, I stopped by her desk in the Volunteer Office and chatted for a few, or sometimes, a lot of minutes. Dolores was not a happy person. Life, she felt, had not been kind to her, especially in her later years. She had a long marriage to a man a few years older than herself. Her husband suffered from Alzheimer's the last ten years of his life. Her time was spent caring for him. When he retired, he chose to receive his pension as a single life annuity payable to him. That meant more income while he was alive. It also meant when he died there was no benefit for her whatsoever. After he died she lived mostly on a small Social Security check. They were not blessed with children.

It wasn't long after her husband died, however, that Louis came along. Louis, too, was recently widowed. Louis dressed sharply, drove a fancy car, and took her to nice restaurants. He fussed over her and courted her vigorously. Louis was a persuasive talker and in a short time, to the surprise and dismay of Louis' children, they were hitched. Louis offered Dolores stability, financial security and a new, exciting life. Dolores offered Louis companionship and eagerly joined in Louis' active lifestyle. Relationships with Louis' children were stressful but the children lived out of town.

Dolores joined Louis' church but they had a falling out with his congregation. They began attending Sunday morning worship with us. Soon they were not just attending worship but also dinners and other events in the life of the church. Louis, who enjoyed public speaking, signed up as a liturgist. Dolores signed up to volunteer in the church office.

One Wednesday morning visit, Dolores confirmed what we all suspected. Louis was in the early stages of Alzheimer's. It had become evident something was wrong a few months earlier. As liturgist, Louis could no longer follow the printed Order of Worship. He became confused every Sunday he served. At first, we joked about it. Louis had a strong pride. He could not admit he could no longer perform simple duties. We recruited other liturgists and 'promoted' Louis to usher. I saw other early signs of dementia in Louis also, disorientation, repetition, inability to come up with a name or a word.

Dolores was devastated and angry. For ten years she cared for her previous husband. She was not prepared to begin the ordeal again. She did not anticipate this turn of events when Louis courted her. Sometimes, in her anger, she wondered if she should just leave him. Let his children worry about him. It would serve them right. But Dolores had nowhere to go. She had been very close to an older sister but her sister recently died. She had alienated herself from all others. Dolores now was alone, except for Louis. She would stick with Louis and care for him the best she could. Nearly every week Dolores and I had long conversations about coping with Louis and Alzheimer's.

So, Dolores brought me a letter to read before she sent it to one of Louis' sons. She composed the letter in response to a letter written by the son. The son's letter was petty and vindictive, accusing his father of being distant and non-caring, of never being involved in their lives. It was not a pretty letter to a father in the final stages of life. The son obviously did not comprehend the seriousness of Louis' Alzheimer's. Louis was not capable of responding to the letter. It was up to Dolores. When she did, she wrote in the same tone as the sender, spiteful, certainly not conciliatory. This was the letter she showed me, the letter the son "deserved."

The following week Dolores came into my office with another letter. She had not sent the previous one. She wanted me to read the new letter. I did. It was beautiful. She spoke openly about Louis' Alzheimer's and his inability to connect relationally at this time in his life. The disease had progressed much beyond his son's understanding. She empathized with the son's feelings of being emotionally distant from his father. She knew Louis was a self-absorbed man when she married him, how that could be hurtful to his children. She did not accuse the son of wrongdoing. She did not ask why he visited his father so seldom. The letter opened the door to understanding and reconciliation. I told Dolores it was a beautiful letter and she should send it. She also sent it to Louis' other two children, along with a copy of their brother's letter. As I spoke with Dolores in the following weeks, she thought her letter lessened tension in the family. They spoke to one another with more civility.

A couple of months after this letter incident our Office Manager told me Dolores would no longer be a volunteer. I asked if caring for Louis was becoming too much. She said "no." Dolores had gotten angry that day. Another volunteer was busy in the Volunteer Office gathering materials to put together folders for an upcoming church event. Dolores said the Volunteer Office was her space Wednesday mornings and she couldn't tolerate others using it when she was there. She would not volunteer anymore. The 'guilty' volunteer was a dear saint in the church. She would be horrified to know she offended someone by intruding into their space. She would have been respectful and certainly come back and work at a different time if she sensed she was upsetting someone.

I called Dolores and talked with her but did not ask her to come back as a volunteer. I have learned in ministry there are some personalities in the church who have a history of estrangement from family, friends and church. It is sad, but they have a difficult time maintaining close, mutually giving relationships. Dolores showed that tendency. I rejoiced she broke from this pattern to write the beautiful letter to Louis' son.

A few months later, I received a call from the dear volunteer who upset Dolores. She often called to check on members of the church family who were absent in worship. She noticed Louis and Dolores missed four Sundays in a row. She called their house to see how they were doing. Louis' daughter answered. Things were not good. Louis had a severe heart attack a week earlier and the damage was extensive. He was in a cardiac care unit thirty miles away. His long term prognosis was uncertain. Dolores visited him the day after the heart attack, left the hospital, and slipped on ice in the parking lot. She hit her head causing a brain bleed. She was now on a ventilator, sedated but responsive. It was uncertain she would live. She was in intensive care on another floor of the same hospital as Louis. The family was grateful for the call from the saint in our church. They did not know where Louis and Dolores attended and did not know whom to call.

I immediately went to visit the family. They mourned the possible loss of their father and spoke with fondness about him. I wondered if Dolores' letter had a conciliatory effect on the children that they were able to grieve the loss of their father amiably. I wondered if I would have encountered a more stressful situation if she had sent her original letter. In all the broken relationships of Dolores' life, I rejoiced she put aside her pride and wrote a beautiful letter to Louis' children.

Damage to Louis' heart was worse than expected and he passed away in a couple of days. Services were held for him while Dolores remained in the hospital, still on the ventilator. I visited with her over the next few days. She communicated with me through blinking her eyes, letting me know she heard and understood what I was saying. It became more probable she would not be weaned from the ventilator. She would never leave the hospital bed.

Dolores had no family member or close friend to make health care decisions on her behalf. Louis' children barely knew her. She hadn't spoken to her closest relative, her younger sister, in decades. I knew of no living will for Dolores. I sought to understand her wishes about remaining alive attached to a ventilator. She was failing and it was hard to communicate with eye blinks. I told her it was okay to let go. God was waiting for her and ready to receive her home. Twelve days after Louis' death, Dolores died. I called her attorney and, after a few days, received permission from her younger sister to have a memorial service to honor her life. Nearly everyone there was a member of our congregation.

It is impossible to reconcile after a loved one has passed away. Can we set aside our pride? Can we seek to sow peace where seeds of division have grown so long, before it is too late? I think Dolores did that in her letter and Louis' children received the gift of reconciliation from an unexpected source.

I learned from a pastoral colleague, after the services for Louis and Dolores, they missed those few weeks before their calamities because they were attending another church. They decided to leave our congregation. That check-up call from the saint in our church enabled Dolores to receive ministry in her time of need from those who cared for her the most. As she gave an unexpected gift of reconciliation to Louis' children, so Dolores received an unexpected gift of reconciliation from someone whom she brushed aside. How beautiful when reconciliation comes! How extraordinary and marvelous when it comes from unlikely people!

CHAPTER 70

We Expected a More Patriotic Service

I shy away from publicity. I prefer others in the congregation serve as spokespersons to promote ministries of the church. It is the actuarial part of my personality. But there I was, leading off both the 10:00 and 11:00 evening news programs on nearby big city television stations.

Our nation was in mourning once again. The unthinkable happened. Twenty first-grade children and six adult school personnel were shot and killed in another horrific school shooting, the third deadliest mass shooting by a single person in U.S. history, the deadliest in a grade school or high school. Although the shooting occurred at Sandy Hook Elementary School in Newtown, Connecticut, hundreds of miles away, our community grieved. The tender age of the victims and senseless slaughter (and, if we are truthful, it also occurred at an affluent white school) touched us.

I sent an email to pastors in our community asking if there was interest in a community prayer service to come together, mourn the loss of precious life, and support one another amidst grief. Perhaps it was the busyness of the Advent/Christmas season but response from pastors was sparse. I sent a second email. It, too, generated little response. I was about to give up on the community prayer service when I received a couple of emails from a member of the congregation urging me to continue. I went ahead and planned the prayer service, inviting the couple of pastors who responded to join me. We sent the usual publicity notifications to newspapers and other churches.

The local newspaper put the announcement on the front page. News personnel from big city TV stations, looking for ways to cover the outpouring of grief following the shooting, showed up unannounced in our sanctuary. Before the service began, news anchors interviewed me and another pastor in front of cameras. They then remained inconspicuous during the prayer service.

Our sanctuary was fairly full, though only a few from my congregation. People came from all walks of life and a wide diversity of churches, some with no church background. They gathered to share common grief and bring their pain before God. We need support from others as we mourn horrific acts. We may find few answers to our many questions, but are comforted by the love and prayers of others sharing our loss. Sometimes grief is personal and lonely, but sometimes grief is public and best expressed through community.

At the prayer service we mourned those who died in the terrible shooting at Sandy Hook. We also remembered the violence against children occurring daily throughout our country, children who die in school, on their way to school, at the playground, or on their parents' front porch. We reminded ourselves of children around the world who live amidst warfare, strife and violence every day of their lives. Horrific and tragic deaths among children are too common. We grieved we live in a world where such loss is too frequent.

In one church I served, two teenaged sisters in the congregation babysat frequently for a family with three young children who were close friends to their family. The family of the young children appeared to be the perfect American family. They had everything. They were beautiful and wealthy. They lived in a fabulous restored area of an adjoining city in a gorgeously remodeled Victorian home. One morning, perhaps in an extreme response to a likely divorce, the young mother suffocated each of her beautiful children, one by one. Her attempt to take her own life failed.

Can anyone ever understand how such unspeakable acts of murder happen? Do the perpetrators really know why they commit such horrendous deeds? Depression? Mental illness? How could we possibly explain the deaths of these beautiful children to the girls in our congregation? Some things can never be explained. They can only be felt and grieved. We hope by talking and listening, hugging and praying, and having faith in the goodness of God, we find healing over time.

No public event in my ministry caused more outpouring of public grief and anguish than the 911 attacks. Nearly every pastor I knew had a prayer service within a day or two of the attacks. Sanctuaries were filled at every church. At no other time in my ministry could I announce a spontaneous prayer service and have the whole congregation turn out on a weekday evening. We are drawn to God in times of hurt and pain, anguish and suffering, questioning and searching.

At the 911 service, people hurt, but they were also angry. They were angry at the 911 perpetrators and Osama Bin Laden. They were angry at Muslims in general and people who looked like them. I sought to address both the hurt and anger in my sermon the following Sunday. I talked about suffering and pain of families of victims and how precious life now seemed to us, how we all vowed to hold our loved ones a little closer.

I also tried to speak to the cause of 911. I said God grieved even more than we did. Those who died were God's children. God knew the pain of loss. In some mysterious way, God witnessed the death of his own Son upon the cross. I said God gave humans the responsibility of living together in respect and love and pursuing peace and justice. In Jesus Christ, God has shown us what that looks like. Instead, hatred, greed, selfishness and prejudice have gotten in the way. The result of all that hatred, greed, selfishness and prejudice throughout the world caused airplanes to crash into the World Trade Center and the Pentagon. Innocent people suffer the consequences of a world gone far astray.

I also said justice had to be done. People who do such horrible, horrible things must be punished. People who delight in killing innocent men, women and children must be stopped. I went on to say Jesus showed us a more difficult way than hating and a far more courageous way than shouting angry words at people who may be different. "But I say to you that listen," Jesus says, "Love your enemies, do good to those who hate you, bless those who curse you, pray for those who abuse you.... Do to others as you would have them do to you." Only love can conquer hate. Jesus says love and forgiveness must enter the world or the cycle of hate will never stop. I said the world was united in its common grief and outrage at the atrocity and my prayer was the tragedy would open new windows of understanding. The greatest strength of America lies in our capacity to love one another and give generously and freely. I concluded with a declaration of faith in the love, grace and power of God. Despite the tragedy, God was still alive and would bring forth God's reign of peace and justice.

Most left the service thanking me for my words, but not everyone. A few voiced their disappointment. "We expected a more patriotic service," they said. They wanted a sermon to rally troops to fight the evil of Islam. They didn't want to hear a "love your enemy" message. They certainly didn't want to hear the fiery message given by an African-American pastor that same Sunday, a pastor in my denomination serving a church far bigger than mine 30 miles away.

While most of America sang "God Bless America" and felt sorry for itself, Dr. Jeremiah Wright preached a powerful and provocative sermon, giving a different cause for the 911 attacks. In the sermon he carefully laid out the history of the United States' intervention in the affairs of other countries —bombs dropped, terrorism supported, and violence inflicted upon innocent people. He concluded, "And we never batted an eye ... and now we are indignant, because the stuff we have done overseas is now brought back into our own front yards. America's chickens are coming home to roost." In a later sermon, "Confusing God and Government," that Dr. Wright delivered at the start of the Iraq War, he detailed numerous lies and deceptions of our government over the years. Dr. Wright drove home the point that governments lie but God does not. Again, while the rest of the nation was feeling good singing "God Bless America," Dr. Wright cried out "God damn America!" "God damn America as long as she tries to act like she is God, and she is supreme!"

Dr. Wright's sermons disappeared into the archives of his church until they were resurrected seven years later when one of his parishioners was running for President. The fiery excerpts were lifted, usually with no context, and played again and again over the internet. Dr. Wright was vilified. The future President came under intense criticism.

I moved to a new church during the Presidential campaign while the wrangling was taking place concerning Dr. Wright. A couple from my new congregation came into my office. They asked what I thought about Dr. Wright's speech. I asked what they thought. They thought Dr. Wright was an abomination. He insulted our country and should be defrocked by the denomination. I explained in our polity local pastors have a great deal of freedom of thought and expression in their sermons. It would be very unusual for a pastor to be defrocked for angry sermons.

They asked what I thought of his sermon. I responded Dr. Wright's style was not my style. My sermons at those momentous times in our nation's history tended to be pastoral. I also said Dr. Wright viewed himself in the tradition of biblical prophets. Biblical prophets were out of step with leaders of the nation and often with the people as well. They were rarely liked and often persecuted. Their allegiance was to God and not their country. They proclaimed their message whether people wanted to hear or not. Dr. Wright, I said, sought to be faithful to the Bible more than to his country. The couple soon left our congregation.

Public grief can get messy. Public grief is not easily separated from politics and personalities of the day. It can, and should, become tied up in issues like gun control and gun rights, religious prejudices and racial bigotry, government lies and government injustice, and much, much more. Public grief isn't simple and we shouldn't make it simple. "Prayers and thoughts" are not enough. Like Jacob in the Bible, what is needed is space and courage to wrestle with these issues, and with God.

CHAPTER 71

Your Sister Is No More

Harvey and Esther usually arrived a little late for the 8:15 am Sunday service in our small, quaint chapel. During the Announcement and Greeting time, they slowly made their way to their preferred seats in the second pew. Esther walked slowly with a cane, but I guess they were late because of Harvey. Esther dressed nicely. She presented herself with modesty and grace. Not so Harvey. The color and pattern combinations of Harvey's outfits astounded us all. He started with a string tie and anything was possible beyond that. I once heard a radio interview with the girlfriend of Bob Dylan as he was breaking into folk singing in Greenwich Village. It appeared at the time Bob gave no thought to his clothes. They looked like items purchased at the local Goodwill Store hastily thrown together as he went out the door. In reality, his former girlfriend said, he spent hours in front of a mirror trying different styles to obtain just the right 'look.' I don't think that was the case for Harvey. I think he chose clothes in about two seconds and probably never wore the same combination twice.

Just as we never knew what Harvey would wear, we also never knew what would come out of his mouth. Nor did we know when it would come, during announcements, prayers, sermons, just about any time. Often it was a joke, a corny joke, one we heard before and wished we would never hear again. Besides his clothes, jokes were Harvey's trademark. He greeted everyone with a joke, usually not just one, but two or three. He never ran out. Though the jokes were often bad, you couldn't help but laugh.

People didn't love Harvey's jokes. They loved Harvey. Harvey never knew a stranger. He was a lovable, adorable old character and a perpetual child. He was simple, transparent, and well-meaning. I don't think he told jokes because he was a frustrated comedian. He told jokes to poke a little fun at himself. He knew his jokes were corny but they broke the ice and put people at ease. We didn't take life quite as seriously when Harvey was around.

Harvey owned a printing business and passed out little cards with funny or clever sayings. The little cards were intended to make people laugh or feel better. I think Harvey ran his print shop not to make money but to make people laugh. Business should be fun. He also owned a Christmas tree farm. For a few years Carolyn and I cut down our trees there. In his later years, Harvey was not able to keep up with trimming. The trees were a bit like Harvey, odd but fun. We have the best memories of those trees.

Harvey wanted me to join his service club and invited me to attend a few times. Harvey was the same funny guy there he was at church, greeting everyone with a joke and interrupting proceedings with an offbeat remark. Everyone loved Harvey there as well.

I belonged to a service club only once. Life as a pastor was busy enough without adding more commitments. I joined that club because a lot of men in the congregation were members. I didn't see several of the men Sunday morning. My weekly Rotary luncheon kept me in contact with those members. Besides, that local chapter wasn't as service-minded as others and fit my schedule better.

At one Rotary meeting the membership secretary went over the stringent attendance requirement expected of active members and the consequences of not fulfilling it. When he asked if there were any questions, I raised my hand. "Could you come to the Congregational Church and give that same talk?" I am not sure my wayward members appreciated my comment.

Despite his playful ways, Harvey also had a deeply spiritual side. Prayer and Bible study were dear. He had an honest faith, a seeking faith, a humble faith. He had a deep desire and passion to know God and be the person God called him to be, but he didn't pretend to know it all, not whatsoever. He knew he hadn't arrived yet but he was on the journey and prayed it was the right path. His relationship with the Lord was the most important thing in his life.

Our church had an active ministry to area senior living communities. A devoted lay member directed this ministry. Harvey enjoyed giving messages at these facilities. I also led services at the senior communities. One Sunday evening, five minutes before seven, I received a call from the piano player. "Are you coming to the service?" she asked. I had forgotten. Carolyn and I were hiking and driving home. The good news was I was only 10 minutes away. The bad news was I was in hiking clothes. I asked if people cared whether I came dressed as I was. She asked and came back to the phone to say they didn't care.

I preached that evening in a T-shirt I received as a birthday present at a family camp in a previous parish. All week long I led morning hikes for the family camp along the Blue Ridge Parkway. The T-shirt was a gift from a couple of clowns at the end of the week. The front of the T-shirt said, "Hike Naked." The back read, "It adds color to your cheeks." Fortunately, when I wore this T-shirt and preached at the senior living community, it was the last time I was preaching there before retirement. Harvey would have loved the story and the T-shirt. I wish he had been around to tell him.

As Harvey's health deteriorated and he knew he didn't have much time, he shared a story, probably from the 1930's. Harvey had a sister much older than himself. His sister was like a second mother to him. He loved his sister, idolized her. His sister became pregnant and wanted to marry the father of her baby. I am not sure why but her own father told her "no." Harvey said one day soon after news of her pregnancy, his father came to him and said, "Your sister is no more. We will not talk about her anymore in this house." Harvey was grief-stricken. He adored his sister.

Harvey found out his sister, unable to marry the father of her baby, had an abortion. Abortions in those days were illegal, performed secretly in back alleys in unsanitary conditions. His sister died during the procedure. Now, to her own father, she no longer existed. Harvey was devastated and never forgot her.

In all my years of ministry I never had a woman come to ask counsel regarding an abortion. Perhaps it is because I am a man and women believed I would have a difficult time understanding. Perhaps they felt I might be judgmental and shame them. I am sorry if I have not been approachable. Such decisions are so personal and heart-wrenching they would be difficult to discuss. I rejoice there are pregnancy crisis centers where women can go. It would be very difficult to think clearly, make decisions, and seek help amidst swirling feelings of anger and fear, grief and loneliness, shame and guilt.

Abortions have been around for a long time. They didn't begin with the 1973 Supreme Court decision Roe vs. Wade. As long as there have been unplanned or unwanted pregnancies, there have been abortions. Since 1973, abortions have generally been safe, performed by licensed medical personnel in sanitary conditions. Women like Harvey's sister have not had to risk their lives to terminate unwanted pregnancies.

People are passionate about abortion. It is murder, some say. No, it is a woman's right to choose, others say. The Bible says God hates those who have abortions. No, the Bible says God has mercy on the afflicted and oppressed. The Bible says life begins at conception. No, the Bible never says anything like that. Unfortunately, rhetoric concerning abortion is often unchristian. Self-righteousness can be strong on both sides of the issue. We vilify those who disagree with us. That is too bad. If both sides could cooperate, abortion rates would surely decrease.

Pro-life adherents advocate for abstinence, an honorable ideal, but it doesn't prevent unplanned pregnancies. People, even pro-life folks, don't follow it. Judging from my own family tree, the first baby arrives less than 9 months after marriage quite often. Abstinence doesn't work. What all studies have shown to prove successful reducing abortion rates is widespread sex education and availability and use of contraceptives. Planned Parenthood is the pro-life movement's best friend preventing unplanned pregnancies, thus reducing the number of abortions.

I think God grieves every time there is an abortion. I think every woman who has an abortion also grieves. We live in a fallen, imperfect world. Unplanned pregnancies will continue. Abortions will continue, whether legal or not. If we lived in a more compassionate and understanding world, both would decrease.

You know, even though I heard hundreds of his jokes, I can't remember a single joke Harvey told. I remember the story that wasn't funny. I can't forget it.

CHAPTER 72

Dammit, I Am Not Dead Yet

Edgar should have died. His heart stopped twice. Twice the response team rushed the crash carts into the Intensive Care Unit and revived him. He spent days on a ventilator, teetering between life and death. Weaning him from the ventilator was not easy but the medical team succeeded. Now Edgar was breathing on his own, assisted only by a small oxygen tube in his nose. Edgar knew he should be dead and was kind of proud he was still alive. He bragged to me, "Everyone thought I was a goner, twice, but I fooled them. I'm too ornery to die."

"When I was waking up," Edgar recounted, "I could hear my kids talking. They were talking as if I was already gone. I yelled over to them, 'Dammit, I am not dead yet!'" Edgar would tell that story again and again. He survived. Dammit, he wasn't dead yet. He beat the odds. He would beat the odds for another six years

His children meant no disrespect to their father by talking <u>about</u> him rather than <u>to</u> him. For many days as he lay in ICU, their dad was sedated and unresponsive. His prognosis for survival was slim. He could not hear their conversations, so they spoke freely around his bed. As he awoke from unconsciousness, they continued that habit. But their dad, in his usual straightforward way, reminded them he was still among the living.

How we talk among the dying, or those who should be dying but are too ornery to die, is important. Too often we who are able-bodied with good hearing assume the patient lying quietly in bed, unable to speak and appearing to be in their final days, doesn't hear us. The truth is we don't know what the dying person hears or doesn't. Physicians tell us the sense of hearing is the last to fail. Aunt Maggie or Uncle Fred may be hearing the conversation better than we think.

When we are in a room with sick or dying patients, it is important to include them in the conversation. Yes, they may not hear us. Yes, it may seem awkward. They may be incapable of communicating back, but we include them. It shows our respect for the living. They haven't passed over yet. They are still among us. Speaking with them and not about them, we uphold their dignity and are mindful of their feelings. If we need to talk about issues regarding the patient we think would make them uncomfortable if overheard, it is best to step out of the room.

If patients indicate their desire to pass on, it can be good to talk about funeral arrangements in the presence of the patient, if they are comfortable doing so. As we talk, we include them in the conversation, even if they are not able to respond. We exchange ideas about favorite music, Scriptures and other things to include in the memorial service. We discuss who might participate. We express our love. We tell of our hope in God. We share memories of good times. We give thanks for ways our lives have been touched. As we speak, we try to honor the life and legacy of the one dying.

I have been in rooms where a dying loved one lingers and family members become impatient for death. The loved one is ready to pass. The family is ready. The medical staff thinks death is imminent, but day after day goes by and Aunt Maggie or Uncle Fred hangs on through no fault of their own. I hear comments around the bedside like 'if she doesn't die today we can't have the service Saturday and I will have to cancel my vacation' or 'if he keeps going a couple more days, my boss won't give me more time off.' Some of us have busy schedules and death complicates our lives, especially long, drawn out deaths. We may have to forego plans and incur inconveniences, but keep those conversations out of the patient's room. Let us not afflict our loved one with unnecessary and undeserved guilt in their dying moments. Celebrate the time you are in the presence of your loved one.

Unless it is clear the patient is longing to be released from this earthly body, always, always, keep hope and be positive. Critically ill patients live on hope. Never take hope away. One young mother told me of receiving news from the oncologist that her six-year-old daughter had leukemia. The oncologist told her it was very serious and they would do everything they could to defeat the disease. He outlined the treatment protocol and what they might expect. He didn't minimize the gravity of the disease but the mother left the physician's office feeling hopeful that just maybe their daughter might prevail. As they walked down the hall after leaving the oncologist's office, a young resident motioned them into a consulting room. The young oncology resident said to them, "I don't know what Dr. So-and-So told you, but I want you to know this form of leukemia is a death sentence for your daughter. She will die. I don't want you to walk out with false hope." This young mother was devastated. She said the only thing she had was hope and this young, know-it-all resident took it away.

I received a call one day that Todd was struck by a bus. With severe brain injuries, he was comatose, not likely to live. If he lived, it was doubtful he would ever enjoy a satisfying quality of life. I performed the wedding service for Todd and Jennifer a year earlier. They were young, bright and ambitious, both of them attorneys. Todd worked for a large law firm in the state capital. He was in the crosswalk of a busy street, walking to the state house on legal business when a bus, turning the corner, struck him. I drove an hour to his hospital and was met by Jennifer's mother in the ICU waiting room. She explained the seriousness of the situation, and then, before I went to see Todd, she said, "When we are with Todd, we are only thinking positive thoughts and we are only saying positive things."

Seeing someone following a traumatic brain injury is very difficult – the shaved, bruised, bloody, swollen head with drainage tubes, IV's, monitors, and wires seemingly everywhere. Jennifer was by his side soothing an arm, telling him how much she loved him and how much she looked forward to his healing. I didn't ask how he was doing. I think I just talked about their deep love for one another and how that love, combined with Christ's love, would bring strength and healing.

Every time someone visited Todd they were reminded to think only positive thoughts and say only positive things. The positive thoughts, prayers, Todd's determination, Jennifer's love, or the excellent medical care worked. Something worked because in the weeks and months following, Todd recovered and went home. He was not able to resume his high-pressured position at the law firm but he enjoyed a high quality of life. He practiced law in other ways. A couple of years later Jennifer gave birth to twins. He was a very proud and thankful dad.

We don't give up hope because we never know when miracles will happen. A miracle happened to Jeremy when he was 11 years old. He was hit by a car and received, everyone assumed, a traumatic brain injury that would soon lead to death. His mother never gave up hope. Jeremy spent months and years in rehab, but he prevailed then, and continues to prevail today.

I met Jeremy more than 20 years after his accident. He talks in a slow drawl and walks with jerks and lurches. Sometimes he shows cognitive impairment and he still endures much pain from the accident. But Jeremy is a determined man. He lobbies before the State House and Congress for better care for victims of Traumatic Brain Injury. Our church supported his efforts and I had the privilege of accompanying him on one of his annual trips to Washington D.C. As I drove to the Capital he was busy working his phone, setting up appointments. I overheard him chewing out an administrative assistant in the Vice President's office for not returning his call. Once we arrived Jeremy walked through the halls of Congress with tenacity and spunk, announcing himself at appointments with a voice of authority. I followed behind with a legal pad to take notes. Jeremy wore a white shirt, coat and tie. I was in shirt sleeves. People knew who was in charge.

Miracles happen every day. Is God answering our prayers? God's power breaking into this world of ours? Positive energy flowing from one person to another? Breakthroughs of modern medicine? Or just plain coincidence? I never know for sure but I always give thanks to God. I never presume to know the mind of God. I simply choose to be grateful for what I believe is the abiding presence of a loving and gracious Savior.

CHAPTER 73

For All the Saints

I looked at the alarm clock by the side of my bed. It was 3:30 a.m. on Holy Saturday, the day before Easter. The phone was ringing. Most calls during the night came from the church's security company telling me, per contract, that either telephone service or electric power at the church building had been interrupted. It was nothing to worry about, just our fire alarm system was inoperative until service was restored. "Hello," I answered in a 3:30 a.m. voice. "This is Ellen. I am at the emergency room. Howard just died." I could only cry out, "No, no, no!" I quickly dressed and rushed to the hospital.

Ellen was Howard's daughter-in-law. Howard was one of the truest saints of the church I ever met, and a dear friend. In the ministry, we don't just bury parishioners, we bury friends. We bury those whom we come to love very deeply. Their deaths leave emptiness not just in their immediate families. It leaves emptiness within the church family and within me. When they die suddenly from a heart attack, as Howard did, the news is shocking and upsetting to pastors, just as for everyone else. We grieve, we hurt, we cry. The pain of loss is very real. Sometimes, we are able to focus on needs of grieving loved ones and how best to minister to them. Sometimes all we can do is grieve alongside the family. Our hurt is so deep. Our eyes moisten during the memorial service. Our voice quivers when we make the Sunday morning announcement concerning their passing.

One difficult struggle serving a church a long time is saying goodbye to a growing number of cherished friends like Howard. Burying friends, with whom we have journeyed over many years, through conflicts and accomplishments, through dreams, plans, service, mission and worship, in good times and bad, can be heart-breaking. Striving together toward common goals, consoling one another amidst losses, celebrating jobs well done and persevering amidst day-in, day-out routines bind us together. When those friendships end in death, grief is real and grows heavy on our souls.

Early in my ministry I made the decision to limit myself to ten years in any particular congregation. I felt ten years was sufficient time to dwell within a congregation and affect change. I felt it would be difficult to sustain creativity and new ideas beyond that time. It would be too easy for the congregation and me to grow into a rut and become entrenched. We would be content with less than what God calls us to be. If I stayed more than 10 years it would be a more difficult transition for my successor. What I didn't realize then, but do now, is the longer we pastors stay in one place, the deeper the hurts when beloved friends in the church pass away. Deep, intimate friendships grow in ministry. Burying friends is a painful part of the calling.

In Howard I buried a friend. I grieved my loss. I also buried a great saint of the church and I grieved the loss for the church. Howard was 89 years old, the youngest 89-year old man I ever met. He was handsome with a full head of beautiful white hair. He stood erect and still walked with a bounce in his step. His eyes twinkled, his smile ever-present. He cared for flower beds and planters around the church. They were always beautiful. Howard loved the church and would do anything for it. He loved his Lord Jesus Christ and would do anything for him. He was humble, sincere and honest, his motives always pure, his comments positive and his love genuine. Every time he was in the church building, he popped his head into my office, smiled, and said, "What's the good word for today?" I loved Howard's interruptions.

In my eulogies, I try to portray the deceased in realistic, familiar terms. I don't try to make a saint out of a scoundrel. But Howard was a saint through and through. In my remarks at the memorial service I rejoiced in a life well-lived, a life to be emulated and followed by others. I sought to paint a picture of a world if everyone lived as Howard. Here are excerpts from my message:

"First of all, the world would be joyful, a happy place. Howard greeted everyone with a smile. Everyone. He was always positive, upbeat, never spoke a mean word against anyone, incapable of holding a grudge. He made it a point to know everyone, took an interest in them. His smile was contagious, the twinkle in his eye infectious, with just a hint of mischievousness. You felt good, happy, and joyful after talking with Howard. His enthusiasm and positive attitude rubbed off on you. Everyone feels special in Howard's world.

"Second, it would be a world without need. I don't think anyone would go hungry. No one would be homeless. Everyone would be taken care of because Howard possessed an expansive generosity. His tender spirit was easily moved. He was willing to give of himself and his resources without holding back. His delight in life was serving and helping others. It was never about himself. In Howard's world every person would be looked after. No one left out. A caring, giving world.

"The world would be a place of humble service. You give not only with your money. You serve with your time and talents and energy. You do whatever needs to be done. And you aren't recognized or lifted up when you do it, because it is very embarrassing when that happens. You turn beet red. Howard always deflected attention away from himself. He just wanted to serve, and was happiest if he wasn't singled out for what he did.

"Next, the world would be a prosperous world. Howard was a hard worker. Raised on a farm, he came about a strong work ethic naturally. He worked hard all his life. Even at age 89, he was keeping up his lawn and flowers at home, at the vacation house, at the Insurance Agency, and at the church. Howard was always in great physical shape. That work ethic served him well as he developed his milk route as a young man, and then as he began the Insurance Agency. He went door-to-door calling on folks. When someone moved into town, Howard was on their doorstep before the moving van left, introducing himself, offering his services as an insurance agent, and also inviting them to church.

"It would be a beautiful world if we were all Howards because Howard loved beauty. With all the flowers that Howard planted each year, Howard graced us with a lot of beauty. He kept the planters and flower gardens at the church looking gorgeous, watering and pruning them until frost in the fall. Every year he said this would be his last year tending the flowers, but the next spring he was excited to tell me his plans for the new year.

"It would also be a world of progress. Howard was eternally youthful, always open to new ideas, active in the lives of young people, wanting to know about what was happening in the world, encouraging people to try things that were new and different.

"Howard's world strives for justice. Howard was concerned for the rights of all people, especially the poor, the forgotten and the oppressed. From the civil rights marches of the 1950's and 60's for Open Housing and Equal Opportunity to the more recent struggles of the LGBT community, Howard advocated for full rights and liberties for all people. Everyone is welcomed in his world, no one excluded.

"And Howard's world would be a world of peace. Howard was a good listener, and sought to understand the feelings and views of all. He never insisted on his own way. Howard would never ever willingly harm another person by word or deed. To do so would have grieved him terribly.

"In Howard's world everyone would know about Jesus. Howard's passion was his faith. He loved the Lord. His greatest desire was to be a steadfast servant of God. He talked about his faith so simply and enthusiastically you couldn't help but want to join and follow Jesus also."

We all wish we lived in such a world. If we all lived like Howard, we would experience such a world. I believe people who inspire us most in life are not ones we read about in books or see on the news. The most inspiring people are the saints next door. When we concluded Howard's memorial service singing "For All the Saints," everyone knew we were singing about Howard. When I closed the committal service with the words, "Howard has received the crown of life, the crown reserved for all who love and serve the Lord," all knew it was true. We were grieving and shedding a tear for one of the truest saints we ever met.

Nearly all churches have some dear saints like Howard. Their faithfulness to the gospel and selfless service blesses and strengthens the whole congregation in ways the congregation doesn't realize. The ministry of the church is carried forward on the faith of these saints.

CHAPTER 74

It's Always about You

The church's retired men's group gathered for breakfast at the local café on the town square the second Tuesday of the month. It was November, season of Thanksgiving. Someone suggested we go around the table and tell what we are thankful for. We talked about families and children, freedoms we have in our country, health and how good it was to be alive. When Guy's turn came, he said, "I am thankful for Velma. I was just an old bachelor high school history teacher when Velma rescued me and brought a great deal of joy into my life."

I nearly choked on my blueberry pancakes. I think others choked on fried eggs, oatmeal or whatever. Velma was Guy's wife for nearly 50 years. To express thankfulness for one's longtime companion seems the natural thing to do. But we all knew Velma. Velma was a holy terror, though it was hard to find much holy about her. There are many names I could use to describe her and none are good. We all felt sorry for Guy for having married Velma. Guy was a sweet man, kind-hearted and giving. We all felt life played a cruel trick on Guy by giving him Velma as his wife. But Guy was sincere in his thankfulness. He loved Velma. How? No one knew, but he did.

When I began at the church, I quickly learned Velma did not like any of my predecessors and she would not like me either. I met politicians in town who received long disagreeable letters from her. A principal of an elementary school, upon arriving at his new school, was given the "Velma folder" containing the correspondence and communication between her and the school. Teachers told how they dreaded having one of Guy and Velma's daughters in their classes. They knew it would mean long, ugly conversations with Velma. A neighbor of theirs told me of the vile language she used when calling her daughters home for dinner.

Everyone in town knew Velma, and everyone was scared of her caustic tongue and scathing letters.

I get along with most people, but not with Velma, not at all. I stopped talking with her one on one or trying to answer her letters. The letters began reasonably with what seemed to be a valid concern. They degenerated into spurious accusations and outlandish ideas. She talked of my unfitness as a pastor. She was going to leave the church. I called together our church's Pastoral Relations Committee to deal with her concerns and mediate her differences with me and the church.

At one such meeting she was upset some women in the church began a breakfast group at the same time as the retired men's breakfast group. Velma wanted to go but Guy and Velma only had one car. Velma said the time prevented her from attending the women's gathering. She asked the women to change the time but they refused. She was not used to people in the church telling her 'no.' I explained to Velma several men gladly offered Guy a ride to the breakfast. She could drive to the women's gathering. That wasn't good enough. She was adamant the women chose the time to exclude her. She said they didn't want her in the group. That wasn't right in a church. I explained she was welcome to attend the women's gathering but they were not going to change the time just because she wanted it.

At a Pastoral Relations Committee meeting, Velma repeated her threat to leave the church. The committee members said they were sorry to hear it, but sometimes people have to change churches to find the spiritual support they desire. Guy always accompanied Velma to the meetings but never spoke. Guy had no complaint with the church. He loved Velma. He also loved the church.

Finally, Guy spoke when Velma said she would leave the church. With his head bowed and tears in his eyes, he whispered softly to Velma, "What about me? I love the church." I am sure it took a great deal of courage for Guy to speak. He looked like a broken, defeated man. He was a sweet, gentle, caring soul and caught between his love for Velma and his love for the church. My heart was breaking for him. He was suffering. He wanted Velma to acknowledge his feelings, desires, and existence so much.

I wasn't prepared for Velma's retort. "It's always about you," she said to Guy rather curtly, "always about you." I think my heart snapped at that point. Was there no compassion, no feeling for this man who loved her so much? How could she be so hurtful to someone who cared for her for nearly 50 years? Life was never about Guy. Life was always about Velma, but that wasn't Velma's view of the world. Domineering people belittle and demean others imputing their own ugly and malicious behaviors on them.

I then told Velma about the retired men's breakfast group and how, when we went around the table expressing our thankfulness, Guy said, "I am thankful for Velma. I was just an old bachelor high school history teacher when Velma rescued me and brought a great deal of joy into my life." Surely, I thought, that would soften her heart, but no. She responded, "Are you trying to make me feel guilty? Is this pick on Velma night?" The meeting broke up. I went to my office and cried.

Velma's words reminded me of similar words I heard one night walking through Chicago's elegant Lincoln Park neighborhood. Our family walked to a restaurant amidst beautiful brownstones, places only the wealthy could afford. A couple in their early 40's walked out of one of the lovely homes and began to approach us. They were tall, slender and both stunningly attractive in their long leather coats. "These are the beautiful people in the world," I said to myself as the couple neared. Then I overheard just one brief excerpt from their conversation as they passed us on the sidewalk. The beautiful woman said to the handsome man, "It's always about you, isn't it?" Maybe life wasn't so grand in the elegant brownstones of Lincoln Park after all.

Velma kept her promise this time. She went to the Methodist church. A short time later she was diagnosed with cancer. Her health declined rapidly. She fell out with the Pastor of Visitation and Senior Pastor, but blessedly connected with the Associate Pastor. I went to visiting hours when she died, and greeted Guy. It was good to see him again. When I greeted one of their daughters she wondered whether cancer was present for some time and made her mother into the holy terror. Being Velma's daughter must not have been easy.

I called on Guy a couple of times after Velma's death. He lived in an assisted living facility where members of my congregation also lived. I couldn't help but think he seemed more peaceful and at rest than I had ever seen him. Perhaps it was just my imagination, though others who knew him said the same thing. We didn't talk about Velma.

I think Guy really loved Velma and saw in her things the rest of us could never begin to see. He had a great capacity for love. Maybe his love was modelled after the love of our Savior, Jesus Christ. How many times have we broken Jesus' heart with things we have said and done? How many times have his eyes moistened when he sees callousness in our hearts? Yet, he never gives up on us. He continues to love us despite our inability to love in return.

CHAPTER 75

No One Should Have to Die Like This

Clayton lay in bed at the beautiful new hospice center. His private room had wood paneling and a large picture window looking out onto a garden and county park. The room offered a foldout sofa for a family member, comfortable chairs, a large flat screen television, pleasing artwork, soft carpeting and gentle music. Decorations and colors were carefully chosen. It flowed together seamlessly to evoke calm and peace. The hospice center had massage tables and whirlpool tubs for patients, quiet lounges and dining rooms for family members. The center offered the latest in palliative care. Staff were carefully trained and chosen to care for the dying. Chaplains offered prayer, counsel and faith. It was a beautiful place to die. In the 3 years the center was open, I sat there with several parishioners as they said goodbye to friends, family and this earthly existence. Clayton, I felt, was receiving the best care available.

Dying evolved greatly in my 30+ years of ministry. Luxurious accommodations did not exist for the dying when I began. Nor did advances in pain management and palliative care. Morphine and other painkillers were used sparingly. Physicians were reluctant to prescribe medication that may hasten the dying process. Death was intended to be natural. Death struggles seemed prolonged. Labored breathing of the dying continued for days. It was heart-wrenching for families to sit at the bedside and watch their loved one suffer.

Now caregivers and medical personnel consider the dignity of the dying. They listen to their wishes. They honor and respect their personhood. Hospice care gives thoughtful and considerate care to the journey of the patient during the final days. Dying does not seem to be the tortuous journey it once was.

So, I was a little startled when Clayton's wife, Nina, said, "No one should have to die like this." Yes, Clayton was struggling for breath. Yes, painkillers did not take away all of his pain. Yes, he thrashed in bed. I saw these things countless times in dying patients. I took them for granted. Even with the best hospice care, suffering and pain were inevitable. Death often didn't come easily. That was the cycle of life and death.

Nina sought an alternative to hospice, something illegal in the state where I lived, but legal in a few states around the nation. Nina sought physician-assisted death for Clayton. Clayton agreed. Drugs and the means to make death more merciful were available. We send pets to their next journey in as pain-free a way as possible. Why can't we do the same for family members? Why can't we die on our own terms in the manner we choose? Why do we have to accept the kind of death our terminal illness dictates? Why can't we say goodbye to family and friends with dignity and grace before the debilitating and ravaging effects of disease make it impossible? Nina preferred another way.

The first time I heard a parishioner wish for something like physician-assisted death was 30 years earlier. Harry and Irene were a childless older couple in the church. I watched as Irene succumbed to the effects of Alzheimer's. In a couple of brief years she went from healthy, intelligent and communicative to babbling in a wheelchair, unable to recognize even her husband. I watched from a distance, but Harry watched at his wife's side every day, seeing her slide into a world of oblivion, no longer recognizable as the woman he loved for more than 50 years. Harry was educated, thoughtful, articulate, and voiced strong opinions. He became angry, angry he could do nothing to help his wife, angry she had to endure the indignities and shame of Alzheimer's. She shouldn't have to endure such a wretched existence.

On visits with Harry I began to recognize he was repeating himself more often. He forgot words, phrases and people. Harry, of course, knew it also. He knew the symptoms of Alzheimer's too well, and he knew its progression. He understood well what would happen. He confided in me, "I am going to be just like Irene soon, and there is not a damn thing I can do about it. That is not the way to live. I should be able to choose to die the way I want to die. No one should have to go through what Irene has gone through." Each visit, Harry got a little worse. Finally, the once-articulate man could no longer carry on a conversation. He sat in his wheelchair babbling, just like Irene before him.

A few years after my conversation with Harry, Dr. Kevorkian began assisting people like Harry to realize their wish of dying with dignity. He spent 8 years in prison for it.

Many times in my ministry I have sat in homes and hospital rooms of parishioners who were asking, "Why can't I just die? Why do I have to go on living like this? I don't want to live if I am not going to be in my right mind. That is not life." Sometimes the parishioner was in the early stage of Alzheimer's or another form of dementia. Sometimes it was another debilitating illness. They were distressed at what lay ahead. They didn't want to endure it. There was no point in enduring it. To them it was not life, at least life of any significant quality. They were ready to die. Why couldn't they just do it now?

And sometimes, they were just tired of living. They had aches and pains. Each day was a struggle. Their friends and loved ones had died. They were lonely. They had no purpose. Life no longer had meaning. Death was a release. They were ready to move on.

I read where the hunter-gatherers, our human ancestors thousands of years ago, had a simple way of dealing with the aged who could no longer keep up with the tribe. A young man would sneak up behind an old woman and dispatch her with a quick blow of the tomahawk. That seems heartless and cruel. It seems to cheapen human life but the demands of getting by were great and resources for coping with the infirmed and aged were limited in such a society. I suppose they did what they had to do.

We have greater resources and means today. Ethical questions surrounding physician-assisted death are many and deep. What does death with dignity look like? What kind of choices do we leave to the individual and what do we reserve for the wider community? Is the taking of life ever justified? How do we value and love our elderly population? How do we allocate limited resources? Do we always do so with efficiency in mind? What kind of unfair expectations do we place on the elderly? Questions go on and on.

None of us wish to end our final days, perhaps years, strapped into a wheelchair in the hallway of a nursing home, slumping over the feeding tray, drool dripping from our mouths, as we yell "Help me! Help me!" to everyone who walks by. I tell my children to take me out behind the barn and shoot me, problematic since we do not have a barn or a gun. I want them to know if there comes a time when they have to make decisions, perhaps life and death decisions, regarding my care and future, they can do so without guilt. They do not need to extend a life no longer worth living. I believe my future is with the God who created me and loves me still. My days on this earth are numbered. They have been numbered since the day I was born.

The family put the following in Clayton's obituary in the local newspaper:

> *"Clayton – a lifelong Republican and a Christian – believed everyone should have the power to determine when and how their lives end. His family and the Hospice cared for him as best they could with the tools available, but Clayton would have chosen an earlier departure if Ohioans had a legal right to die – something he and his family support."*

His wife, Nina, hopes the law is changed when her time to die draws near.

CHAPTER 76

Blink Your Eyes

We looked into Norma's eyes and reviewed her condition once again. "You fractured your spinal cord when you fell. You understand that? Blink your eyes once if you understand." Norma blinked her eyes. She understood. "The injury is permanent. There is nothing doctors can do to fix it. You understand that?" Norma again blinked her eyes. "You will never again be able to move your body below your neck. You understand? You will never walk again." Again, Norma blinked. "A ventilator is breathing for you now. You know that?" She affirmed she knew. "For as long as you live, the ventilator will need to do your breathing. For as long as you live you will have feeding tubes. For as long as you live you will be confined to bed. You understand all that?" Yes, she did. "Your mind is sharp. There is nothing wrong with your mind." Yes, she knew that also. "Do you want to remain on the ventilator and continue to live? If so, blink." She did not blink. "If you are taken off the ventilator you will probably die in a short time. You understand that?" And she blinked. "Do you want to be taken off the ventilator?" Norma blinked. Norma made it very clear what she wanted. She was ready to move on and see what God had in store for her.

It was the Monday after Father's Day. Carolyn and I drove three hours to Indiana after Sunday worship to spend Father's Day evening with my dad. When Lawrence called on my cell phone, we were having breakfast at Bob Evans with my parents. Our intention was to drive the hour and a half further and have lunch with Carolyn's parents before returning home. Instead we canceled lunch and drove directly to the hospital to be with Lawrence and Norma.

Norma was nearly 89 years old. She and her husband, Lawrence, lived active, full lives. They enjoyed satisfying careers, pursued many hobbies and interests, travelled to more than 80 countries, and were blessed with many dear friends, children and grandchildren. In recent years Norma was finding it difficult to slow down even though her body was telling her otherwise. Her eyesight was failing fast. She walked with a cane and sometimes a walker. Still, she and Lawrence did as much as possible. They continued to enjoy Road Scholar trips and frequently attended concerts and community events. They were in church every Sunday. Norma didn't like the physical limitations of growing old. She didn't think of herself as old but she couldn't deny what was happening to her body.

As Lawrence and I sat by Norma's bedside, Lawrence said to her, "I always knew you were feisty." Norma tried to shake her head as best she could. "You're not feisty, Norma?" I asked. "No," she tried shaking her head again. Lawrence often accused her of being feisty, but she always denied it. If feisty means having exuberance for life, Norma was feisty. She was gutsy. She would try anything. Life was to be full and lived with passion. She had a glint in her eyes, liveliness in her step, and playful spirit in all of life. She also had tenacious stubbornness and dogged perseverance. Norma always asked for "My Way" to be played at her memorial service. Perhaps there was feistiness in her request.

As much as someone can be feisty when paralyzed from the neck down and hooked to a ventilator, Norma was still feisty. She knew what she wanted. She understood the risks. She understood the life and death decision she was making. As much as she enjoyed life and pursued it with passion, she was now willing to say goodbye. She knew her time on earth was complete. Living attached to a breathing machine and feeding tube was not what she wanted.

During my ministry, I have sat with several families at the bedside of loved ones when they were disconnected from a ventilator. We sent the loved one to the Lord bathed in prayer, with faith God would receive them safely on the other side of death. Sometimes in a few brief minutes, sometimes through interminably long hours, the patient passed away. With Norma it was different. No other parishioner was conscious. They were all considered 'brain dead.' The family made the decision to remove the ventilator, not the patient. The family was honoring what they believed to be the desire of their loved one, to release them from the captivity of their body so they could pass on to the Lord. Those patients were not able to blink their consent at the final point of decision.

I have also sat with numerous parishioners who knew they would pass away within 24-48 hours. Death was soon and inevitable. They were perfectly lucid and fully aware within two days they would be gone. These parishioners, too, were different from Norma. There was nothing they could do to sustain their lives. They were accepting the inescapable.

Norma, fully aware and lucid, chose to have her ventilator disconnected. She could prolong her life. Some might argue it would not be much of a life paralyzed and attached to a ventilator. Others would say life is always better than death, the knowable preferable to the unknowable. Many persons have lived that way and through grit, determination and care from loved ones, discovered a satisfying quality of life. Perhaps if Norma were a younger woman she would not have been so firm in her decision. Maybe, also, Norma was willing to make this decision because she had pursued life to the fullest. She did not have regrets.

Norma was ready. She made the decision to move forward with courage and faith. With Norma's consent we set the time to disconnect the ventilator for the next day, Tuesday. The next 24 hours would give an opportunity for all her children to be with her and all her grandchildren to give her one last phone call. Tuesday the last child arrived from California to be with her mother. When the phone call from the last grandchild ended, Norma nodded she was ready. We went to the nurse's station and told them it was time.

Unfortunately, the attending physician had yet to sign the order. He was busy on rounds with his residents and was not available. The family had been perturbed with his gruff bedside manner the day before and waited impatiently for him to arrive. It was an odd period of time, patient and family ready to move on to death but unable. The physician was not welcomed by the family when he arrived followed by his entourage of residents. The family preferred he not see Norma at all. They didn't want her disturbed at this time. But he was firm saying he needed to make sure of Norma's consent before he signed the orders. He agreed to leave his entourage in the hallway. The physician was quick. He signed the orders and, as the nurse stood by with the sedating medication, we had a prayer of commitment for Norma. The children each said a final goodbye and the respiratory therapist unplugged the machine. I have always felt sad for therapists who have the duty of unplugging the respirator. I am not sure of ethical and professional procedures in such situations but it seems physicians and nurses are not permitted to do the final act.

Norma did not expire quickly. Waiting was difficult on the family. I ran into the physician outside the elevator. He asked how things were going. He seemed genuinely concerned. I sensed he felt badly his relationship with the family had not gone well. Norma finally passed away and took her feistiness on to heaven.

We were not able to hold her service in the sanctuary. Our church was in the midst of a large construction project and much of our building not accessible. The family understood and was content to have the service at the funeral home. There, we listened to Frank Sinatra sing "My Way" over the speaker system, and fondly remembered Norma.

Not many of us will have decisions to make as Norma did. Death will come on its terms and not ours. I pray if I ever have that final decision to make, I will be able to make my final decision, whatever it is, with faith and courage, trusting in the goodness of the God whom I have proclaimed all these years.

CHAPTER 77

I Have Paid My Debt to Society

I visited with Roy in the gathering area of the old rooming house where he lived. At one time the rooming house was the residence of one of the leading families in the community. It sat amidst other once-stately houses where other members of the family once lived. I don't think any of the houses were single-family homes any more. They were rooming houses, apartments or offices. None were restored except for the old original family homestead, lovingly preserved as offices for the family business.

Roy's rooming house was home to 8 – 10 men living in small single rooms, most with bathrooms down the hall. As Roy and I talked a few men gathered on the porch. Others came and went, always greeting each other cheerily. They seemed to know each other well. I sensed the house was more than a place to lay one's head. It was also a supportive community.

Roy was in his mid-70's, slender and reserved. He called and introduced himself shortly after I arrived at my new parish. He called to tell me he was a registered sex offender. He served his time in prison and now was seeking to rebuild a shattered life. As Roy said, "I have paid my debt to society." Roy attended our early morning chapel service.

The interim pastor who preceded me told me about Roy. Knowing the concerns a congregation might have about a registered sex offender in attendance Sunday morning, Roy sought permission to worship. The church offered an early morning worship service in our chapel. Generally, children did not attend the service. The interim pastor and Roy signed an agreement he would attend that service only, entering and leaving through the door next to the chapel. He would not enter the Christian Education hallways where children might be present. The rules were meant to protect not just the children, but also Roy from false accusations.

I told Roy I was happy he was attending worship. He was welcome and I hoped he would continue his weekly participation. After our meeting, I checked the online sex offender registry and saw he was convicted of the rape of a mentally disabled adult.

Sex offenders are perhaps the greatest outcasts and pariahs in our society. They are required to register at each new address. There are restrictions on where they can live. Laws are designed to protect the innocent, especially children, to prevent them from harm by sexual predators. Parents and caregivers have a right to know if neighbors present a risk to their children. But how do we protect our children and also give those who "have paid their debt" an opportunity to begin anew? It is a difficult topic: protecting the innocent while giving hope and new life to the felon and miscreant.

In my preaching I sometimes craft stories through which I seek to capture the spirit and message of the biblical passage. I find stories break down the self-defenses that argue for our own righteousness and innocence. Stories open us to new insights and understandings through the leading of God's Spirit. About 15 years before meeting Roy, I wrote a story for a congregation on Luke 18:10-14, the story of the Pharisee and tax collector going to the temple to pray. The Pharisee gives thanks for his own righteousness and goodness. The tax collector beats his breast, standing far off, pleading for mercy as a sinner before God. For Jesus, the tax collector went home justified before God and not the Pharisee. "For all who exalt themselves will be humbled," Jesus says, "but all who humble themselves will be exalted."

In the story I created, people come to the church to offer prayers on a Day of Repentance proclaimed by feeble-minded Pastor Hinklemyer. I used the characters of Salvation Sam, Feminist Felicia and Rotary Ron as pharisaical types in our own times. Each, in their own way, went home from church feeling satisfied and smug, content with their life and themselves. In their world they were good people, ones who had it all figured out and did the right things. For the tax collector types, I used Raunchy Ralph and Silent Sylvester. Silent Sylvester was a sex offender released from prison. Just as the tax collector was the greatest outcast in Jesus's day, I thought the sex offender was the greatest outcast today. Sylvester was scared as he entered the chapel and treaded lightly toward the altar. Church was an alien place for him. It was a holy place, too holy for someone such as himself. "Have mercy on me, O God!" he whispered and darted from the chapel.

I concluded the sermon saying I didn't know who went home justified before God after Pastor Hinklemyer's Day of Repentance. Only God knew. But Jesus tells us sometimes those who are justified before God are not ones we might expect. I thought I might receive critical feedback from the congregation for casting a sex offender in a possibly positive light, but I didn't.

I sensed in Roy a true humility. He was sorry for what he did. He sought God's mercy. He paid his debt. He lost his family and everything dear to him. He wanted very much to begin anew. I wanted the church to be on his side.

I serve in a denomination priding itself on welcoming all persons. No matter who you are or where you are on your journey of faith, you are welcome in our churches. How far do we extend our welcome? Welcoming everyone has risks. It has risks because it may upset our comfortable world. It may challenge us to re-think stereotypes or re-imagine the stepping stones of our faith. When we invite everyone to worship we risk disturbing many equilibriums around us. Welcoming sex offenders, we risk something more precious, the safety of our children. Can we include registered sex offenders? If so, will our children be safe? What will their parents think?

Roy brought a friend to worship one Sunday, a handsome 30-year-old man, Justin, who lived in Roy's rooming house. He, too, was a registered sex offender recently released from prison, as were several men living in the rooming house. The owner of the house felt called to a ministry of helping these 'pariahs of society' get a fresh start when they left prison. Lodging was difficult for a sex offender. This landlord offered a safe and welcoming place to call home. It explained the close-knit, supportive community I observed when I first visited Roy.

When I checked the sex offender registry on Justin I discovered his presence was more problematic than Roy's. Justin was not only young, his offenses were perpetrated against children. I visited with Justin in the rooming house and he agreed to the same terms as Roy, terms to isolate Justin from children in the church. After a couple of weeks, Justin expressed interest in attending our contemporary service because of his preference for its type of music. This was a service where children were present. As a pastor I must protect the safety of our children, but I also wanted to work toward restoring Justin to society. Justin had taken positive steps in that direction, returning to college to complete his engineering degree even though his tainted background may preclude him from meaningful work in the engineering field.

I told Justin that to attend the contemporary service, I would recruit someone who would be with him from the time he left our chapel service to the time he left our property. Again, it would not only protect our children but also Justin from false accusations. I approached a retired Superintendent of Schools in our congregation. I knew he would understand the seriousness of welcoming a young man accused of sexually predatory behavior against children into our worship. If he agreed to be Justin's companion he would carry out his duties diligently. He was also an easy-going and compassionate man who might be a good friend for Justin. When I approached the retired Superintendent with the idea he was honest, as usual. He spent his whole career protecting children from sexual predators. Children were precious and he wasted no sympathy on those who would abuse them in any way. He said he would have to do a lot of praying and soul-searching before he said yes in welcoming such a person to worship where children were present. I understood. In the meantime Justin found a job keeping him away from church on Sunday mornings. He also soon found a church home where his parents worshipped. The last time I saw Justin he completed his engineering degree and was working as an intern with the hope of being hired permanently.

Protecting the innocent and vulnerable from predators while giving hope to sex offenders is not easy. If we err on the side of leniency without proper safeguards, we risk the safety of our children and others. If we err on the side of judgment, we deny hope and reconciliation to those who need it most. Unfortunately in the church, I think we err too often on the side of judgment with respect to lay folks and on the side of leniency when it pertains to pastors. Too many pastors betray the sacred vows of their calling, abusing and taking advantage of the vulnerable, without proper discipline and restitution to those who were harmed. It has been far too prevalent in all traditions of the church. We have not been honest with parishioners and have set a double standard, one for laity and one for clergy. It hurts our witness to the gospel of Jesus Christ and diminishes the integrity of the church.

Roy continued to worship at the chapel service. I don't know if others knew his background, but he found a spiritual home with us. After a few years, Roy moved to a nearby city and had increasing health issues, including hip surgery. Attendance at worship became more difficult for him. When he was able to attend, I enjoyed seeing him limping through the door to his usual place in the pew. During my final Easter season at the church, Carolyn and I stopped to see Roy and deliver an Easter lily. He seemed happy. His relationships with his children had been restored and he was on friendly terms with his ex-wife, caring for her in her battle with cancer. Roy lost so much. It took many years to get it back. I sensed Roy felt blessed. I am thankful the church was able, in some way, to be with Roy in his journey back to wholeness.

CHAPTER 78

The Finest People I Have Ever Met Have Come through These Doors

The first thing you noticed about Tom was goiters drooping from his chin and cheeks. They were huge. I had never seen anything like it before. The second thing you noticed about Tom was his gentle, humble smile. That smile made you forget the first thing.

Tom was sitting in the back of the small chapel when I walked in half an hour before the 8:15 am service was to begin. It was my first Sunday at the parish. I couldn't think of a better person to see so early in the morning. Tom painfully rose to shake my hand. His knees were in bad shape and he would soon have double knee replacement surgery to ease the pain. Tom's smile welcomed everyone to worship. He introduced himself, and proudly said he had been a member since 1944. He ushered for more than 50 years before he retired, head usher much of that time. He still ushered for the small chapel, but not the larger sanctuary service. I knew instantly I would love Tom.

He then said words I would hear him repeat many times to new member classes over the years, "The finest people I have ever met have come through these doors." In the next eight years I served the congregation I came to know those folks who came through the doors well. I also heard stories of those who came through the doors before I arrived. Tom was right. Some of the finest people I ever met came through those doors. I met folks who were humble, kind, hard-working and had a deep love for Jesus. Their love was evident for others and for God's world.

They worked hard to make the church and the world a kinder, gentler, more giving and forgiving place. They blessed me as they blessed so many. I also heard stories of wonderfully grace-filled and kind-hearted people who were before me.

What Tom didn't say, and what Tom would never say, is some of the biggest S.O.B.'s also walked through those doors. They were judgmental, petty, self-righteous, and self-centered. I met some of them, too, and I heard stories of some who came before me. Tom would never talk in derogatory ways about anyone. He focused on what was good, uplifting and positive.

As head usher for many years, Tom greeted everyone who came to worship. He knew their names and made them feel welcome. Being head usher was a great privilege for him. His simplicity and humility represented the church well. The church was blessed to have him. A few years before my arrival, after Tom retired from ushering, the church initiated an award named after him. Each year the church presented the award to a member or couple who exemplified the years of hard-working, humble service Tom gave to the church. Generally, I am not fond of awards in the life of a church but I was grateful the church chose to honor Tom. During the years I served the church, it was a joy to present the award to those whom Tom called "the finest people I have ever met."

As Tom aged and his health became more debilitating, attendance on Sunday mornings became less frequent. Some Sunday mornings it was just too hard to get going that early. I always knew if Tom was going to be there, I would see him when I walked into the chapel a half hour before service time. Tom kept his habit of arriving early and greeting everyone who passed through the doors. Everyone looked forward to Tom's smile and "Good morning."

Churches with greeters like Tom are blessed. Established worshippers enjoy seeing the familiar face. New worshippers feel not just hospitality but warmth of Christian love. It creates an infectious atmosphere of caring and joy on Sunday morning. Another church I served also had a long-time greeter like Tom. His name was John. He stood outside the entrance Sunday after Sunday, year after year, greeting each worshipper. I heard stories from adults recalling John welcoming them when they were children. Long-time members often said he was the first person they met the first time they visited. John's ministry of hospitality was remembered years after he died. The church put a plaque at the spot where John stood greeting. The plaque read, "Always Ready with a Warm Hand and Heart."

One Easter Sunday Tom and another usher brought the offering forward. The little chapel was filled, including the front row. When Tom lifted his arms to give me the offering plate he had a wardrobe malfunction. His pants dropped. Quickly, considering his bad knees, he bent down and brought his pants up. Fortunately the crowded chapel prevented anyone, except the other usher, and perhaps a couple of people in the front, from seeing the wardrobe malfunction. I heard no gasp or laugh from the congregation when it happened. When I entered the chapel the next Sunday, Tom opened his jacket and showed off his new purchase. He smiled and said, "I got suspenders."

Tom's wife and son attended the nearby Lutheran Church where they served as custodians. When Tom and his wife were married more than 60 years earlier, they each loved their own church and agreed to continue worshipping in their church home. As they were faithful to one another, they were also faithful to their churches.

I received a call one day that Tom's son died. When his son didn't come over for dinner on time, Tom was concerned. Tom's son was punctual like his father. He also inherited the same thyroid condition Tom inherited from his father. He was single and relied on the emotional support of his parents. When Tom and his wife went to his apartment they found him passed away, apparently from a heart attack. When I visited Tom the ready smile was still there, but it was hard. He experienced perhaps the greatest loss we can endure, the loss of a child. As his simple trust in God always gave him strength to see the world with hope and grace, he found comfort amidst tragedy and trusted in the goodness of God.

Tom continued faithfully to attend our New Member classes. I was always happy to have Tom there offering his simple words about the "finest people" he ever met. His big smile, with big goiters drooping down the cheeks, summed up what was best about our church. It summed up the gospel of Jesus Christ. Evangelism isn't about slick marketing plans. It isn't about putting on a false front to appear successful and happy. In recent generations many churches have become inauthentic places to worship and grow in our walk with Jesus. Everything seems a little too polished for me. Tom offered a humble servant's heart, not showy or pretentious. When we said in our worship service, "No matter who you are or where you are on life's journey, you are welcome here," people sensed we meant it.

I needed Tom. It is easy to become discouraged, even bitter, serving churches. Church fights and disagreements can take a lot out of us. We become skewed in our view of the church. We become sour and dour. I needed Tom's smiling face and his positive outlook greeting me each Sunday to remind me "the finest people I have ever met" were coming through the doors of our church.

CHAPTER 79

Did You See the Front Page?

"Did you see the front page of this morning's paper?" the church financial secretary asked as I walked into the office. "No, why?" "Here," she said, "you better read it." Her voice sounded ominous.

The lead story told of an infant girl named Aria found dead in her crib by a cable TV technician. She had been dead for more than a month. Police picked up her father and older sister, Isabella, at a shopping mall in a nearby city. He was charged with abuse of a corpse, possession of drugs, and endangerment of a minor. Police said that further charges might be forthcoming. Aria had another sister who also died in her crib a few years earlier. I read the article but the connection to the church didn't register. The financial secretary then said, "That's our Isabella." Then I knew.

For the last few months Isabella attended our church with her grandfather. They sat in the very first row. Isabella was a cute, sweet six-year-old girl who quickly captured your heart. Carolyn taught her in Sunday School. Since they sat in the first row, I greeted her grandfather, Arthur, every Sunday during the Passing of the Peace. He was a personable, out-going, distinguished looking man in his late 60's. Our church had a Breadmakers hospitality ministry. Women baked bread on Monday afternoons. Drivers delivered the hot, freshly-baked bread to visitors, the recently hospitalized, the grieving, and others who could use a little pick-me-up from the wonderful aroma of bread just out of the oven. The man delivering bread to Arthur told me Arthur lived in a big house with a lake in the front yard. A couple of other men in the church knew Arthur through business connections. He was successful and well-respected by his peers. I didn't have Arthur's phone number or email. I never had more than a brief conversation with him.

We broke the news to our Director of Christian Education. Aria and her father had been to the church once, she said. She remembered meeting them. Aria stayed in our nursery.

I drove to Arthur's house that afternoon and rang the doorbell. I could see Arthur on the telephone in his study. I waited on the front steps until he was free. He had been on the phone all afternoon talking with attorneys, attorneys to represent his son and attorneys to gain custody of Isabella. The mother of Isabella, Aria and their late sister was a drug addict living in New York. Her cocaine addiction probably brought on the "failure to thrive" deaths of Aria and her next older sister. Arthur did not want Isabella returned to her mother. He and his wife would happily raise Isabella. She spent much time with them already because of their son's troubles. Their house had been her home.

Arthur was happy to see a friendly face. It was a stressful day, the kind of day no parent or grandparent should endure. Reporters and cameramen from big city news stations parked trucks with big satellite dishes in his long driveway all morning. It seemed like a heartless intrusion into the private life of a grieving grandfather but I suppose they were just doing their job. To them, it was sensational news. National news outlets picked up the story. It dominated headlines of our hometown newspaper for days. People relish stories with a hint of the macabre or scandal.

Arthur and Isabella continued to attend Sunday morning worship and sit in the front row. Isabella was the same bright, incredibly cheerful little girl. For all she experienced in her short life, I was amazed how well-adjusted and composed she seemed. I sent an occasional card to let them know I was praying for them. I delivered a poinsettia at Christmas. I assured them they were very welcome in the church and we wanted to help in any way possible. Arthur was appreciative of the prayers. The coroner's office kept little Aria's remains for months. Aria's father was under arrest in a secluded, unknown location. A memorial service did not seem appropriate just yet.

I had lunch with Arthur a couple of weeks before I retired. The trial of Aria's father, delayed many times, would begin shortly after my retirement. Custody arrangements for Isabella were not finalized. Those decisions would be forthcoming also. A memorial service for Aria still had not been observed. I would retire from the church soon and pastoral ethics required me to give up pastoral contact and support.

The trial filled the front page headlines for several days. Isabella's father was eventually convicted on drug charges and abuse of a corpse. During this time I adhered to pastoral ethics and did not contact Arthur.

Relationships in pastoral ministry are multi-faceted and complex. They grow through trust, prayer and honest dialogue. They are nurtured over time. A pastor is not a counselor offering advice or a chaplain offering a prayer. A pastor's role is not neatly defined. The relationship a pastor has with each parishioner is unique. It is more a ministry of presence, inviting God's comfort and Spirit to enter distressing or difficult situations. Pastors mediate a connection with God and God's grace. Often, one pastor simply cannot take over where the other pastor left off. It takes time for a pastor and a parishioner to grow trust and respect.

Perhaps some of the pastoral ethics regarding contact after termination of a ministry should be re-examined. Questions guiding the discussion should have nothing to do with egos and authorities of pastors. It should have everything to do with caring for the parishioners' needs. Discussion between previous and present pastors can resolve most ethical concerns and determine the best care and support for parishioners. If the previous pastor does not intrude or interfere and the present pastor respects their counsel, the ethics of pastoral involvement may be determined with the benefit of the parishioner in mind. Of course, pastors are imperfect. Sometimes previous pastors cannot give up reins to the church. Sometimes new pastors fail miserably offering loving pastoral care. Thus, conflicts occur.

I have said 'no' many times to former parishioners who called for funerals, weddings and other services. In nearly all cases I felt saying 'no' enabled ministry between the new pastor and my former parishioner. In the long run it was best the parishioner look to the new pastor for pastoral care.

On one occasion I received a call from a former parishioner asking me to preside over the funeral for his wife. Although I had not spoken with the couple in the nine years I was absent from the church, they entertained Carolyn and me at their country club several times in the years I served. We got to know them well and became close. Our daughter still has the little stuffed polar bear named 'Snowy' they gave her on her first birthday. The couple had not attended my former church for several years. They never met the new pastor. They lived nearly an hour's drive from the church and were in declining health.

I told my friend and former parishioner pastoral ethics prevented me from doing the service. He became angry, told me they wouldn't have a memorial service then, and hung up. My friend had been a high level executive and not used to hearing 'no.' I called the present pastor of the church and explained the situation. He gave my friend a call, offered his pastoral services, and above all listened to his grief and concerns. After his conversation, the pastor thought it best if I performed the service. The present pastor's grace in reaching out to the widower and permitting me to perform the service healed some of the tension the widower felt toward the church. I pray it re-connected him. Through dialogue I think we were able to provide my friend with the best possible pastoral care.

Perhaps we should see pastoral changes as transitions taking place over time rather than a sudden and abrupt passing of the baton. The present model of saying goodbye to an exiting pastor, hello to an interim, goodbye to the interim, and then hello to another pastor, all within a short period of time, can give the congregation a bumpy ride. It may not be best for the continuing health of the congregation or the pastoral needs of its members. If pastors can put aside egos and engage in thoughtful dialogue, transitions might happen more smoothly. The congregation will be served more compassionately.

In the meantime, I continue to pray for Arthur and Isabella. I think praying for former parishioners is still allowed in pastoral ethics.

CHAPTER 80

I Love My Country, but I Am Not Always Proud of It

No one died. I had no funeral or memorial service to plan. No death was imminent and no one seriously ill. But still I was grieving. I tossed and turned the whole night. Sleep didn't come until the wee hours of the morning. My stomach churned. My head ached. I dreaded facing tomorrow, the day after that, and the day after that. I couldn't believe it was actually happening. I was grieving for our country. We just elected a man to be President who spent his life not just disobeying, but mocking and belittling the teachings of Jesus, and was proud of it. What good could possibly come from such a man for our nation?

I spent years in ministry, teaching and preaching the good news of God. I sought to lift up the life and teachings of Jesus, calling people to walk in his footsteps. I proclaimed Christ's message of grace and acceptance. I urged people to flee greed and self-centeredness, to pursue justice and peace. Now we had a President-elect whose life and message ridiculed those values. He gained riches, and now gained the Presidency, through bullying, lies and demagoguery. Greed, adultery, deception and self-righteousness were the foundation on which he built his life. He lacked a moral compass. His message was fueled by hate and fear. Citizens of our nation, not a majority, but enough, believed his lies and joined his deceptions to put him in office. So I grieved. My heart ached for what was to come for our country. My heart ached for those who believed in decency and justice for all people. My heart ached for Jesus.

The Bible is clear where the heart of Jesus lies. The gospel of Jesus Christ is not one of fear but hope, not one of hate but love, not one of exclusion but inclusion, not one of greed but compassion and generosity, one where we value every person as a child of God and treat them as such. The gospel of Jesus tells us we are to serve and not to be served, we are to treat others as we would have them treat us. The gospel of Jesus brings hope to the least among us, the oppressed, poor, sick, and disabled. Those whom everyone else rejects and derides, Jesus touches with healing, grace and compassion. We need to hold our nation to these principles. We failed on election night.

I grieved. I knew I did not grieve alone. Tens of millions of others shared my grief for our country. The election proved we were no longer a nation where Christian values matter. Many Christian leaders, with right-wing ideologies, endorsed him and saw, in this anti-Jesus demagogue, a sort of Savior. How Jesus must ache for the church and his people! How easily we are led astray! How we flee from his teachings! How ironic that those who profess Christianity deeply initiated a post-Christian America. "For what will it profit them to gain the whole world and forfeit their life?"

During a mission trip to Honduras our team was stopped every day going in and out of the city of San Pedro Sula on the way to the village where we built houses. Sometimes it was the police, sometimes the army. A governmental leader was assassinated before we arrived and the government clamped down on security. The police or army captain asked a few questions. Our mission host responded we were building houses for the poor. They let us pass. One day was different. The police captain looked at the bracket around our front headlight and said it didn't pass code. Our mission host assured him it passed safety inspections. The police captain insisted it didn't. He would write a ticket and send us to the downtown traffic court to pay. He said it would probably take all day waiting around the court to pay the fine.

Then he offered us an alternative. We could pay him 30 lempiras. Lempiras were the Honduran currency and, at the time, 30 lempiras was about $2. Our mission host reluctantly paid the police officer and the officer waved us on. As we drove away our host was very embarrassed. We just saw a part of his country he wished we hadn't. He then said words I always remember, "I love my country, but I am not always proud of it." I love my country, but I am not always proud of it.

That is the way I felt election night. I love my country very much, but I was not very proud of it that night. Our faith is reflected in our politics. Our beliefs are revealed in what we do. We clearly said 'no' to the gospel of Jesus and I grieved. Our nation willingly let itself be deceived.

I am a white, middle-class, educated male. As such, I am a person of privilege in our country. There is much I take for granted. I wasn't grieving for myself alone.

I was grieving for the poor who cannot afford adequate health insurance, for the African–American who lacks basic civil liberties, for undocumented aliens whose families would be torn apart, and members of the LGBTQ community who would face harassment. I grieved for children and grandchildren who would inherit a world of global warming brought about by lies of the naysayers of climate change spreading their views through shameless greed.

I grieved for our nation at other times. I grieved when we started the Iraq War based on deceptive lies of weapons of mass destruction. I grieved during the war when we tortured prisoners and demeaned them at the Abu Ghraib prison. These were not actions of a nation founded on the teachings of Jesus. I was not proud of our country. I was not proud torture was sanctioned by the highest levels of our government. The injustice our government perpetrated sending thousands of soldiers and hundreds of thousands of civilians to their deaths in a war initiated on contrived grounds made bribery by the Honduran police officer seem rather petty. I grieved and I think the Lord Jesus Christ grieved also.

Grief comes from loss. Loss comes not only from death but from the loss of many things: relationships and friends, jobs and wealth, dreams and opportunities, innocence and youth, physical and mental health. We grieve what we will never have again. I grieved for my country because I felt I lost the nation I loved. I prayed our nation would not be lost forever.

I was not only grieving for our nation. I was also grieving for the church. The election revealed the church in America deserted the teachings of Christ. Persons professing faith in Christ led the national vote for an anti-Jesus candidate. Perhaps, for too long, too many in the church have proclaimed a message rooted in fear and not love, a message appealing to our self-centeredness and debased nature. It plays into our prejudices and greed. It lifts us by demeaning others. Followers of Jesus reacted to fears heralded by our future President again and again and, despite the teachings of Jesus, voted for values contrary to the gospel. It is so easy to be led away from following our Lord.

Church leaders, like all leaders, are corrupted through power. Sometimes they proclaim a disingenuous gospel to maintain control and authority. Jesus called religious leaders of his day 'hypocrites.' Many religious leaders in our nation today are guilty of the same sins as those in Jesus' day. I give thanks through the centuries, in times of ecclesiastical abuse and waywardness, God raises up saints and martyrs to speak the truth and challenge injustices in the church. I pray such leaders will rise in our generation and the church enters a time of reformation where we return to the teachings of Jesus. We are wandering in the wilderness. We appease people through a false gospel that appeals to self-interest over service, a gospel that makes us feel good rather than do good, a gospel that elevates us by denigrating others.

I think some Christians are looking for a savior besides the Lord Jesus Christ.

We look for a savior in a charismatic pastor who tells us things we want to hear. We look for a savior in those who profess to be Christian but simply reinforce prejudices and biases. We look for saviors in political leaders as well. In the search for saviors, we Christians can be gullible. Naiveté and a propensity toward intolerance make us easily persuaded and manipulated by those offering false hope and deceptive lies.

The gospel is not just about personal salvation, a ticket to eternal life at the banquet table of God. The gospel is transformative. It declares a world of justice for every person, a world of peace for every nation. It decries injustice, greed and deceit at every level. I don't expect every person in our country to embrace the Christian faith as I have. I do expect all Christians to embrace and follow the teachings of Jesus. As a Christian, I pray our nation will uphold the values of Jesus. I think values similar to those taught by Jesus undergird most other major religions. Disregarding those values is where our nation fails.

I pray our nation grieves what it is losing. I pray our nation repents. I pray our nation will strive to be great by pursuing the ways of Jesus.

Conclusion

George and Winny were the two cutest kittens you ever saw. We adopted them one spring from a local animal shelter as birthday presents for our children. Romping and rolling, chasing and jumping, biting and scratching, they always entertained, bringing forth laughter and smiles. They were brothers but didn't look alike. George was hefty and orange, Winny slender and grey. They played hard and then collapsed on the floor curling next to each other, totally exhausted. Nothing aroused them when they slept.

Kayla was a two-year-old girl whose family attended our church and lived in our neighborhood. Kayla loved going on walks with Mom or Dad and stopping by our house to play with George and Winny. Her face lit up and she shrieked delightedly whenever I brought the kittens out for her to pet. Nothing, it seemed, would ever change Kayla's delight seeing George and Winny. Summer came to a close and so did Kayla's walks in the neighborhood. The following spring Kayla and her parents resumed their walks. She and her dad stopped for a visit. I fetched George and Winny and brought them for Kayla to pet. It was six months since her last visit. Kayla looked at George and Winny, now one-year-old cats and no longer kittens, and said, "No, I want kitties." I explained to Kayla these are the kitties. George and Winny grew up. But Kayla kept saying, "No, kitties! I want kitties!" George and Winny were no longer cute little kittens. Kayla didn't want anything to do with them.

After Kayla left I looked at George and Winny and said, "Well, boys, I guess you can't stay young and cute forever. One year old and already over the hill." Our journey to the grave begins the day we are born. We have one continuous, unrelenting journey from birth to death. Most of the time we are not aware of death as our destination. We are just living, taking care of business and pursuing life from one day to the next. We don't think of ourselves getting older. We just hit the significant milestones in life, 16, 21, 30, 40 or whatever. Most of us aren't thinking of dying. We are preoccupied with getting by, or getting ahead.

There comes a time, though, when our thoughts turn more and more to death. We look in the mirror and don't recognize the person looking back. Where did the wrinkles come from? Where did the hair go? I look like my grandparents or great-grandparents. I don't feel old inside. Inside, I still feel like the small child looking at the world in wonder and terror, trying to figure out what life is all about. My bones, skin, heart and lungs tell a different story, the story of a body wearing out, a body that will not last forever.

Some of us enjoy wonderful lives. We find meaning and joy in loving relationships, fulfilling work, close friendships, and delightful adventures. Many childhood dreams come true. We are blessed by wonderful surprises along the way. We are spared much of the pain and suffering common to human beings. Life is good. We are not ready to give up on it just yet. For a few of us, pain and suffering is more than we can bear. Life has been unfair and unjust. We have borne the weight of oppression and abuse. Death, no matter what follows life, will be better than our existence on earth. It will be the relief we have longed for.

The journey to the grave, although common to all, is also unique for each of us. No one else can travel it for us. Dying is the most personal thing we do. We long for a good journey. We pray our physical and emotional pain is bearable. We pray our relationships are strong and life-giving. We pray we have time to get our affairs in order and follow many of our dreams. Death remains the great unknown so we pray for faith, faith to believe the Creator of this world is alive, loving and forgiving, and will welcome us home, or at least to the next step on the journey. We pray we have courage to say goodbye to loved ones with grace, strengthened by the bonds that have grown between us.

The journey to the grave is generally not easy. Even though death is inevitable and will come whether we are ready or not, dying is the most difficult thing we do. On the journey we will probably encounter the greatest physical and emotional pain we have endured. We will say goodbye to those who walked alongside us and shared their lives with ours. Above all, we will need to draw upon more faith in God than ever before.

I try to make regular trips to a fitness center to ward off some of the weakening effects of growing old. I have never been much of a swimmer but occasionally I included swimming in my exercise routine. Swimming was always a little humbling as swimmers in other lanes lapped me again and again. The few times I kept pace with another swimmer, quite proud of myself, I realized the other swimmer was not using either legs or arms. My pride was short-lived.

In one of my parishes I had a member who was a swimming marvel as a young man. He held national records and even an unofficial world record. When I knew the man, he was in the senior years of his life. He experienced debilitating strokes making it difficult to swim and walk. I often thought it took more persistence and will-power, courage and determination, to swim then than as a young man with stands full of spectators cheering him to new records. Our battles, as we age, become more demanding and there is no one telling us we are doing a great job. We pray we have accumulated the strength, courage and faith to help as we encounter challenges and stumbling blocks on the way to the grave.

In his letter to the Philippians the apostle Paul writes, "I want to know Christ and the power of his resurrection and the sharing of his sufferings by becoming like him in his death, if somehow I may attain the resurrection from the dead. Not that I have already obtained this or have already reached the goal, but I press on to make it my own, because Christ Jesus has made me his own. Beloved, I do not consider that I have made it my own; but this one thing I do: forgetting what lies behind and straining forward to what lies ahead, I press on toward the goal for the prize of the heavenly call of God in Christ Jesus."

Paul writes this passage late in life. He is imprisoned, awaiting trial, contemplating his own death. His destiny is tied to Christ Jesus, both in suffering and resurrection. Suffering and resurrection, for Jesus and Paul, are inseparable. We strive amidst our suffering and pain to know the power of resurrection in Christ.

One summer vacation, our family stopped to visit Eleanor and Jane. Members of our congregation and retired school teachers, they lived together for many years. They spent summers in their little cottage on the shore of Lake Michigan. We stopped on the Fourth of July, joined the neighborhood party, then watched fireworks over the lake.

The next morning we walked the beach. Amidst the dead alewife washed ashore cluttering the beach, we spotted something round quietly flopping on the sand. We walked closer. It took a moment or two before we realized it was a sea gull. The gull apparently mistook a shining silver lure for a fish. Barbs of the lure were hooked into its beak and feet. The fishing line twisted around its wings and neck wrapping the gull in a tightly wound ball. The gull must have fought a long time to become free but the battle only imprisoned it more. Exhausted, the gull now feebly tried in vain to flap its wings entangled in the line.

I hate to see suffering in any creature. I turned to walk away and let nature take its course. The gull surely did not have long for this world. Eleanor also hated to see suffering in any creature. Rather than walk away, she picked up the ball of feathers and, turning to me, said, "Maybe we can set it free." I did not like to see the gull suffer but the last thing I wanted was to mess with this bird. Flopping, flapping, pecking birds unnerve me. I avoid them. Not so Eleanor. Nothing rattled her. She was calm and practical, focused on the issue at hand. She had a slow and steady 'let's deal with it' mentality. She was Dean of Girls at the high school for many years. I think she was probably pretty good.

For the next 30 minutes, while Eleanor held the bird, I attempted to unwind the fishing line. It was difficult to follow the path of the entangled line. It was difficult to avoid tightening the line and hurting the bird even more. It was especially difficult because the bird did not want me messing with it. I tried to be gentle. I tried to be patient. I tried to hide my discomfort and annoyance brought into this hopeless task. I tried my best not to let a 'damn' escape my mouth when the bird's beak struck pay dirt on my hand. The bird pecked at my hand every chance it got. Barbs on the fishing lures got under my skin. I did all this for a bird I knew never had a chance. If we succeeded disentangling the bird it would be unable to fly and still die there on the beach.

Finally, the line was free, the lure disengaged from its beak and feet. Eleanor held the gull up high, and let go. I was ready to see it fall to the sand. But the bird flapped its wings and sailed down the shore, flying with the effortless ease of any other bird. Two hundred yards down the beach it joined a flock of sea gulls resting on the sand. If it looked back and said 'thank you,' I didn't see it.

Sometimes I think we are a lot like that sea gull. We see something that looks shiny and attractive and we go for it, naively thinking it will bring happiness and satisfaction. We are mistaken. Instead, we become entangled in its snares. The more we fight to become free, the more entangled we become. Finally we are hopelessly ensnared and can't escape. We must rely on someone else to set us free. Even then, when our Rescuer comes, we continue to fight, still not knowing what is best.

Perhaps death is that moment of freedom when we are released from the lures and lines entrapping us. We fly unconstrained down the beach joining the flock awaiting us. All fighting and struggles have ended. God has rescued us. We are free to enjoy what God has prepared.